Chicken Soup for the Soul.

My Wonderful, Wacky Family

Chicken Soup for the Soul: My Wonderful, Wacky Family
101 Loving Stories about Our Crazy, Quirky Families
Amy Newmark

Published by Chicken Soup for the Soul, LLC www.chickensoup.com
Copyright ©2022 by Chicken Soup for the Soul, LLC. All Rights Reserved.

The publisher gratefully acknowledges the many publishers and individuals who granted Chicken Soup for the Soul permission to reprint the cited material.

Front cover photo courtesy of iStockphoto.com/nattanan726 (©nattanan726)
Back cover and interior photo of Meerkats courtesy of iStockphoto.com/KimMarriott (©Kim Marriott), photo of picture frame courtesy of iStockphoto.com/TPopova (©TPopova)
Photo of Amy Newmark courtesy of Susan Morrow at SwickPix

Cover and Interior by Daniel Zaccari

Publisher's Cataloging-In-Publication Data

Names: Newmark, Amy, editor.
Title: Chicken soup for the soul : my wonderful , wacky family , 101 loving stories about our crazy , quirky families / Amy Newmark.
Description: Cos Cob, CT: Chicken Soup for the Soul, LLC, 2022.
Identifiers: LCCN: 2022944301 | ISBN: 978-1-61159-097-5 (print) | 978-1-61159-334-1 (ebook)
Subjects: LCSH Families--Humor. | Family. | Self help. | BISAC SELF-HELP / Motivational & Inspirational | HUMOR / Topic / Marriage & Family | FAMILY & RELATIONSHIPS / General
Classification: LCC PN6231.F3 .N49 2022 | DDC 814/.6--dc23

Library of Congress Control Number: 2022944301

PRINTED IN THE UNITED STATES OF AMERICA
on acid∞free paper

27 26 25 24 23 22   01 02 03 04 05 06 07 08 09 10 11

101 Loving Stories about Our Crazy, Quirky Families

Amy Newmark

Chicken Soup for the Soul, LLC
Cos Cob, CT

Changing your life one story at a time ®
www.chickensoup.com

Table of Contents

❶

~Sometimes You Just Have to Laugh~

❷

~Relatively Embarrassing~

❸

~Happily Ever Laughter~

❹
~We're All Nuts Here~

❺
~Dad Did What?~

6

~Not So Grave~

7

~Family Fun~

8

~Grand & Great~

❾
~Mom Did What?~

❿
~In-Laws and Out-Laws~

⓫
~Family Bonding~

⑫

~Kids Will Be Kids~

Sometimes You Just Have to Laugh

Queen of the Cautionary Tale

When your mother asks, "Do you want a piece of
advice?" It's a mere formality. It doesn't matter if you
answer yes or no. You're going to get it anyway.
~Erma Bombeck

My mother was the Queen of the Cautionary Tale. I think probably everyone's mom is, really, but when I was growing up, none of my friends' moms could deliver a "Don't Let This Happen to You Story" like Frances J. Mark.

First of all, she was a great storyteller, but she also understood that line from Hemingway that "every true story ends in death" and made sure to impress that on all of us kids. I can't remember a single cautionary tale that didn't end in death, no matter how simple the lesson might be. You didn't want to clean up your room? Well fine, but you'll just end up like little Bobby Samuels who tripped over the blocks he left on the floor and struck his head on the dresser. "They later found him — dead."

That was the final word of every story — "dead" — and always delivered with emphasis. Ma was from Saco, Maine, and so these stories were all delivered in her broad New England accent, which always made them sound more ominous. They resonated with the tone and authority of a Puritan preacher. You didn't want to wear socks with your shoes? "Well fine, but remember little Johnny Whitaker who did that same thing? Developed a blister on his heel that burst, and he got blood poisoning. They found him later in an alley — dead."

This applied to any situation in life where she felt one needed to exercise some degree of caution — which seemed to be pretty much everything — but periodically focused on an actual potential danger like crossing the road after getting off the school bus.

"You wait until the bus driver tells you to cross and make sure he can see you. Remember what happened to little Sally Ann. It was the day of her first report card, and she was so excited to show her mommy that she ran off the bus and started to cross. The driver didn't see her and ran her over. They found her under the wheel of the bus, still clutching her report card — dead."

There really wasn't any reason for Ma to add "dead" to these stories after a certain point in our lives. We already knew that would be the conclusion of every tale. That didn't matter to Ma though, and the "death stories" continued into our teenage years. When my younger brother Jason and I began driving, there were more tales, now tailored to our age and experience, like the one about the importance of clearing the exhaust of the car in winter after a snowstorm and not sitting in the car while it warmed up unless we had done so.

"You don't want to wind up like the Stevens boys. They went out one morning to clear the snow from their dad's car. It was cold, so they got in while it was warming up. But they hadn't cleared the exhaust, and they suffocated on carbon monoxide. They were later found in the front seat together — dead."

That story had a very strange conclusion after the "dead" line because, apparently, the two boys were propped up in car seats or something at their funeral as a warning to other parents not to let their kids clear snow off a car — or something. I never could understand why two kids young enough to need car seats were clearing snow off a car without any parents around, but you learned not to question the logic of Ma's tales — or even if they were actually true. You just accepted the lesson and promised you'd do as she asked.

The stories went on even after I was married.

"Make sure that you and Betsy always take vacations together. You don't want to wind up like poor Mr. Collins. He and his wife used to take separate vacations, and she met another man and ran off with him. Mr. Collins took to drink. They found him in his lawn chair clutching a bottle — dead."

It seemed like sound advice, but I could think of plenty of scenarios where a married couple took separate vacations that didn't end with infidelity and suicide-by-whiskey. Still, even as a married adult, I never questioned the stories. I'd just nod and agree.

Looking back, I remember these tales fondly, but, when I was a kid, they could sometimes be annoying. And there were plenty of times when I was a teenager that I thought Ma was more than a little crazy. How on earth could she possibly know so many dead people? And, if the stories were all made up, how were we supposed to keep believing them? It seemed like any time anyone did anything, they wound up dead.

But, for the most part, I loved the stories, and so did my brother and sisters, Carol and Charlotte. I can still remember sitting in the back seat of the car next to Jason while Ma told us one tale or another as she drove. Both of us would look at each other and silently mouth the word "dead" when she came to it and try to clamp our mouths shut to stop the laughter.

I'm sure she did make up most, if not all, of the death tales, but that never really mattered. Even when I was a teen and thought she was crazy, I knew she only told us these stories because she loved us and wanted us to be safe. And it seems to have worked because we're all still alive all these years later. I'm sure her crazy stories have had something to do with that. To this day, I always clear the car's tailpipe first after a winter storm, keep a clean house, and look both ways before crossing a street. And I never, never wear shoes without socks because, as Ma would say, I don't want to wind up like little Johnny Whitaker.

—Joshua J. Mark—

You're Ruining Your Divorce

You can't choose your family, but you can ignore their phone calls.
~Author Unknown

"Tell your mother to reevaluate her priorities," Dad told me over the phone. I could picture his tight mouth.

"Why do you say that?" I pried, twisting the phone cord around my fingers.

"She repainted the bedroom." He paused for a deep breath. "Purple."

I tried to imagine that purple room, one of two small bedrooms in his beige-and-brown house, and I knew what Dad meant: Mom had repainted his room in his house with her color choice. Mom and I had lived in many rented apartments, and I knew that repainting with a crazy color was not a path to pleasing your landlord.

Then I burst out laughing. "Gee, Dad, I hope you're not talking about divorce."

Dad laughed, too.

In fact, my parents got divorced when I was five. Now Dad was calling me at college to complain that Mom was a terrible roommate. It was unnatural for the two of them to live under the same roof again after so many years apart.

Of course, their divorce was not "normal" from the start. They parted ways as friends, what celebrities call "conscious un-coupling." I know they did this in order to share custody of me in an amicable way.

Mom simply rented a nearby house. Halfway through the week, I could walk a few blocks, past an empty field, through Old Town Goleta, and right on over to Dad's place.

As I grew older, Mom found an apartment downtown. They split my time as equitably as possible.

Mom's place was open for her friends to gather; she liked to play country-western music and let me watch *Fantasy Island*.

Dad was a fan of classical music, which he blasted from a clock radio sitting on top of the fridge. We watched *NOVA* and planned our next camping trip.

When Mom bought a new stereo, Dad came over and helped her set it up, connecting the speakers and turntable. When Dad bought a suit, Mom helped by hemming the pants.

When Mom's brother Howie died, all three of us flew to Oakland for the memorial. Dad drove the rental car, while Mom read the map and sniped at him for missing the exit.

"No problem," he said, nonchalantly. "We have one stop to make before we get there."

Mom looked as confused as I felt until he turned down one street filled with dilapidated houses.

"Oh, my God," she said, covering her face with her hands, and then laughed with him, mischief in her eyes.

He pulled over in front of an ancient house with boarded-up windows.

"There it is," he chuckled, looking at me over his shoulder. "The house where you were conceived!"

Cringe.

At Thanksgiving, it wasn't unusual for them to each bring their significant others. I remember Dad cheerfully introducing himself to Gary, who would soon become Mom's second husband. Their wedding was meant to be held at Alice Keck Park in the middle of Santa Barbara, but it poured that day. Dad elbowed me under the umbrella and whispered, "We should take this production somewhere else. I've got a great idea."

Pretty soon, the whole wedding party was caravanning to an office complex a few blocks away. There, in the breezeway, outside the realty and insurance offices, Gary and Mom said their vows. Dad snapped the wedding photos. Over dinner at China Palace, Gary raised a glass. "I can't believe I'm saying this, but a huge thanks to my bride's ex-husband for rescuing this wedding from the rain."

By the time I finished high school, I watched their paths diverge even more. Mom took to wearing wild clothes Dad would've hated. She relished her freedom in fashion.

Dad liked to go hiking. Before smart phones, he wanted to know the air temperature at all times, and often wore an outdoor thermometer on a leather boot lace hanging around his neck. Even strangers tried hard not to comment.

At least my parents didn't need one another's approval, but they often called one another for advice anyway.

So, when Gary divorced Mom, she called Dad to ask if she could keep the Winnebago in front of his house. This was Gary's parting gift to Mom. She had no job, but she could have a place to stay, if only she could find a place to park.

Away at college, I was horrified. Poor Mom! Poor Dad! Then I had a second thought. Maybe at nineteen I was receiving the surprise gift that every child of divorce supposedly craved: My parents would be back together. Hurray?

The fantasy lasted about a week until Mom called to ask me questions about Dad: "Does he ever vacuum the house?"

"Sorry, Mom. It bothers his asthma. Don't you remember?"

"No. I probably vacuumed anyway."

That's when it dawned on me that she was out of the Winnebago and now living in Dad's house.

Soon, the calls from Dad started in earnest. "Why does she go shopping when she has no money? That makes no sense."

I shrugged. "She's bored," I told him, unable to explain why a trip to the mall was entertaining to Mom and me.

But I could see the serious rift beginning to grow, and not long after that, I had to put Dad on call-waiting while I answered a call from Mom.

She said he was uptight.

He said she was irresponsible.

She said he ate weird, organic food.

He said she drank a glass of wine every single night.

"I can't take this anymore!" I yelled at them both, shocking them into silence.

I took a deep breath and said, "I can't stand the two of you under the same roof. Mom and Dad, I love you, but this is too close for comfort. Living together is ruining your divorce," I blurted out.

When the conference call ended, I felt wiped-out and weary, but a slow smile snuck onto my face. I love each of them dearly, but I don't love them together.

When peace had finally been restored, I felt satisfied that they had been as good to each other as they could possibly be. They didn't need to be sharing a household, and they really couldn't if they still wanted to share me.

— Robin Jankiewicz —

Hot Pants

*Sometimes, you've got to just put
on your sassy pants and move on.*
~Author Unknown

I s it just me or has anyone else noticed how small men's suits have become over the past few years? Whenever I watch the news (which is as rarely as possible), I notice those tiny suits, especially on the weathermen. They all seem to be wearing jackets that are tight in the shoulders, snug on the biceps and short in the sleeves, making the wearer look like he put on his junior-high graduation suit by mistake but decided not to change because his mom said he looked just fine.

At first, I figured I was simply watching channels that didn't pay their staff enough to buy decent-fitting suits. Then I saw several other celebrities sporting that same too-tight, too-short suit, and it dawned on me that they were dressing that way on purpose.

I'm guessing designers are going for the two-sizes-too-small look because they're saving a lot on fabric. What I can't understand is how any man willingly wears a suit that looks like it might be one of Pee Wee Herman's castoffs.

Fashion is a funny thing. It is always interesting to look back at a decade and think, "We wore THAT?" But, while you're wearing it, you're mightily impressed with yourself for being in vogue. The 1980s and 1990s are excellent examples of such delusional thinking. Just check out a television show like *Miami Vice* or *Magnum, P.I.* if you don't believe me. The pastel outfits Don Johnson sported made him look more like a Good Humor man than a hardened vice cop, and those itsy-bitsy shorts Tom Selleck ran around in were plain embarrassing.

Leather was also popular in the 1980s, another hard-to-comprehend trend, but it was big, even affecting my husband, Mark, who has never been a slave to any fashion. For some reason, Mark got it in his head that he needed a pair of leather pants. I don't know if this was the influence of the then-new channel VH1 or if all the leather pants displayed in the window of the Chess King clothing store at our local mall caught his eye. However, the bug got in his ear, and leather pants were what Mark wanted for this birthday.

We found the ideal pair for something like eighty dollars, which was a lot of money for pants, even leather ones, back in those days, but Mark had his heart set on them. On his birthday, we decided to go out for dinner, and I suggested he wear his newest acquisition. Mark agreed and vanished into the bedroom to put them on.

When he hadn't reappeared in ten minutes, I went to investigate. I found him wearing the leather pants, a polo shirt and a worried expression.

"What's wrong?" I asked.

"These pants. I'm not sure if I like them."

"Why not?"

"They seem… tight."

"Stand up and let me see." Mark stood up, and he was right: They were tight. As in David Lee Roth tight.

"They didn't look that tight in the store," I said.

"They didn't feel this tight in the store. I can't wear these in public. Can we take them back?"

"No, we can't. We had them hemmed, remember?"

"Well, I'm not wearing them." Mark peeled off the leather pants and replaced them with comfortably worn and decently loose Levis. "That's better. Now I can breathe."

Those leather pants accompanied us on several moves since neither of us could bring ourselves to donate them, and we didn't know anyone we could give them to who would actually wear them and not laugh at us. Finally, after about twenty years, I suggested we try to sell them on eBay. Much to our surprise, those 1980s leather pants sparked a bidding war that netted us a lot more than our original eighty-dollar investment. They finally landed in California where the happy buyer wrote "Hot Pants!" on his review, thus ending Mark's sole foray into high fashion.

I have to think life is much simpler when you wear the same thing season in and season out, ignoring what's in and what's out, and focusing instead on what fits and what doesn't. That said, I'll be very happy when the tight-suit look is passé, and weathermen go back to wearing suits that actually cover their wrists again so I can stop worrying about their blood circulation.

— Nell Musolf —

A Cure for Practical Jokes

I love practical jokes, but I don't like being scared.
~Mitt Romney

When my son was eight years old, he loved to play practical jokes on me. Every time I walked into a room that had a door to it, a shower of stuffed animals fell on my head. He put fake flies in the ice-cube trays, ants in the pleats of my lampshades, and whoopee cushions everywhere. You never knew when or where he would strike. I admired his ingenuity, but I have to confess there were days when it got old.

One weekend, we decided to go to Moonshine Beach for the day. Beaches in southern Missouri aren't like beaches in Florida. There isn't any sand; it's crushed rock. When you go into the water to swim, you must wear shoes or you'll cut the bottoms of your feet.

After a long day at the beach, we headed home. Everyone was exhausted.

When we got home, I put the blanket we'd sat on in the wash. I'd throw it in the dryer the next morning. When I pulled the blanket out of the washer the next morning, a huge, brown tarantula fell at my feet. I figured my son had struck again. I picked it up and was amazed at how lifelike it looked. It was as big as the palm of my hand. Whoever made this toy spider really went all-out for detail. It even had hair on it like a real tarantula. I took it inside and found my son watching television. I stuck it in his face and said, "Very funny, Adam."

His face turned pale. He backed up and said, "Mom, I didn't do that. It's real." At first, I didn't believe him, but then I saw the look on his face. I screamed, he screamed, and the tarantula went flying across the room. We both ran out of the house. When we got the courage to go back inside, it was still lying where it had landed, dead. We both started laughing so hard that we were in tears. That day cured him of his practical jokes; he knew he could never top that one.

— Brenda Beattie —

Chicken Soup
for the Soul

Sorry for the Inconvenience

*Recreational shopping is the shortest distance
between two points: you and broke.*
~Victoria Moran

With the last cup of morning coffee in my Have a Fabulous Day mug, I walk to my office and flick on the monitor. First, I check e-mail. Delete. Really? Ignore. A quick peek in Facebook to see what's new and then a review of our bank account and credit-card statement.

$6,279.00! What? How? When?

I follow the screen down. Twenty-one line entries. All online purchases. Each worth $299.00. I race the mouse up and down, but it changes nothing. My finger jerks across the keyboard to open My Online Orders tab.

And there it is. The list. Giant Jumping Bouncy Castle with Slide. Twenty-one times. To be delivered to my daughter's house. Tomorrow.

What have I done? I only ordered one.

A thought niggles in my head. A recollection that the quantity read 2 on the initial order, but I know I changed it to 1. Didn't I?

Not a problem. The online chat people will help. They're wonderful. I tap the icon to start the conversation.

Order Desk: Hello, how may I help you?

Me: I need to cancel order #701-4152852. I only want 1 giant bouncy castle. The order says 21 are coming.

Order Desk: Let me check. Please stay connected.

Me: Thanks.

I send a quick text to my husband: *21 bouncy castles being delivered tomorrow.*

Husband's response: *Why?*

Order Desk: May I ask why you want to cancel the order?

Me: I made a mistake. I only want 1.

Order Desk: I understand. Return is so easy. Do you wish to cancel the entire order? Or only 20 of them?

Me: Whatever is easiest.

Order Desk: Stay connected. I will proceed with the cancellation.

Me: Thank you.

Order Desk: I'm sorry, but I tried to cancel 20 for you, but the system would not allow it. I tried to cancel the entire order, but I cannot do that either. But you will be happy to know I cancelled 7.

Me: What? If you cancelled 7, why can't you cancel them all?

Order Desk: I am sorry, but you must realize we only have the ability to cancel the purchases that have not been assigned shipping tags.

Me: But I only want one. You can't deliver 14. They'll fill her whole driveway.

Order Desk: I am sorry, but please understand there is nothing I can do about the delivery. They are now waiting for the carrier.

Me: If they haven't even left yet, please go stop them.

Order Desk: I am sorry, but our procedures are such that we cannot affect the delivery once the shipping label is attached to the package.

Me: Then go rip the label off.

Order Desk: I cannot do that, but you can refuse the delivery once it arrives.

Me: I don't want them to arrive.

Order Desk: I hope you understand our technical limitations. I'm sorry if this causes you any inconvenience. When they arrive, you can easily return them.

Me: So, there's really no other way to stop this?

Order Desk: That is correct.

Me: What am I supposed to do with all of them? Each one is the size of a pickup truck.

Order Desk: Our company is very good on returns. I suggest you refuse the shipment when it arrives with the carrier. We'll issue a full refund. For your reference, I'll e-mail the link with the carrier contact information.

Me: What if I call the carrier now? Can I stop it then?

Order Desk: I am not sure. That is out of our control.

Me: Thanks. I'll call them.

Order Desk: If you are unable to refuse the shipment or return the packages, please write us. We will provide prepaid return mailing labels and accept the return at our expense as an exception for you. I hope this helps.

Me: Yes, it does. Thank you.

Order Desk: Thank you for contacting us. Please click the End Chat icon on the top right corner of this window to close this session and have a grand day.

I text my son: *14 bouncy castles possibly being delivered to your sister's tomorrow! My fault. $4,000.*

Son's response: *Are you having a heart attack?*

Me: *What good would that do?*

***

I punch in the carrier's phone number.

"Hello." I smile for no other reason than to start this conversation off on a good foot.

"Good afternoon," a perky lady says. "How may I help you?"

I learn that her pleasant voice comes all the way from a dispatch office in Nova Scotia—a very long way from Calgary, Alberta.

As I relay my problem, I add inflections, attitude and hand gestures, which I'm sure carry through to her. After I finish with my dilemma, there's silence.

"Hello?" I press my phone harder against my ear.

More silence.

"Are you still there?"

Loud, high-pitched laughter pierces my eardrum. It makes me grin despite the fact my entire family will think I'm totally out of control.

When the laughter stops, I say, "Yup, major fail on my part."

There's a snort and throat clearing.

"This is the best screw-up I've heard in a while," she says.

"Thanks. I usually don't have to work so hard at it."

"How about we don't stop the delivery? Let it arrive at your daughter's, and you sit across the street, video it all and send it to me."

I almost choke.

"It'd be hilarious." She laughs. "Imagine the poor sap hauling those giant boxes out of the truck and up the driveway. Stacking them. The look on your daughter's face when she sees it."

"It would be funny." I sigh. "But I'd never live it down. I can't."

"Are you sure?"

"Positive."

"Okay. I'll issue a pre-cancellation order. That will stop the delivery from getting on the truck. Then I'll issue a cancellation order followed with a confirmation number. Give me a few minutes and then have a pen ready to write down the numbers."

"Thank you so much. You're the best."

Elevator music fills the line as I congratulate myself on dodging a bullet. She comes back and rattles off the numbers.

"Thank you," I say. "You saved my butt."

"No problem, but I'm telling everyone about the lady in Alberta who ordered too many bouncy castles."

"Great. Guess I'm never coming to Nova Scotia."

***

At noon the next day, my phone pings. A text from my daughter: *14 giant boxes in my driveway wth.*

No!

I phone the carrier, mention yesterday's call, and tell him all the boxes are now sitting on the driveway.

"I had confirmation numbers," I whine.

"Sorry, ma'am," he says. "Sometimes, we make mistakes. It happens."

"You have to go pick them up and take them back."

"We can't do that. You'll need to contact the vendor to arrange for the boxes to be returned."

"You're kidding?"

"No, I'm not. I'm sorry for your inconvenience." He pauses. "Please, have a nice day."

My phone bings again.

It's a picture of my grandson amidst all the boxes, and he's wearing the biggest smile. The biggest, most expensive smile.

— Barbara Wackerle Baker —

Chicken Soup for the Soul

Sleep Deprivation

Motherhood: Powered by love.
Fueled by coffee. Sustained by wine.
~Author Unknown

Four-month-old Grant and I snuggle into our big rocking chair. The glow of the television is the only light illuminating the toys scattered across the living room floor. I rock and kiss the baby's head while giving him his bottle.

Out walks two-year-old Harrison. Harrison has decided that 1:00 A.M. feedings are the perfect time to get in some extra mommy snuggles and playtime. Harrison crawls into my lap. I kiss him on his head and snuggle him close. He quickly hops down and begins playing with toys. I sit mindlessly rocking and flipping through channels trying to find something to keep me awake long enough to finish feeding Grant and get both boys back in bed.

Becoming engrossed in a medical drama, I lose track of what Harrison is doing. I look over just in time to see Harrison come from behind the couch. Behind him is a four-foot, slithering creature. I let out a scream that would make a horror-movie director proud. I grab Harrison and pull him into the rocking chair with me.

When I pull Harrison into the chair, the slithering creature jumps in the air and lunges toward us. I let out another blood-curdling scream while frantically kicking and slapping at the creature, trying to keep it away from my babies. At this point, Harrison is crying because his mother is screaming. Grant is crying because his bottle has fallen out of his mouth. My husband, eyes wide with alarm, runs into the living room asking what is wrong.

I look over to see the remnants of a crochet project lying lifeless on the floor beside my foot and a crocheted piece clutched in Harrison's sweet, pudgy hand. I smile sheepishly at my husband and reply, "Sorry, sweetie. False alarm." In a very sleep-deprived state, under poor lighting, the beginnings of a crocheted blanket can look like a rather large and extremely fierce snake.

Grant and Harrison can rest assured that their mother will fearlessly protect them from crochet projects for the rest of their lives.

— Marie Loper-Maxwell —

Trying to Fit In

Why worry? It's not the end of the world.
And if it is, why worry?
~Robert Brault, rbrault.blogspot.com

y aunt Gertrude was an awesome woman. An English war bride, she left all she knew to come to America to be with the man she loved. Having grown up eating English fare, Aunt Gertrude had a hard time fitting in with our Italian-American family. No matter how she tried, nothing she made tasted Italian. She was loved, but her cooking was not.

But one holiday, she demanded the family come to her house for dinner rather than to the home of one of her husband's siblings. She knew that every major dinner had lasagna as one of the many dishes. She worked diligently on inserting all the spices and cooking the sausage and meatballs as she had been instructed. The noodles would be no problem to cook, so she left the tomato sauce simmering as she went to have a smoke to relax. She went outside to catch a cool breeze and reached in her shirt pocket for her pack of cigarettes. But her pocket was empty!

She searched high and low for that pack, but it was nowhere to be found. Sighing, she gave up and went back to her cooking. The lasagna was baking in the oven and the first guests arriving when she finally found the missing cigarettes—at the bottom of the pot of sauce. She stood there with the soggy wrapper and stared at the bits of tobacco floating in the red liquid before her.

There was no time or ingredients to redo this meal. She chucked the package in the trash and sadly sighed as she brought the food to the table.

She waited for the usual forced smiles as everyone took their first bite and slowly chewed. And chewed.

For the first time in all her married years, she watched people take seconds of her cooking attempts. Compliments flew around the table as every bit of sauce was sopped up on a hunk of bread. Her husband beamed from the end of the table as he raised a glass to salute her.

"To my wife, who made the greatest sauce anyone ever made!"

Gertrude waited two years before confessing.

— Camille Regholec —

The Fine Art of Curmudgeonry

*Every family has that one crazy person in it. If you're
missing one, I seem to have a few extras.*
~Author Unknown

"Where's that waitress?" Sadie snapped. "I want more coffee. I'm dying of thirst." Sadie was treating her daughter June, my young son Gene, and me to a restaurant buffet lunch. She adored my son, had placed me firmly in her heart since my marriage into the family, and felt she needed to include my mother-in-law June in the weekly ritual.

Catching our young waitress's eye, I gestured her over.

"Where the hell's my refill?" Sadie barked.

Over the top of Sadie's blue-white curls, the girl's amused gaze connected with my chagrined look. She filled the cup and bent toward me, whispering, "I'll keep her cup full. I've got an old granny, too," before scurrying off to her other tables.

Our waitress returned with plates for the buffet, refilled Sadie's cup and hustled off.

June brought out Fourth of July pictures, and as we passed them to each other, our waitress checked Sadie's cup again, topping it off with a tiny pour.

Sadie squinted suspiciously at the slight, dark-haired girl. "What are you trying to do? Fill me up with liquid so I won't eat as much?"

***

As the elevator rose, I shifted the box filled with bubble-wrapped glasses. It was Gramma Sadie's moving day. She was leaving the house that she and her daughter June had purchased in the 1940s for a modern, senior high-rise nearby.

A half-dozen teenaged grandchildren gathered to haul furniture and tote boxes. Sadie's grandson Randy was with me in the elevator, standing next to Granny's recliner. I had my arms full with a cardboard box. At the rear was a stranger, about our age, carrying a small grocery bag of possessions for some elderly relative.

The door slid open on Sadie's floor. I eased out, and Sadie shuffled forward to meet us. "Careful with that box," she instructed me, with her eyes on Randy, who was trying to maneuver the chair into a lifting position.

As he struggled, Sadie shouted, "Careful of that arm. Look out! Look out! Jimmy, you lazy bum," she added, "help Randy out."

I scanned the hall for her son Jimmy. Where had he come from?

"Jimmy, sommanabitch, give Sharon that bag and help Randy." Sadie's arms pantomimed giving me the bag.

"Gram, that's not Jimmy!" I stage-whispered. The young man waited, caught behind the struggling Randy and the recliner.

"Well, whichever the devil one he is, he can start to do a man's work."

"No, Gram, he's not one of our family!" I could hear the "Oh, no, this guy must think we're nuts" tone in my voice.

"Well, it won't kill him to carry a chair for a poor, helpless, old lady," she retorted as the grocery bag came my way.

— Sharon Boerbon Hanson —

Please, Not Me!

Good news: The holidays are about family.
Bad news: It has to be your own family.
~Author Unknown

Some people might call her thrifty. Others might call her frugal. Or economical. I just call her cheap! There is no other way to describe her. She's the one who once bought a used "floor sample" computer that who knows how many people had fooled with at the store and then wondered why she had problems with it. She's the one who still, to this day, has an old box TV, not a flat screen. The color is bad and the sound's not great, but she can still see a fuzzy picture, so that's good enough.

We are not related, but we have been "family" forever. I'll call her "Auntie." She doesn't have any family living anywhere near her and doesn't travel, so she has "adopted" my family as her own and spends all holidays and special occasions with us.

That includes Christmas. She has money, not millions and millions, but she is very comfortable. She can certainly afford to buy some nice gifts. Now, I'm not talking about gifts like yachts or diamonds, but how about a nice sweater, some wineglasses or even a book? Books make great gifts. Something useful. But no… she regifts! And the way she does it is to find something in her house that she has no use for and give it away. It doesn't have to be new. It doesn't have to be clean. It just has to fit in the old, used box she wants to use.

Our family had gotten to that place where no one needs anything, so last year we decided, for the adults, to draw names for gift giving. We still would get gifts for all the kids, but we would only have to get one gift for one adult. And the name you drew was to be kept a secret until Christmas night when the gift was opened.

Our holiday meals are potluck-style. That way, all the food preparation doesn't fall on one person. Everyone makes and brings something. Everyone has their favorite things they like to cook, and they tend to bring them year after year. Auntie can't cook. Her favorites are nobody's favorites: either a green Jell-O salad or a puree of spinach with a "secret" ingredient. One is worse than the other and she alternates — one year, one green thing, the next year, the other green thing. The Jell-O salad is the kind with cottage cheese and chunks of something mixed in it. And the secret ingredient in the spinach is disgusting. I shudder to think of what it could be.

We've tried to tell her she doesn't have to bring anything, but she says she doesn't want to disappoint us. Oh, if only she would!

One year, Auntie was coming and had drawn a name for the gift exchange. Along with her dish, she said she would bring a bottle of wine to share. Oh, I couldn't wait to see the lovely bottle of wine she would bring. I wondered where she got it and how old it was. Old enough to have turned into vinegar? Did she find it in her garage along with all the other treasures lurking there?

On Christmas Day in the late afternoon, our family gathered at our house. The holiday music was playing softly, the tree was lit and beautiful, and we all had a lot of holiday spirit. It was so nice to be together. Although no one said anything, we all wondered what "special" gift Auntie had dredged up for some lucky family member and which savory, tasty dish she would bring… the spinach or the Jell-O?

Auntie arrived bearing her "gift" and her "dish" to share. Wonderful… It was spinach this year. She was beside herself because she had forgotten the bottle of wine by her front door. She'd just walked out without it.

The kids were excited and wanted to open presents before we ate. Each child, one at a time, picked a gift from under the tree and gave it to the person whose name was on the tag. We all knew which box Auntie had brought and were anxious to see who the "lucky" recipient would be. I hoped that it wouldn't be me.

One by one, the gifts were distributed. And then came that special box. Toward me. *Please, not me!* But it wasn't for me. My husband, sitting next to me, was the poor sucker who got Auntie's gift. The look on his face was priceless.

We went around the room, opening the gifts one at a time so everyone could see what the other people got. Then, it was my husband's turn. The anticipation in the room was palpable. Oh, how he was dreading this. The room was silent as the excitement grew. What was in that slightly dented box that was wrapped in obviously used paper?

It was a bathrobe! An old, never-been-used bathrobe… probably for a woman since it was pink. Very fashionable, to say the least… maybe fifty years ago. We thought it had never been used because it still had the tags on it, but you never know. We knew it was old because of the yellowing of the white parts and the smell. You know that old, musty, dusty closet smell… We all made the appropriate ooohs and aaaahs, and Auntie was very pleased with herself.

After the gift exchange came dinner. The table looked beautiful with all the decorations, including my collection of Santas and Christmas candles. I served buffet-style. The food was on the island in the kitchen; we ate in the dining room. Everyone knew they had to take some of Auntie's spinach with the secret ingredient. You didn't have to eat it, but you had to take some. Auntie always checked. And if you had "forgotten" to put some on your plate, she would happily bring you another plate with a heaping portion on it. That was much harder to hide since it was on a separate plate.

Each time I went into the kitchen, and when no one was looking, I took another serving-spoon-size portion of the spinach out of the serving bowl and stashed it in a secure place where Auntie wouldn't look. This would make it look like people were actually eating it, although it was being hidden under turkey or potatoes or vegetables that were already on their plates. Believe me, we had learned over the years that Auntie looked, and if enough hadn't disappeared, she would bring the serving bowl to the table and serve each of us another portion. That happened to me once, and only once. I never made that mistake again.

I do love the holidays. And, in reality, I think having Auntie and her special treats with us each year makes things even better. It's kind of like a tradition in an off-beat kind of way. I only hope she doesn't draw my name for the gift exchange next Christmas!

— Barbara LoMonaco —

Relatively Embarrassing

White Elephant Shenanigans

*Nobody will understand the craziness
of your family better than your cousins.*
~Author Unknown

'm sitting in a booth at my local Panera Bread avoiding the eyes of patrons staring at my shirt. I'm waiting for my cousin Adam to join me. It is a cold January day. Christmas has come and gone. For the second year in a row, our family has decided to skip Christmas festivities due to concerns about Covid-19, but Adam and I are meeting here today. We know what must be done to keep tradition alive.

He doesn't know I'm wearing the shirt — his shirt — well, not his exactly. It's my shirt, won fair and mostly square during the white elephant exchange at our last family Christmas party. It is a short-sleeve, burnt-orange, button-down shirt with his smiling face emblazoned across the front, back, and down the sleeves. Approximately forty-two Adam faces (I counted) smile back at the curious onlookers.

When Adam arrives, he takes one look at my attire, gives a thumbs-up and exclaims, "Oh, it's on!" Then he disappears to his car and returns with a gift bag. When it's time, he's ready to push the button on his phone so we can pull up Facebook Live and let the family enjoy our antics from afar.

In 2019, we gathered for what would be the last extended Gordon Family Christmas Party. We had no idea a pandemic was barreling down on the nation, ready to take away so much from so many. In our pre-pandemic bliss, we ate buffet-style casseroles, tortilla roll-ups, and potato salad. We watched the elder statesmen of the family — my aunts, Jan and Sherri, and my father, Larry — huddle at a table and open gifts from each other. We watched the kids unwrap their goodies. Finally, it was time for the adults to participate in the white-elephant exchange. I remember someone asking Adam, "What is DaniMichelle going home with this year?"

My first name is Dani, and my middle name is Michelle, but on this side of the family, it's all one word: DaniMichelle. Legend has it that my paternal grandmother — a spitfire of a woman who was almost legally blind but kept an immaculate home and made the best grilled-cheese sandwich you've ever tasted — didn't like the name Dani. She said it sounded like a boy's name. It was 1971, so she wasn't wrong. My parents were hippies, nay, visionaries. Grandma announced she was going to call me Michelle instead. Mom and Dad swiftly rejected the idea. Without missing a beat or losing the argument, Grandma referred to me as DaniMichelle, and everyone followed suit for years, long after she was gone and to this very day.

Back to the party. If you're not familiar with a white elephant exchange, these are the basic rules in an otherwise lawless game. You purchase a nondescript gift that anyone (or no one) would like to receive. Participants are chosen by numbers drawn from a red plastic cup. We don't get fancy about it. During the first round, when a person's number is drawn, he or she chooses a gift from the pile, unwraps it, and shows the group. Maybe it's a calendar with horses, a bottle of booze, an oversized mug, or the holy grail of white elephant gifts — the Starbucks gift card. In round two, numbers are drawn again, and the person can steal/trade his/her gift with someone or keep it. When the second round is finished, what you're left with is what you're leaving with, thanks for playing.

Three years earlier, my white elephant fate was sealed when I opened a large, decorative pillow with an equally large picture of my cousin Adam's face. It was simultaneously amazing and awful. The family loved it but not enough to steal it, so it was mine. The next year, I let my youngest child choose for me in the first round. To my delight, I started unfolding a soft blanket, only to reveal a full-body picture of Adam lying semi-provocatively (but clothed, thank God) in a bed of leaves. "Dang it, Adam!" The family howled with laughter. I went home with the gift — again. The third year is a blur. I'm pretty sure the game was rigged because that's the year I ended up with the orange, button-down shirt. I started calling these items the Adam Henderson Home Collection.

Adam insists he never intended for me to be the one to give these items a forever home. But if he's being honest, he's delighted that I wind up with them every year. Though I am fifteen years his senior, we're both adults, so the age gap doesn't seem as wide as it used to. We are political sparring partners. He is a devout Catholic who leans conservative. I am an LGBTQ ally who leans so far left that I'm afraid it will affect my posture. We don't see eye-to-eye on many things except the importance of family — and maybe potatoes, because they can be cooked in so many delicious and versatile ways. Family and potatoes, that's it. Everything else is a potential landmine, but we love the hell out of each other.

In 2020, for the first time in anyone's memory, we skipped the Gordon Family Christmas Party due to the fear of Covid-19. Adam and his family dropped by one Sunday after church to deliver the gift he was going to submit to the white elephant exchange. It was the one I surely would've wound up with: a black-and-white bathmat with, you guessed it, his smiling face hovering in the air, staring (seemingly) from the great beyond. There were no Gordon family giggles and no big reveal. A few days later, on New Year's Eve, we lost our matriarch, my beloved aunt Jan. She would've adored that ridiculous bathmat.

Which is why Adam and I are both standing at Panera Bread on a chilly Saturday afternoon with people gawking at us and one customer even asking me, "Did he pay you to wear that?" Soon, we'll sit and catch up over lunch. We'll chat about our lives, our kids, and maybe the latest news headlines. We'll tread carefully there.

But first we must tend to business and keep tradition alive. As Adam presses the button on his phone to record the video for Facebook

Live, we know our families will be watching. It's not the way we want to do it. There won't be hugs, casseroles, or in-person conversations, but they'll be there, virtually, when they see me open the gift for the first time. They'll be there to laugh right along with us (and our fifteen new friends at Panera Bread) during the big reveal when I unfold... a shower curtain with a shirtless Adam standing in the woods, leaves raining down like confetti. Behind the phone, he will proudly (and loudly) declare, "This is my greatest creation yet. That's the best thirty-four dollars I've ever spent."

Another item to be cataloged in the Adam Henderson Home Collection. We almost have enough accessories to furnish a very quirky, Adam-centric guest bedroom and bath.

Nah, I'm a good sport but not that good.

— Dani Michelle Stone —

11

Aunt Vee's Hat

A great hat speaks for itself.
~Author Unknown

I was in my front yard playing with my sons when Aunt Vee came walking up the street, waving. She lived around the corner and would often stop by for a quick hello.

"Yoohoo! Donna, come see my new hat!"

Perched on her head was a large straw hat with a floppy brim and a flat top with an indent in the center. It didn't look like a stylish hat — at least not one that I would wear. Then again, Aunt Vee is not one to worry about being fashionable. She is the family character who marches to the beat of her own drum.

"I got it on sale at the Five and Tenny for only $1.49," she boasted as she entered my yard. "You should go get yourself one!"

"Um, that's okay. I don't really like to wear hats."

"It's got this large rim that really protects your face and neck from the sun. And look at this feature." She whipped it off to show me the inside. "It's lined with plastic so it's waterproof!"

At that moment, I realized why her "hat" looked so funny. I struggled to hold back my laughter.

"Um, Aunt Vee, that's not a hat."

"What do you mean it's not a hat?"

"Well, it isn't designed to keep water out but to hold it in. That's why it's flat on the top, or rather, the bottom." She looked confused, so I continued, "It's a plant holder. You put a plant that's in a plastic

Relatively Embarrassing | 33

container inside this to dress it up, and when you water it, it won't leak out."

"No, that can't be right. They had a great assortment all stacked up, and they even had children's sizes."

Rather than argue, I walked into my house, picked up a philodendron plant that was in a very similar holder, and brought it outside to show her. I could almost see the light bulb clicking on.

"Ohhhh…" she said as she compared her "hat" to my plant holder. Again, I bit my lip to keep from laughing. Then, she added, "That explains why people were looking at me funny in the store."

"What do you mean, Aunt Vee?"

"Well, I spent about twenty minutes trying them on for size!"

"You did what?" Oh, my goodness, I could just imagine her trying on all the straw plant holders in the store. I'm sure those who witnessed the scene firsthand found it hilarious. At this point, I couldn't stop myself. I howled with laughter.

She shrugged. "Now that you mention it, they were in the garden center by the plants. I thought they were for gardening."

"I can't believe you tried them all on!"

"I didn't try all of them. Some looked like those fez hats, but they wouldn't provide much protection from the sun. I thought they were for men, so I didn't try those ones."

I was having trouble catching my breath as a sharp pain stabbed my side from laughing so hard.

"Oh, well, I still like it." With that, she plopped it on top of her head, the price tag dangling from the brim, and with a wave marched off. Once again, to the beat of her own drum. My giggles followed her.

To this day, if I see a straw plant holder, I call it "Aunt Vee's hat."

— Donna Anderson —

12

My Zombie Sister

*If you don't understand how a woman could both love
her sister dearly and want to wring her neck at the
same time, then you were probably an only child.*
~Linda Sunshine

Mom just didn't understand. Not only was I strictly forbidden to watch scary movies, but I was instructed to stay far away from *Night Gallery*, *The Twilight Zone* and, for all I knew, any potentially thrilling *Gunsmoke* reruns.

"You'll have nightmares," Mama said matter-of-factly, with historical evidence to back her up.

But I might not. *This* time.

I was banned from even peeking at *Dark Shadows*, the daytime vampire soap opera that featured Barnabas Collins, a delicious creature whose persona and talents spanned from vampire to werewolf over the course of the series. *Dark Shadows* came on at 4:00 in the afternoon.

When Mama was at work.

I watched it regularly, often from behind the living room couch, hiding from the vampires.

Then, one delightful Saturday night, Mom and Dad went out for the evening. They would be out "quite late."

Quite late!

I devoured a heady murder mystery in the afternoon, finishing up with cautious glances over my shoulder even though it was daytime. Then, filled with my success at catching every episode of *Dark Shadows* that week, I stayed up late to watch an Alfred Hitchcock film on TV.

With my sister.

Sir Alfred did what he did best. By the end of the show, I was ready to flee at the first sign of the supernatural.

Time to get ready for bed. I went to the bathroom. This was an old house and had a small lavatory sink in the kitchen, just outside the bathroom door. My sister, Vampira, began her nighttime routine out there at the sink. Inside the bathroom, I heard only silence outside the door and was faced with a dilemma.

Had nighttime creatures carried Vampira away, lifeless with eyes open and cold, to their kingdom in the graveyard? I was afraid to open the bathroom door.

And then, I heard a trickle of water in the small sink. That gave me hope. I reached for the doorknob, hoping fervently that the trickle involved water and not human blood.

I opened the door. My sister stood there with a ghastly, pasty white face. The holes for her eyes and mouth looked horrible and dark.

THEY GOT HER!

The evil ones had body-snatched my sister.

Luckily, I was still holding the belt I'd worn earlier. A weapon!

I couldn't let Mom lose two children in one night — especially if one of them was me. I acted with the speed of panic and terror.

"AAAAIIIIIGGGHHHH!!!" I launched into my fright dance, flogging the creature with my belt as my instincts screamed, "Kill it! Kill it! Save yourself!"

The creature responded.

She came toward me, hands outstretched, making a hideous wheezing sound.

My zombie sister was laughing at me from beyond the grave.

My screams increased in pitch, and my efforts with the Belt of Death increased.

Kill the creature!

The creature came forward again, hands outstretched.

And spoke. A horrible sound issued from its quivering lips.

"It's me! It's me!"

How horrible! She was trying to call to me from beyond death. It was too late to save her. I flogged on. I must escape.

Fortunately, I was too frightened to get close enough to do much harm. As a rule, zombie sisters are fiends for retribution.

As I danced the dance of terror and rained blows down on the air around her, she wheezed out a message from across the cosmos. "It's me! I have night cream on my face."

Night cream?

Night cream didn't sound like something a creature of the night might say. I was pretty sure the undead came by their pallor naturally and had no need to resort to pasty white creams for special effects.

I paused in my flailing. The vampire zombie creature paused its hideous screams and leaned against the sink, gasping for breath, wiping tears from its eyes and snort-laughing until coughing fits took over.

My head seemed to be intact, and my brain, though not functioning at full capacity, was still contained inside.

"I'm washing my face," the creature wheezed. "Stop beating me, or you're never watching Alfred Hitchcock again."

Identities were confirmed, and we took ourselves to bed, although I didn't sleep well that night.

In the days that followed, I tried to forget about the incident, but snickers from around the house reminded me that random incidents of terror-fueled beatings could be used for blackmail.

Then, on another Saturday night, Mom and Dad went out for the evening. Alfred Hitchcock's masterpiece, *The Birds*, would be on TV that night.

We watched *Bonanza*.

—Amy A. Mullis—

Opera Night at the Movies

Surprise is the greatest gift which life can grant us.
~Boris Pasternak

I had a lovely, eccentric great-aunt named Margita. She always wore colorful clothing and had a colorful personality to match. She was spunky, beautiful, gregarious, and generous. Despite her humble beginnings, she graduated from The Juilliard School of Music in Manhattan, having studied professional opera singing. She went on to teach voice at Juilliard and later toured the world as a member of the New York City Opera company. Although I had never attended one of her professional productions, I was eventually treated to an impromptu, semi-private, solo performance by her.

While I was visiting her as a young girl, she surprised me with an outing to see the movie *Mary Poppins*. The movie theater was large, spacious, and lined with ornately designed, wooden balconies and private boxes. We were seated in the front row at ground level of the packed-to-capacity house. Toward the end of the movie, the lead actor sang a cheerful song with uplifting lyrics, "Let's go fly a kite, up where the air is light…"

After the first refrain, a background chorus in the movie joined in singing. Precisely at this moment, my great-aunt popped out of her seat, then turned and faced the audience. I instantly slipped down in my seat, unsure of what was happening. Then, right on cue and in perfect harmony, she sang along with the chorus, loudly and robustly, in her Julliard-trained operatic soprano voice. As she raised her arms wide open, she graciously shared her gift with all the moviegoers, from ground level to the upper tiers. She confidently and powerfully sang the entire song facing the audience along with the chorus, as though she had been personally invited to do so.

When the song was finished, she calmly turned around and sat back down. As though on cue, the entire audience stood up and gave her a thunderous standing ovation! I slowly slid back up in my seat and cautiously looked around me. My little self was absolutely stunned by her magnificent voice, which I'd never heard before, and the crowd's ecstatic response. I instantly shifted from being slightly embarrassed to feeling immensely proud of her. It was a wonderful surprise, one of those great gifts that life sometimes hands us.

— Pamela Dunaj —

14

Free Shipping

The manner of giving is worth more than the gift.
~Pierre Corneille

y husband's cousin Kyle was having a baby with his wife, Beatrice. As supportive family members, we celebrated in the joy of a new life. But we also had busy lives of our own, and we never found the time to check out their baby registry. Then the baby shower was approaching, but we weren't fretting. We could pick something and get it shipped in time.

We had not anticipated that far more thoughtful family members would have already cleared out a large chunk of the registry. Luckily, there was still a baby stroller that would be both useful and in our price range. Add that to the shopping cart, check out and... We were two dollars short of free shipping, and shipping costs were twelve dollars!

My husband and I are nothing if not economical. We just needed to dig through the registry and find a pair of baby socks for a couple of dollars and we could get free shipping.

Well, drat, the only small item we could find was a pair of four-dollar little red... pacifiers? We weren't quite sure what they were, but they earned us free shipping, so into the cart they went.

A few days later, we were dressed to the nines at the family baby shower. We were a little disappointed, though. We had received a notification that the baby stroller had been delayed in shipping and would arrive a few days late. Though disappointed our gift wouldn't be unwrapped in front of the family, we knew we would simply explain the situation to Kyle and Beatrice, and all would be well.

After telling us they would be welcoming a little girl, Beatrice began to unwrap their gifts. She lifted one small package and read off our names. That was not a baby stroller-sized package at all. My husband and I looked at each other, bemused. Beatrice ripped into the gift packaging we had requested, and then her smile went from courteous to mildly confused.

She swallowed.

She looked at us.

She looked at our grandparents in the crowd, at the young children looking up at the wrapping paper in her hands.

"Thank you… for the nipple covers."

The *what*?

Beatrice politely shuffled the wrapping paper over the pasties and moved on to the next package, but it was too late. Nipple covers rippled through family and friends as they, too, turned to look at us as if searching for answers, and our faces provided none.

We had never once considered that the two items we ordered would be shipped separately. We had never once considered double-checking what we had purchased.

We were able to explain the mix-up to Kyle and Beatrice, and Beatrice laughed until she couldn't breathe. As the years have gone by, Beatrice and Kyle's family has grown, and they still give us a look at their baby showers and ask where the nipple covers are.

—Nan Rockey—

15

Night Sounds

Snoring keeps the monsters away.
~Judy Blume

Uncle Bob and his wife, Aunt Sue, didn't have any children, but they did have a Boston Terrier named Princess. That black-and-white dog was just as spoiled as her name implied. Uncle Bob and Aunt Sue took her everywhere except to work and church. Every time they came to visit my widowed mother and me, they brought Princess with them. I don't know that they ever asked Mom if they could bring Princess in the house, but she came inside anyway.

In their home, Uncle Bob and Aunt Sue had a special corner of the living room for Princess. Since they were gone all day at their jobs, she would lie in her corner with her blanket between her paws, snorting and making odd sounds while she chewed the blanket to shreds. She got a new blanket every year. Her heavy nasal sounds reminded me of an old man in deep slumber. Even when she napped, she lay curled up with her blanket snoring so loudly that it was sometimes difficult to carry on a conversation with my aunt and uncle.

Uncle Bob passed away the year after I graduated from high school. After my mother remarried and I started college in another town, I sometimes spent the weekend with my petite Aunt Sue. Princess greeted me each time but slept in the bedroom with Aunt Sue. Amazingly, Princess never roused when I needed to get up in the night. As I passed Aunt Sue's bedroom door near the bathroom, I could hear the familiar snoring that I had grown to associate with Princess.

When I married my husband, Morris, his job took us out of state, Thankfully, Aunt Sue and Morris got along so well that she told me, "Mary, any time that you and Morris come back to Oklahoma City to visit, I want you to stay with me."

That assured her of the opportunity to visit with us in the evening or in the morning even when we had other demands on our time during our visit.

The first time we stayed with Aunt Sue, Morris asked me, "What's that awful noise coming from Aunt Sue's room? It could lift the roof off this house!"

I assured him, "That's Princess! She has always made that sound."

"That's awful!" he lamented. "I don't see how Aunt Sue can sleep with that racket going on!"

"She's done it for years. I guess she's used to it!"

After a few more visits, we received news that Princess had died. The little dog must have been about thirteen years old when she passed away. That wasn't astonishing news since Boston Terriers have an average lifespan of ten to fourteen years.

On our next visit, Aunt Sue's house seemed quiet without the spirited Princess to greet us when we entered. Her favorite corner appeared empty without her tattered blanket.

The next morning, Morris was laughing while we dressed before breakfast.

I had to ask, "What's so funny?"

He declared, "Princess is still alive!"

"What?" My face must have reflected my puzzled state of mind. "What do you mean?"

Morris explained, "I had to go to the bathroom during the night, and when I passed Aunt Sue's room, I could still hear that awful racket that you always said came from Princess. It never was Princess! It was sweet, little Aunt Sue all along!"

— Mary Hunt Webb —

16

Christmas Ghosts

Remember, as far as anyone knows,
we're a nice, normal family.
~Homer Simpson

y mother and I had recently returned to live in south Mississippi amid our extended family. We had been invited to join one of the adult boys and his family for Christmas. It would be a group of about ten ranging from toddlers to young adults, middle-aged adults and senior citizens, the perfect Christmas mix.

With full stomachs and contented hearts, we watched the children play with their new toys and kept half an eye on the football game airing on the big screen in the living room.

The first tornado alert came about 1:00 P.M. Multiple cell phones chimed. Throughout the afternoon, the warnings came, although we saw no sign of a twister where we were. The children played, oblivious to any threat. The adults kept a tense watch on the skies until the alerts ended.

Later, we got word that a tornado had passed through the county about twenty miles away. One of the young women volunteered to check the conditions for those of us who would be heading home shortly.

She reported back about electricity being out in the vicinity of our house. The shortest way home was blocked by fallen trees, but she saw no other signs of damage out our way.

We stayed a few more hours, hoping to give the authorities time to clear the roads and get the power on again.

It was darker than usual as we drove home, due to the blackout. The only light came from other cars on the highway. I decided to take the long way around in case the trees were still blocking the shortcut, so I followed the interstate north into town. Once I left the highway and accessed the local road to the house, it was pitch black. I kept my focus on the twists and turns of the road. Cattle and chickens had been known to escape their enclosures, and I didn't want to be responsible for killing someone's animal, not to mention damaging my car.

All of a sudden, my mother shrieked.

"What's wrong, Mama?" I asked as I hit the brakes.

"It's ghosts," she yelled, pointing off to her right. "Ghosts are coming after us."

I looked off to the side of the car and caught my breath. After a moment of reflection, I had to bite my tongue to keep from laughing. We were driving past a fenced field. The black cows pastured there were approaching the fence, possibly drawn by the car lights against the dark night. The only visible parts of their bodies were their white faces floating eerily above the ground as they neared us.

"It's okay, Mama. It's just cows," I assured her.

She watched them for another moment until the outlines of their bovine bodies began to take shape in the glow of the headlights. Then she sighed.

"Thank heaven," she said. "I didn't want to be a Scrooge."

We laughed the rest of the way home, glad our Christmas spirit had spared us the necessity of a visit from Christmas ghosts.

— Mary Beth Magee —

17

Salty Mouth, Loving Heart

Why use profanity in real life and writing?
Because sometimes "darn it" just doesn't cut it.
~Jacqueline Patricks

Most of the members of my father's family were people to shy away from, and we didn't have much contact with them when I was young, except for my father's younger brother, Donny. Donny was a big guy with an easygoing, friendly nature, and everyone's favorite out of my father's family. But my heart was won over by his rough-around-the-edges wife, Margot.

Margot had a good heart to match her husband's, but people felt uneasy around her because of her incredibly filthy mouth. In all my life, I have never known anyone to so casually use profanity as Margot. She dropped swear words with a nonchalance that was simply amazing. On others, such a demeanor would have been unacceptable; but I thought that, with Margot, it fit.

Margot was rail-thin, with dirty-blond hair that "looked" dirty. Her usual attire was a pair of faded blue jeans and a wrinkled T-shirt, not to mention the ever-present cigarette that hung from her lips. Margot was a hard worker, unafraid to tackle the roughest jobs, and her calloused hands showed it — no manicured nails and polish for her!

Margot was fluent in all the various dialects of profanity, but her favorite swear word, by far, was the "F word." Margot seemed to find it such a suitable word because it was extremely versatile. That one word could express anger, astonishment, amusement, sadness, or even, amazingly, tenderness. One memory I will never forget is Margot hugging her daughter, the two of them crying over the daughter's broken heart, while Margot repeated over and over, in a surprisingly comforting voice, "I am so f****** sorry, baby."

That was just how Margot was, a woman with a loving heart behind a salty mouth.

As enchanted as I was with Margot's ways, and as lovingly eccentric as I found her, plenty of other people were exasperated with the constant profanity. During one of the occasional visits that my brother and I undertook to see our father and the family he had with his second wife, Janie, this exasperation gave rise to a family legend. I do not have much in the way of good memories, as far as my father's side of the family goes, but this visit provided golden fodder for reminiscence.

My stepmother, Janie, had had enough of Margot's mouth and was complaining loudly about it to me and my brother: "Margot can't say three words without saying f***, and I am just sick of it! I swear, the next time that I hear her use that word, I am just going to haul off and tell her to f*** off!" And, if anyone doubts that God has a sense of humor, let me provide what happened next as evidence to the contrary.

As if on cue, the phone rang, cutting into Janie's tirade. And, of course, who should be on the line but Margot. We plainly heard Margot's cheerful greeting to our stepmother: "Well, Jane, how the f*** are you?" And our stepmother, as she promised, answered right back, "F*** you, Margot!" Such a response might have offended some people, perhaps prompt someone to slam down the phone in anger. But Margot, being Margot, and clearly having no problem with a liberal use of profanity, took it all in stride: "I know how you feel, Jane."

And thus, a golden memory, a family legend, was born. But the story didn't end there, because Margot came over and accompanied all of us to the supermarket. No sooner had we gone in and gotten a shopping cart than a rather fastidious woman approached and engaged Margot in conversation. "I really hope to see you tomorrow, Margot. The church could really use an extra pair of hands." Now *this* was quite a surprise to us. We never imagined Margot to be the church-going type.

But Margot answered enthusiastically that she would be there, adding that she hoped it wouldn't be so f****** hot and that she sure hoped there would be more f****** people to help than last time. My stepmother and brother had stricken looks of horror on their faces, and I could not help but wonder if they were more shocked over Margot's swearing in the middle of the grocery store or over the image of Margot in a church setting.

But the fastidious lady handled it all graciously, with a bright smile lighting up her face, although she did add, "Margot, please try to watch the cussing tomorrow. You know how people get sometimes." Returning the bright smile, Margot answered, "Yeah, I'll try, but no promises. I ask the good Lord for help with my dirty mouth, but I guess he has more important things on his mind." With a conspiratorial wink, the woman gave Margot a squeeze on the shoulder and wished all of us a good day, calling back as she left the store, "Thank you for your help, Margot. I'll see you tomorrow."

As soon as the woman was gone, Janie turned on Margot, the irritation evident in her voice. "How could you talk like that to a *church* woman, Margot? It's bad enough that *we* all have to put up with it, but a woman from the church…" Janie's voice trailed off, at a loss for words over the outrageous situation, but Margot was as unaffected as usual. "Oh, that's Sister Daniel, you know, the pastor's wife. She says I'm probably the only person whose cussin' God always tunes in for."

And with that, the matter was clearly over, at least as far as Margot was concerned.

But I like to think about that day and our ideas of what counts as holy and dignified behavior. In a world where so many people like Aunt Margot are judged for their coarse speech, I have to wonder if, after all is said and done, the only thing that really matters is not so much what a person says but what that person actually does. Perhaps that is the truest measure of a person.

And that is how I like to think of Aunt Margot — a woman with a salty mouth but a loving heart.

—Jack Byron—

Happily Ever Laughter

A Sink Full of Dishes

*Sometimes, I wonder if men and women really suit
each other. Perhaps they should just live
next door and visit now and then.*
~Katharine Hepburn

My parents had a complicated relationship. Dad was a disabled veteran. Mom took care of him and everyone else. She devoted her life to the family business, an adult foster-care home founded by her mother. They had up to sixteen residents at a time to cook, clean and care for.

When Grandma died years before, Mom moved into her apartment at the care home and took over the business. Dad stayed in my childhood home a few doors down. They still saw each other every day and lived as a married couple, just in separate houses.

Dad has always had an aversion to housework, but the inequity in the division of chores was never more obvious than when Mom moved out and stopped cleaning his house. At some point, Dad decided Mom should have to come home and do dishes for him because he didn't want to do them anymore. Mom refused because Dad didn't work and didn't have anything better to do — plus, they were *his* dirty dishes!

She worked her tail off running the care home, mostly by herself, and didn't have time to wash more dishes. When she refused to do Dad's dishes, he protested by letting the dirty dishes pile up all over the kitchen. Soon, both sides of the sink were full and overflowing onto the counters. Still, he refused.

Every time Mom came home, she would remind him to do the dishes, shame him for leaving dirty dishes all over the place, and even threaten to box up all the dishes and make him eat on paper plates. They argued about those dirty dishes for so long that they became a metaphor for all the power struggles in their forty years together.

I remember vividly when my dad bought those dishes for my mom for Christmas. She picked out a stoneware set in a department-store catalog. She loved it because it matched the wallpaper border she hung in our dining room when I was a kid. It had little white geese with blue ribbons around their necks. Dad bought every piece of the set, right down to the salt and pepper shakers. I helped him wrap the boxes and hide them at my grandma's house. Mom loved that set of dishes. She was so proud of it.

One day, after one of their talks about Dad's dirty dishes, my dad decided to reclaim the kitchen counter once and for all. One by one, he carried those dirty dishes to the back door and tossed them into the weeds. He did this until all the dirty dishes were gone.

When Mom discovered he threw all the dishes outside, she was furious. He expected her to be mad enough to go out there and get them, clean them and put them away. Turns out, he was wrong about that. If that was his plan to get her to take care of his dishes, it completely backfired. She left them outside for him to clean up.

Mom died unexpectedly a couple of years ago, but if you go to my dad's house and poke around in the back yard, you can still find those dishes out there in the weeds. Neither of them ever bothered to retrieve them.

As much as it drove him crazy sometimes, he loved my mother's tenacity. She was stubborn as a mule and tough as an ox. She was barely five feet tall and not quite 100 pounds. He was six-foot-one and 250 pounds — and still afraid of her because, as crazy as Dad was, he knew Mom was just a little bit crazier.

— Renee Dubeau —

19

That's Amore

I love being married. It's so great to find one special
person you want to annoy for the rest of your life.
~Rita Rudner

I can't sleep like this!" announced my husband Larry. "It's too bright." All the lights in our bedroom had been turned off, but the streetlights still shone through. I got out of bed and closed all the blinds except for one on a small window. Then it was pitch black.

If we could keep the sun out until late in the morning, maybe Milot the cat would not awaken us too early.

We settled down for the night. The bedroom door remained open so Milot could wander in and out without disturbing us.

I slept soundly until approximately 5:00 A.M. when I heard my husband mumbling.

Talking in his sleep again, I thought. It was a common occurrence. I pulled the covers over my head and rolled over.

A few seconds later, I heard him again, still whispering but more distinctly.

"Come here, sweetness. Come on closer."

Not having had enough sleep, I pretended I didn't hear him. I adore my husband, but there are times when a woman simply needs her privacy and rest.

I tried to ignore him.

"You are so pretty, my little muffin. Come here, baby," he cooed.

How could I resist those tender words of love? So, I turned over to his side and gently wrapped my arm around his chest, hoping this would hold him until later. It came as a shock when I felt his hand on my arm, firmly flipping it off him.

"Come on, Eva. Not now!" he snapped.

Well, I didn't care for that one bit, but I thought, *Okay, I will deal with this tomorrow. But at least now I'll get more sleep.*

That wasn't the end of his affectionate chatter. A minute later, he was at it again.

"Come to me, pumpkin. Let me hold you. Let me pet you. You know you are my beautiful baby girl, don't you?"

Never, ever had he used those amorous words with me! I was getting more than outraged. If it wasn't me to whom he was talking so lovingly, then who was he dreaming about?

The daylight started peeking through the mini blinds on the small window. I opened my eyes and looked at Larry, who was now sitting up in bed still expressing words of love to someone other than me. He was looking to the other side of the room toward the bedroom door. Oh, he was only talking to our cat, sitting by the door. I was relieved and amused. The cat was not responding to his loving words. *Probably waiting for her breakfast,* I thought. *You know cats!*

I could see it bothered him. I watched furtively as he slowly got out of bed. In the partially lit room, he quietly crept to the doorway, still mumbling tender words. "Baby, you're my baby. Yes, we will eat soon. Come back to bed with Daddy. Let me hold you, honey bunch."

I watched as he bent over to pet the cat. It didn't move. I suddenly realized that what was by the door was not the cat after all but Larry's gray gym bag, which he had left on the floor the night before. It was the same size and color as Milot.

There was not enough light in the room for me to see the blush of embarrassment on his face, which I'm sure was there. I didn't laugh. I just whispered gently to him, "Come back to bed, darling. Milot and I are right here for you."

Sure enough, Milot was curled up and purring at the foot of the bed on Larry's side — grateful, I assumed, that the chattering had ended, and she could get to snooze some more.

It was still too dark to see clearly, and I don't know if it's possible, but I could have sworn that cat was smiling, too.

— Eva Carter —

Never Come Between a Man and His Underwear

Why do men like intelligent women?
Because opposites attract.
~Kathy Lette

For longer than I care to admit, I've felt immersed in a sea of testosterone as a wife and mother of sons. In my household of men, I'm often deemed responsible for a missing article of clothing, an important document, or some other random item they think I have mentally catalogued to retrieve within seconds of their request.

Even if it's been missing for weeks.

Why should pieces of their lives strewn across the floor, under a heap of papers on the dining room table or hidden behind a glass in the kitchen be my responsibility?

Because I'm a woman?

I am the chosen one who does most household chores — yes, I am guilty of making their little messes disappear. I do it so often that it's a mindless task. Half the time, I don't remember what I've done with their stuff.

I've thrown a few important things in the trash — leading to their thirty-minute garbage excavation.

I'm sorry, but a tiny piece of paper with an indecipherable list or telephone number doesn't look important to me on a Saturday morning when I'm trying to make the house resemble a normal home.

If I had a dollar for every time I said, "If it's important to you, please put it in a place where you can find it," I'd be richer than crème brûlée.

Truth be told, all this is partially my fault. A stay-at-home mom for fourteen years, I didn't know any better. When everyone returned home from work and school, the house was spotless. I prided myself on keeping everyone's life organized.

Once home, they had nothing to do but mess it up again — and I had nothing better to do but clean it up again. So it seemed.

What year was this anyway, 1950? No, it was the mid-'90s.

Then everything and nothing changed. I went to work outside of the home. My entire house crumbled to the ground. Everyone continued creating their messes. Those little messes snowballed into big messes until the daily chaos assaulted my senses.

I wasn't home all day to make them disappear, but I hoped it would register that I couldn't do it all. It didn't.

I didn't realize the unspoken expectation to carry on as if nothing changed without a blip was the expectation. It became next to impossible to manage.

I wondered how women work, cook, clean, help with homework, attend sporting events, take part in PTA, volunteer for field trips, keep track of bills, schedule doctors' appointments, assist with a home-based business and remain smoking hot — ready to pounce.

Please, I was smoking hot — exhausted.

Was this a sure path to a nervous breakdown? No wonder my grandmother used to get up at 4:00 in the morning. With lots of love and patience, I survived those days.

Fast forward to a year ago. With one foot inside my front door from a hellacious two-hour commute, I glimpsed my husband standing over a pile of his dirty laundry with a quizzical expression.

Before I could slip out of my black Louboutin flats, he asked, "Where is my red underwear? The new pair I just bought."

"Hi, honey. Smooches! Thank you for asking. I had a great day. How was yours? Did you check under the bed, bathroom floor, or the laundry basket stored in the chair behind the bedroom door where you throw most of your stuff?"

I walked straight into the kitchen, opened the refrigerator door, and grabbed the wine bottle. I wasn't about to get roped into spending the next half-hour searching for his red underwear after a hard day's work.

What is it about a man who thinks a woman should always know where all his belongings are?

I guess a man who grew up with his own stay-at-home mom.

"I looked everywhere. Are you sure you didn't do something with them?" he prodded.

"Um, no, Boo, I promise you I'm not harboring your underwear."

"I can't understand it. I just bought them." He padded back and forth down the hallway to the bedroom at least three times, his footsteps sounding like a spoiled child's deliberate thud with each foot landing on the hardwood floor.

What a beautiful monster I had created.

I shot him a side eye as I took a gulp from my wine glass. I'm way past the cutesy sipping stage.

"Isn't this the same underwear you couldn't find last week? May I ask what's so special about this underwear? Don't you have any others that float your boat as much? Is there a secret compartment inside that takes you to a cheerful place?"

With a raised bushy eyebrow, he said, "I don't know what could have happened to them." His concern was disconcertingly sincere. I almost felt sorry for him.

By this time, the empty washing machine was on full throttle. He had started it in anticipation of washing his clothes and got distracted by the missing treasure.

Nature called. He disappeared into the bathroom as I exhaled during my reprieve from cross-examination about his unmentionables.

I overheard him chuckling to himself behind the bathroom door and thought he'd surely lost his mind. I grabbed the bottle off the coffee table and poured another glass of wine.

When he emerged from the bathroom booming with laughter—with his pants scrunched around his knees—I sprayed Chardonnay all over the armchair where I sat watching my own reality show. Whoop — there it is! His red underwear. He was wearing them the whole time.

— Toya Qualls-Barnette —

The Lumpy, Bumpy Wedding Cake

Overachievers don't think reasonably,
sensibly, or rationally.
~John Eliot

Mark and I sat on the overstuffed floor pillows I had made from fake fur and talked about our wedding plans. Flipping through a *Brides* magazine, I casually mentioned that I planned to bake and decorate our wedding cake.

"What? You've never even decorated a birthday cake," Mark said.

"How hard can it be?" I asked. "I've baked and frosted lots of cakes."

"Those were cut-up cakes," he said. "And they were covered in coconut."

"Everyone loved them, including you when I made the race-car cake for your birthday."

"There's a big difference between decorating a one-layer cake covered with coconut and a three-tier cake with roses made from frosting," he said. "It's a lot of work to take on the day before our wedding."

Mark, an engineer, is practical by nature. He's logical, a planner, extremely intelligent, but not a risk taker. Me… I find something I'm interested in and jump in with both feet.

Mark could see the determination in my eyes — the same look I had when I decided to make our bridesmaids' dresses.

"It can't be that hard. If the frosting doesn't work out, I can always decorate with white coconut," I said.

Mark looked at me as if he felt a storm brewing.

The next day, we armed ourselves with parchment bags filled with icing and made frosting roses. My flowers resembled wilted, lopsided cabbages; Mark's flowers looked like the ones on bakery cakes. So, we chose to make sweet peas because they're easier to make, and our version resembled flowers.

We decided our three-tier cake would be cherry chip. The groom's cake would be chocolate oatmeal, which was Mark's favorite.

During the week before the wedding, I baked the cakes and placed them in our freezer and Mark's father's freezer. And I made hundreds of frosting sweet peas.

On Friday, the day before our wedding, I got up early and started enthusiastically working on the cakes. I slowly applied layer upon layer of frosting to a cake, striving to make it perfectly smooth. Uninvited air bubbles and cake crumbs dotted the frosting. So, I applied more frosting, trying to cover the blemishes. Eventually, my enthusiasm wore thin, the frosted cake looked lumpy, and the buttercream frosting was one-inch thick in areas.

In the meantime, Bill, my future father-in-law, and Mark traveled in and out of the apartment, moving in boxes of Mark's things, a bed, a dresser and a coffee table. Their voices and the sound of furniture and boxes gently bumping against the wall should have been signs of merriment. But my head throbbed. I found myself captive in the nightmare world of frosting and cakes.

Every time Bill entered the apartment, he checked my progress. I looked down to avoid eye contact and pretended to be concentrating on icing a cake.

The clock indicated our rehearsal would start in five hours. There I sat, stiff as a board, attempting to smooth frosting on the final cake. I hadn't even gotten to the decorating part yet.

I blinked back tears, trying to control the panic I felt. I could feel Bill looking at me and wished I could disappear. Then Bill said, "I know where we can get help."

After the rehearsal, we loaded the cakes, frosting and frosting flowers into Mark's orange hatchback and journeyed to Maxine's. She was a friend of Bill's and had agreed to decorate our cakes.

The next morning, I woke up smiling in the bed that Mark and his dad had delivered. *It's really happening. Mark and I will be married today,* I thought.

After dating Mark for three years, I knew he was the man I wanted to spend the rest of my life with. Every time I saw him, I felt like I was smiling all over.

I looked at my wedding dress, which hung on the door, and smiled. *Today is going to be perfect,* I thought.

Then I heard footsteps on the stairs, which stopped outside the apartment door. It was Mark—a very tired-looking Mark. His normally well-groomed, red hair was disheveled and hung over his flushed face.

"You're not supposed to see me today. It will bring us bad luck," I said to him, frowning when I saw he carried a cake that looked vaguely familiar.

"Don't worry. We'll be okay," he said and hesitated. "Our cakes need help."

I looked at the pink cake on the platter he held. The frosting was in a pile at the bottom of the cake. Mark confessed that he didn't think about the temperature the prior night, which exceeded over eighty degrees. He left the cakes in the car.

"It was hot. The frosting fell off the side of the cakes," he said, looking contritely at me. "Do you have any frosting flowers left?"

After we spent a couple of hours doing cake restoration, Mark delivered our one-of-a-kind cake to the reception hall.

I looked around the kitchen and dining room. Cake humps, frosting, and pastry bags cluttered our kitchen counter and table. The forgotten groom's cake sat on the counter unfrosted. I was on the verge of tears when my neighbor unexpectedly dropped in. She looked at the chaos and immediately started cleaning as she told me to get ready.

During the reception, Mark and I looked at our wedding cake with the lumpy, sagging frosting. Some flower garlands slid down the side of the cake. Yet, the cake was perfect. Our cake adventures gave us a peek as to what it would be like living together as husband and wife.

Mark is an easygoing, take-charge man, who is patient and supportive of his overeager wife.

My behavior didn't surprise Mark. He'd seen it before when I jumped into projects. I'm his determined, hard-working wife, who is just a little bit high-strung.

Our lumpy, bumpy wedding cake showed us that life is not perfect. Sometimes, imperfections are fun.

— Michele Sprague —

22

Bedside Blunder

*Things could be worse. Suppose your errors
were counted and published every day,
like those of a baseball player.*
~Author Unknown

'd never broken a bone in my body. That record was shattered in the early morning hours of our fiftieth wedding anniversary. I loved my private morning time while my husband still slept. That was my "me time." So, with my latte in one hand, I headed to my garden to pick berries.

I never made it. I became dizzy and woke up several yards away by our kitchen sink, with my favorite cup broken, my hair soaked with latte, and my arm badly skinned. The marble floor was not forgiving. When I tried to stand, I couldn't. I shouted for Steve. He couldn't find me at first. He didn't think to look on the kitchen floor.

It was not quite the fiftieth anniversary we'd planned. I dozed in a hospital bed. Steve was in a chair. Forty-eight hours later, back from surgery, I greeted Steve, saying, "I've been screwed!" In his sleepless stupor, he didn't get it. "Imagine," I explained, "they used a screw to bind me together." My humor faded quickly as I learned my fate: six weeks in a wheelchair. Even gently stepping on my right leg was forbidden.

Truth was, my hip never pained me, not when it happened, not afterward. However, I was a wreck emotionally because I was immobile. I was accustomed to being in charge. Now, Steve cooked, cleaned, and helped me from bed to the bedside commode. The poor guy had to empty it, too.

I felt useless. Steve never complained, though.

One morning, I slept late, woke up, and had to pee. Steve was already up, working somewhere in the house. *I can do this,* I told myself. How proud I was to slowly maneuver out of bed, balance on my left leg, grip the bed, and hop, hop, hop to the potty a foot away.

I plopped down on the seat. I sighed. I closed my eyes in relief. I peed.

I hadn't put in my hearing aids yet, but Steve's shouts registered as though from another world. I swung my head around. I saw his face with exaggerated expressions of terror — really? His mouth moved in anguished shouts.

I panicked, mirroring his reaction. "Are you okay?" I shouted. "What's happened?"

Then, I saw his outstretched hands. They held the pot in which the pee was to go. He'd been dutifully washing it out…

Luckily, our Persian rug didn't show stains. My brain, though, had a picture imprinted on it: Steve, my meticulous husband, on hands and knees mopping up my pee, then scrubbing, then drying.

Finally, that night, when Steve turned out the lights and we lay in bed, we could finally laugh about it. And still do.

— BB Brown —

23

Grease Generously

Keep your eyes wide open before marriage,
half shut afterwards.
~Benjamin Franklin

My husband Bill and I have a happy, healthy relationship based on mutual respect, trust and understanding. We have always been comfortable discussing any topic. We freely express opinions, and we do not keep secrets from one another.

When I saw an e-mail addressed to Bill from a company I did not recognize, with a "rush" delivery date in the subject line, I figured it was another one of his online purchases. He's always looking for the latest gadget. He spends hours thoroughly researching the pros and cons before he makes a purchase. I am not interested in his great buys, but they sure make him happy.

This man of mine has purchased new and improved mouse traps for the tool shed. I no longer have to hard-boil eggs on the stove in a pan of water because he makes them in his electric cooker. There's no more patting ground beef in the palm of his huge hands to make burgers. He has a five-piece, red plastic device that makes uniform patties for his grill.

Since my guy is a late sleeper and I am an early riser, I knew he wouldn't mind my snooping at his "rush" e-mail. I wanted to know what the driver of the Amazon van would soon be delivering. My eyes widened in disbelief as I read the first few words.

"Your order for sanitary lubricant, non-toxic, edible, petrol lube has shipped…."

I Googled the product description: Safe, edible lubricant can also be used on dairy cows.

What the heck?! We live in suburbia, not on a cattle farm. We get our milk in cartons from the store. Granted, my big guy does drink two and sometimes three gallons a week.

My imagination was running wild as I reread the e-mail. Then I thought, *What sort of secret life has he been leading? I'd better not discover he has a secret heifer somewhere.*

I'm certain my blood pressure was sky high by sunrise when I heard my honey waking up. I resisted the impulse to pounce. I sat impatiently waiting for him to complete his morning routine and come into the study.

Cheerful as ever, my husband of twenty-five years walked in and laid his big hand gently on my shoulder. He kissed my neck and said sweetly, "Good morning."

Laying it on thick, my suspicious mind thought.

I swiveled around in my office chair and looked up at him. I stared straight into his eyes. "Is there something you want to talk to me about?" I maintained my composure, but inside I was quivering.

"No, not really. You doing okay?" His smile lit up his big Irish face. He ran his fingers through his curly mop. His grin faded as he waited expectantly for my reply. I continued to stare at him.

He asked, "Everything all right?"

I said, "I don't really know. Is there something I need to know? Do you need to tell me anything?"

"I love you?"

"No!"

"You want to go out to breakfast?"

"Nope."

"Then what? What would you like to know?" His smile faded.

"I need the truth. I want you to tell me why you ordered personal edible lubricant off the Internet." My words were thick. I was holding back hot tears, devastated by the thought of my decent, devoted husband cheating on me.

He stared. "Oh, um, that…" He looked confused.

I wanted to shout, "Don't you dare lie to me!" Instead, I said, "Do not say, 'Um.' You are using a stall tactic. Please be honest with me."

He looked hurt. "I've never been dishonest with you."

"Well?! Tell me why you need that lubricant."

His smile broadened. "I need lubricant for the new meat slicer that was delivered yesterday. The drive gear, pivot points, and blade all need to be generously lubricated before and after using it. The brochure said to use Vaseline, but when I went to the store to purchase a jar, I read the label, which stated the product was not to be used orally. And, honey, your facial expression doesn't compare to the young pharmacist's when I asked him if they carried edible Vaseline behind the counter. The guy was speechless. When I explained the intended use, he said, 'Try Amazon.'"

Tears started rolling down my cheeks as I laughed myself silly with relief. I could envision the poor pharmacist, whose imagination had probably been running as wild as mine.

I am going to order my gadget man a white bib apron for when he uses his latest device. He now purchases hunks of meats instead of pre-sliced products.

We've eaten so much shredded ham, sliced beef, and shaved turkey that my butcher is soon going to need a new tube of lube.

— Linda O'Connell —

24

In a Pickle

Never say, "Oops." Always say, "Ah, interesting."
~Author Unknown

As I recited my shopping list in my best broken Italian, I noticed the grocery clerk's face turn deep red, then almost purple. Was he having a heart attack right in front of me?

We had just moved back to Italy, and I was trying my best to learn Italian. We had lived here for a short time years earlier, so I had already learned some words and phrases. But this time around I wanted to study the language in earnest, using every spare minute to listen to lessons and watch videos. I even put Post-it notes on objects in the house, labeling everything in sight in Italian. By hook or by crook, I was determined to learn quickly.

We kept a grocery-shopping list on the kitchen wall, adding items as needed until we made a trip to the store. I encouraged my husband to write things down in Italian so I would get used to reading the language and speaking to the clerks in Italian.

We had kept in contact with the Italian friends and acquaintances we had made from our first stay in Italy, so we decided to get reacquainted with them by holding a housewarming party. At the gathering, they all seemed charmed and amused at my efforts to learn their language, noting the Italian labels I had plastered all over the house and my Italian grocery list. I spoke to them in my broken Italian throughout the party and marveled that I was already able to understand and participate in simple conversations.

The next day, feeling confident, I grabbed the shopping list and headed to the grocery store alone. Once there, I managed to translate most things on the list and find them on my own. But there were some things on the list I just didn't understand.

So, I searched out a clerk and tried to talk to him in Italian, sounding out the strange items on the list to the best of my ability. That's when his face turned fifty shades of red.

Quickly composing himself, he asked in perfect English to see the list I was holding.

"Perhaps someone has been playing a trick on you," he said. "There are items on this list that are not available in any grocery store."

Then the penny dropped. While hanging around the kitchen eating snacks and having drinks, our guests from the party also "adjusted" my shopping list with some salty language. I explained it to the clerk, who had a laugh about the whole thing.

However, he said, there was one item that he could fulfill, which would turn the tables and get the last laugh. The final item on the list was for "pickles the size of my husband's manhood." He would get me a large container full.

So that's how we ended up with a huge jar of the tiniest baby pickles.

Buon appetito!

— Donna L. Roberts —

25

The BU Tie

To achieve the nonchalance which is absolutely
necessary for a man, one article
at least must not match.
~Hardy Amies

My husband has an amazing number of excellent qualities. Fashion sense is not one of them. Most of the time, he wears blue jeans or khakis, so this is not a problem. On Sundays, however, I am often consulted about which ties go with which shirts and pants. My husband loves ties and has a huge collection. Somewhere along the line, however, he acquired one (from where, I do not know) that I kindly refer to as the "butt ugly" (BU) tie.

The BU tie has a brown background covered with a pattern of gold foliage. Every so often, he will trot out this tie and ask if it goes with whatever he is wearing. My answer is always the same.

"No, that tie doesn't go with what you're wearing. It doesn't go with anything you own." For that matter, it probably doesn't go with anything anyone else owns either, but I refrain from saying this.

"But I have on a yellow shirt," he will attempt to argue.

"You're also wearing blue pants. The brown does not go with the blue. Maybe if you got some brown pants, you could wear that tie."

"I don't like brown pants," he will say.

"Then you really don't have anything that goes with that BU tie."

He will look hurt for a moment. "I like this tie," he'll mutter.

You're the only one, I will think but never say.

So, the tie goes back into the closet for another few months before the ritual is repeated.

A while back, my husband's brother and his wife came to visit for a few days, and my brother-in-law forgot to bring a tie for church. My husband told him to take his pick from the multitude of beautiful ties hanging in his closet. Guess which one he picked? Seriously.

"Hah!" my husband crowed. "Look at which tie David picked!"

"Not the BU tie." I couldn't believe my eyes. "Well, at least he's wearing brown pants."

"What's wrong with this tie?" my brother-in-law asked.

There was nothing I could say. Obviously, the lack of fashion sense is a genetic defect that runs in my husband's family. You can't explain that to people who just don't get it.

— Ellen Fannon —

26

For Better or For Worse

Family: we may not have it all together,
but together we have it all.
~Author Unknown

I scanned the room, taking a final sip of water as Olivia, the maid of honor, finished her speech and hugged her sister at the head table. So many of these faces were people I had known for years, and yet I was nervous. Standing up, I glanced at my date, who smiled encouragingly as she held my phone to record my words. I looked at Mike and Brooke as I accepted the microphone from Olivia. Mike's eyes were steady and trusting. I took a deep breath, faced the guests, and began.

"In most sets of wedding vows, there's a line or two about taking one another for better or for worse…" I met the eyes of several people who leaned forward a bit, wondering exactly where I was heading with these words. You see, Mike's choice of a best man was a little odd. In addition to choosing a woman, which isn't completely unheard of, he had chosen his ex-wife, which absolutely is. Nearly half the people in this room — his family members — had celebrated at our wedding reception twelve years prior. And while it is not uncommon for former spouses to maintain cordiality and cooperation, particularly when children are involved, it is uncommon for them to be closer as friends than they were as romantic partners.

We had known each other since age twelve, dated in junior high, lost touch, and reconnected in our late twenties after I had left the

Army (or so I thought). We fell into a comfortable relationship, and he proposed. Ten days later, I received orders in the mail recalling me to active duty for service in Iraq. We rushed a wedding, and I left for seventeen months. Our daughter was born two years after I returned from Iraq. While we experienced a brief period of contentment in our daughter's earliest years, we spent the rest of our marriage in triage, attempting to bandage the wounds between two best friends who were incompatible as partners.

Divorces are phenomenally painful, even when they are the best and perhaps only option for a couple. I felt at times that it would have been easier if we had not been such good friends. We loved each other deeply without being in love. As a result, the dissolution of our marriage was agonizing. We recognized that we both deserved real love and happiness, but we grieved the end of our marriage like a death in the family, and we grieved the future that would no longer exist.

On my first night in my new house, as my daughter played with toys in our new living room, I locked myself in the bathroom and, sobbing uncontrollably, called Mike.

"I think I was wrong," I gasped through my tears. "This was a mistake."

"You weren't wrong," he replied in his typical, rational fashion. "You saved us. We actually get along now!"

He was absolutely right: Our marriage was over, but we were developing a connection far more real than we had experienced thus far. It wasn't always easy. A personable, attractive, charismatic police officer, Mike did not wait long before kindling a romance with a woman he had known for some time. I was far more affected than I had a right to be; after all, I had initiated the divorce. I couldn't clearly identify the problem. I wasn't jealous, and Brooke was devoted to Mike and kind to my daughter. Perhaps I struggled because she was my exact opposite. Perhaps I struggled because I felt I had been too easily "replaced."

I didn't struggle long; Brooke is kind, considerate, and generous, and I was very blessed that Mike found real love in the form of a woman who has treated our daughter like she is her own. It would take longer for me to experience that same type of true, enduring love, but when

I did, it reinforced Mike's assertion that I hadn't been wrong to think that we both deserved better than we were able to provide for each other. Setting our pride aside and focusing on love allowed us to heal together and continue to live in a different kind of partnership.

It has been three years since our divorce and eighteen months since Mike's wedding. Several of my friends joke that our lives would make an engaging Friday night sitcom. Mike and I have access to each other's homes and are regular visitors. It has not been an uncommon occurrence for me to return home to find my kitchen cabinets all open or a plastic spider sitting in my microwave. Ever the prankster, Mike has not allowed his affinity for surprising me to wane. We help each other with projects, adjust comfortably to changes in logistics for our daughter, and even vacation together on occasion. Mike and Brooke's son is my godson and being a part of his life has brought me much joy.

Instead of opening a window when God closes a door, he sometimes builds an entirely different structure. Unbeknownst to us, when Mike and I took our marriage vows, we were committing to a lifelong friendship that would navigate both the "for better" and "for worse" times. By adapting to change readily, we've cemented a bond that continues to enrich our lives and the lives of our families. Eighteen months ago, as I raised my glass, toasted the happy couple, and met the shining eyes of the groom, I had no idea that I would one day be writing about my divorce with a joyful, grateful heart.

—Marissa Mitchell—

We're All Nuts Here

27

Pepper Roulette

Life expectancy would grow by leaps and bounds
if green vegetables smelled as good as bacon.
~Doug Larson

I drove excitedly down the barren street of the little Michigan town. It had been a decade since I had been back to visit all my family in the great mitten, and I was so excited for my husband to finally meet my Michigan family. I wanted him to see all the beauty of this state, which had captured my heart from the first moment I had visited during my childhood.

We had coordinated to go out the same time as my grandparents, which made it a special opportunity to spend time with them, as well as visit with the rest of the family, some of whom I had never met. It was a journey down Family Tree Lane, and it was more than I could stand that morning, as I wasn't sure if I would be able to remove the giant grin from my face as we drove to visit one of my pairs of great-aunts and -uncles.

"Now, how are Shirley and Gary related?" my husband inquired.

"This is my sister, the only living sibling I have left, and her husband," my grandfather explained.

"Wow, the size of the plots here for the houses is incredible," my husband commented as we pulled into their driveway. This was a more rural suburbia than we were used to in Denver. There was space out here; you felt as if you could breathe.

As we made our greetings, we ended up out back chatting with my great-aunt and -uncle, my grandparents, and some other cousins and family members who had made their way over to visit. I found myself wandering in the garden that Uncle Gary had growing, which was the size of our entire back yard. I was admiring rows and rows of Hungarian wax peppers when my great-uncle came up next to me and remarked, "It's about time for a pepper fry."

"A pepper fry?"

"Don't tell me you have never been to a pepper fry before?" Uncle Gary looked astounded.

"I can't say I have ever had a fried pepper, just roasted for green chili," I responded.

"Well, we are going to have to fix that!" he exclaimed. Next thing I knew, he had retrieved the deep fryer from the garage and had it plugged in on the back porch, warming up and getting ready to fry up some peppers. We all went out together and picked a bucket full of peppers. By the time we had picked them and placed them in the bucket, the fryer was ready. We dropped them in one by one, and my great-aunt Shirley had a serving plate out and waiting for them.

We all sat together around the big wooden table in the back yard. Aunt Shirley had brought out plates and beers for everyone. As we all gathered a gaggle of peppers onto our plates, my great-uncle prefaced our fried pepper snack with a small warning: "Now, these peppers are like Russian roulette. Tasty, but you never know the bite they are going to have until you bite into one, regardless of whether you remove the seeds and veins. But don't worry; it's never unbearable." He winked at us all, biting into his first pepper without any trepidation.

We all nodded in understanding, had our beers at the ready, and began to dig in. The first bite of the fried pepper was heavenly: tasty and juicy with a little zip. Perfection. The conversation flowed as we caught up with each other's doings.

The next pepper I bit into was the same. We continued to catch up, eat our fried pepper snacks, and drink our beers.

The third pepper I bit into... *Holy smokes!* I thought. *Is this a ghost pepper?* I had never had anything light my mouth on fire like this! I chugged my beer and discreetly got another one, thinking, *What I really need is a glass of milk!* But there was no way I was going to let anyone know what a sissy I was.

I pushed the insanely hot pepper off to the side and reached for another one to test, hoping it was less fiery and more heavenly — like the first two. As luck would have it, it was a tamer pepper. As I looked around, I saw the rest of my family members silently suffering and doing the same. A drip of sweat ran down the cheek of my second cousin, and tears were in Uncle Gary's eyes. Aunt Shirley was wise and only ate out of a jar of pickled Hungarian wax peppers, which the rest of us reached for as well in hopes of alleviating the fire in our mouths.

It was quite apparent that everyone was suffering from the fire of one pepper or more on their plate, but no one said a word about it. We continued eating fried peppers for hours that evening, drinking beers in attempt to put out the fire, and catching up on conversations long overdue.

Finally, one of the younger children at the gathering came tottering over to the table and reached for a pepper.

"No! You can't eat that," one of my family members exclaimed with a sense of urgency.

"Oh. And why is that? You all seem quite content sitting there and eating them yourselves," Aunt Shirley said mockingly.

"Well, because some of these peppers are hot as heck!" Everyone burst into an uproar of laughter. "I don't know why we keep eating them," one of my uncles exclaimed heartily. Tears streamed from his eyes, more likely from the heat of the peppers but definitely doubled by the laughter that was now resounding around the table. My great-aunt laughed along as well, and we finally gave up the gambit and brought out some perch caught earlier that morning.

Every year when we plant a garden, we are always sure to include some Hungarian wax peppers. We continue the pepper-fry tradition when we have guests.

— Gwen Cooper —

28

That's Italian!

The big lesson in life, baby, is never be scared
of anyone or anything.
~Frank Sinatra

Growing up in my house was kind of like living out a sitcom where the Italian stereotypes were so strong that you could smell the garlic:

- Fitted clear plastic covers adorned our living room furniture. They made noises when someone sat on them, but that was rarely allowed.
- Every adult relative in my life smoked cigarettes except my three grandmothers.
- Each of my three grandmothers lived past ninety, shrunk as she aged, wore pajama-style housecoats daily, and occasionally wore hairnets all day long in the house and out. They did not drive nor did they own jeans or sneakers.
- Talking was done loudly with grand hand gestures.
- Price dropping happened; if it was expensive, that made it good.
- We always said what was on our minds.
- A good argument made life a little more interesting.
- Curse words were common practice.
- If things went wrong, LOUD quitting seemed appropriate!
- I was not raised to wait for others to stop speaking or even to swallow my food before sharing my thoughts.

- There was always extended family around.
- The refrigerator was always emptied for unexpected company.
- Relatives guaranteed a good kiss or two. Everybody was getting a hug!
- There was amazing food around all the time, and everyone ate every meal until they were Thanksgiving-full. (I was thirty years old before that unhealthy habit caught up with me.)
- We had a basement kitchen where most of the cooking was done.
- Planned company meant a lot of everything—the bigger the better!
- If someone had an Italian name, then he/she was probably a little better than anyone else.

My father was Pete the Barber in his own shop. My mom, Marie, worked part-time jobs to pay for our family's insurance because my father was self-employed. It was the dawning of the "latch-key generation." Not for my brother and me, though, because my paternal grandmother lived with us.

Pete was a "guys' guy." He knew everybody by name and introduced everyone as a friend. If he overheard that something needed getting done, he had the connection and the resources to get it "settled." He "knew a guy..."

"You need your sink fixed? I gotta guy," he'd say, always ready to hook up his "friends" with other friends who could be "of service." And when he met someone for the first time, it didn't matter what that person did for a living or what hobbies were mastered. My dad had been waiting for just that skill for a long time!

"You're a dermatologist? You don't say? See, I've been wondering about this mole here."

"You're a pipefitter? Hey, could you line some pipe in my basement? We've got a slow leak from somewhere."

"A teacher? My son could really use some help with his math homework."

"You play guitar in a band? I have a customer who's getting married, and he's looking for entertainment for the wedding."

"What kind of car do you drive? I'll bet you need a good mechanic."

What's even better than knowing the right person for every job is "paying" for services with spaghetti sauce! Certain that no neighbor could acquire an Italian dinner quite as good as my mother or my grandmother (and probably accurately so), my parents would often offer pasta in return for a favor.

The neighbor cleaning his gutters would soon be climbing our ladder to pull leaves out of our gutters as well. Later, he'd get about a hundred of Grandma's meatballs and a pot of sauce. The driver who took Grandma home from the grocery store on Mondays received monthly lasagnas. The lady two doors down, affectionately known as "Mrs. Mary," who exquisitely wrapped gifts for my mom, was fond of homemade Chicken Vesuvio, and whenever Mom made it, plenty was shared with her.

Today, my father still gives dinner to the young neighbors next door every time he makes a pot of sauce. They think he's kind but don't realize they are being reimbursed for occasionally shoveling Pete's driveway and tending to his technology mishaps.

None of this ever struck me as funny until I was well into adulthood. I also did not realize how well or how much we ate.

Friends invited for dinner would warn each other (and later my prospective boyfriends) not to say, "That's all right," when asked if they wanted more of anything that was being served. "Always say, 'No, I'm full!'" Seconds always meant another plateful, and dinner with the Farellas was not for wimps.

Another thing that would catch dinner guests off guard was the grandmothers' open use of colorful language. I remember one of my childhood friends observing, "Wow! Your grandmother swears." I didn't know to be embarrassed then. Doesn't everyone's grandmother speak like that?

It took years for me to realize the quirks with which I'd grown up were classically funny. The stories of how I grew up, where I came from, and what the big personalities of my life had been through and put me through were more like party entertainment.

Only expensive collectors' pieces (like Lladros and Waterford) were allowed in the living room. The china cabinet was huge and jammed with Italian china. White and gold were accent colors throughout the entire house. Name brands were always purchased and often referred to by price. Less was never more. Less was just less.

God was responsible for all that was good. My mother was not afraid to go down on her hands and knees and praise our Lord, or colorfully blame Him if she wasn't happy with something. Mom and the grandmothers also had many religious statues and rosaries. The children would someday marry good Catholic-Italian spouses and inherit their own set of Lladros and rituals. When my mother confronted me on the phone (I was in my thirties at the time) because she'd heard that I was "dating a red-haired Irishman," I knew there'd be holy water tossed in all directions on that one. And I also knew that, despite that, he was in for a really good meal!

—Gina Farella-Howley—

29

I'm Stuck

I don't have awkward moments. I have an awkward
life, occasionally interrupted by normalcy.
~Robert Pattinson

How does a woman get wedged between a toilet and a tub, with tears streaming down her face, laughing so hard that she has to clench her muscles to not pee herself? Funny you should ask...

It was our last night in Florida. We had gone on an impromptu girls' trip — my aunt, cousin, sister and me. For four days and three nights, we had done nothing but laugh the whole trip. My aunt and I met my cousin, who flew in from college, and my sister, who flew in from Tennessee, and the trip began.

On the day of our arrival, we were trying on bathing suits in one of those stores that sells a little bit of everything Florida: knickknacks made from seashells, T-shirts, postcards, key chains with Florida logos, and racks and racks of bathing suits. The dressing room consisted of a few booths along the wall of the store with drapes running across the front for privacy. My sister and I went into the booths to try on suits while my aunt and cousin looked around. My sister decided right away to buy hers, but I was unsure. It didn't seem to fit right. I came out into the store for some help, and the store owner burst out laughing, telling me I had tied the bikini bottom on as a top. "I just thought I was built lopsided!" I told her as she handed me the actual top.

Later that day, my cousin and I did cannonballs into the pool, making huge splashes and embarrassing my sister and aunt. Whether they were embarrassed because we were doing cannonballs into the water or were plugging our noses while doing them, I'll never know.

We teased my aunt as she got hit on by a good-looking, older gentleman in swim trunks. We teased each other about our younger handsome waiter until he started talking in a squeaky voice, and we all burst out laughing after he walked away.

One night on the beach, we convinced my aunt to climb on a chained beach bike for pictures. It was huge, with tires as tall as we were, and it was made for riding on the sand. We took turns taking pictures on it, ignoring the signs warning people to stay off. My aunt, a rule-follower, was reluctant and the last to go. When she finally agreed and climbed on the bike, the flashing lights of the beach police came driving up the beach. We all took off running, leaving my aunt there by herself to climb down and get away.

In another souvenir store, my cousin and I were reading off magnets with funny sayings. I read one wrong and realized that what came out of my mouth (rather loudly) was not what was written but instead an offensive and inappropriate word. I ran out of the store, leaving her there to pay for the items with an offended clerk. My cousin came out of the store glaring and found me both mortified and doubled over in laughter.

On the last night, we were hyped up on vibes from a great trip. We talked about everything we had done. I swam in the ocean for the first time and exclaimed over the saltiness of it. We lay in the hot sun and let the warmth melt away the stress. We watched dolphins frolicking along the shoreline and watched sunrises and sunsets with the sound of the ocean waves serenading us. We found beautiful seashells to bring home to our children and bottled up some sand to remind ourselves of the beauty we had found. We caught up on each other's lives, laughed so hard our stomach muscles ached, and made great memories. It had been the perfect vacation, and we weren't ready for it to be over.

My cousin, with her video camera out, was asking us questions and recording us while we packed to go home the next day and get ready for bed. My sister went into the bathroom to brush her teeth, and we decided we should scare her. My cousin tiptoed to one side of the bathroom door with her video camera ready, and the door opened just as I reached the other side. "Boo!" I yelled, as loudly as I could. My sister screamed and fell backward, arms pinwheeling.

My aunt came running, and we all stared down at Jessica. My sister was red-faced, hands clutching her chest, tears streaming out of her eyes, and shoulders heaving with gasps of laughter. She stared up at us, firmly wedged between the tub and the toilet.

"You guys," she exclaimed, "I'm stuck!"

—Tia Marie Ruggiero—

30

Psychic Baby Babs

*Obviously, if I was serious about having a relationship
with someone long-term, the last people I would
introduce him to would be my family.*
~Chelsea Handler

My two daughters were attending college in Boston. Now, in my fifties, I was free to ignite all my newfound passions. Among them was my desire to attend clown training and entertain children in my city's annual Thanksgiving parade. So, I diligently practiced my slapstick routines and learned how to pull twenty-five-foot, coiled paper streamers out of my mouth to amaze the masses.

The Barnum & Bailey and Big Apple Circus pros explained the dos and don'ts of clowning. You have seconds to get a laugh and move on to the next group along the parade route. Keep your distance with the marching bands as a courtesy to musicians who are afraid of clowns. Work independently instead of in "clown gangs" that can intimidate children. Beware of the teenagers who like to pull off wigs. Stay away from string-streamer sprays that stain the expensive, rented costumes. Don't use mouthwash; the scent makes parents think the clowns are drunk. And on and on... Who knew?

After days of intense training, my character, Baby Babs, was ready for the mission ahead. I had researched the many faces of clown make-up and knew that keeping it simple was best. I'm 5'2", so I could pull off a baby-doll costume complete with pink hair, a huge baby bib, bottle and pacifier, colorful ribbons on my sneakers, striped stockings, short white gloves, and a ruffled pink-and-white dress with lots of pockets to carry my props.

Although I didn't have to be there until 10:00 A.M., I set my alarm for 6:00 A.M. to prepare for the nine hours ahead, gently stretching out my calves, quads, back, neck, and arms like a contortionist warming up for a circus act. I would need my stamina to squat every few yards to put children at ease by being at their eye level.

The oil-based grease paint had to be put on in strategic layers, setting each one with baby powder so it couldn't wash off with water or perspiration. We were taught the trade secret of filling a white tube sock with baby powder and gently patting the face after each application. Then the eyebrows had to be evenly drawn on the forehead, and only the bottom lip got colored. During one training workshop, I made the mistake of not using a clean part of the sock and smudged pink and purple "bruises," making me resemble an abused clown. I had the arduous task of soaking cotton pads with baby oil to wipe off the entire face and start over.

Signing in at the parade tent, I found a magical place filled with bagpipers, police officers, acrobats on stilts, uniformed bands, dance teams and, of course, Santa with Mrs. Claus and Mr. Jingles. I could only take small sips of water and eat a small snack since there was no stopping along the route for bathroom breaks.

We were divided into groups of about a dozen clowns and transported in golf carts to our assigned starting points to warm up the crowd and walk the 1.5-mile route of the parade. Once the giant Scooby-Doo balloon appeared, it was time for my two friends and me to commence our practiced skits for young and old. My friends had volunteered for years and had recruited and coached me; one was even certified to visit children in the hospitals. I felt confident in the company of these seasoned pros.

Walking the pavement, I kept hearing children call out, "Baby clown! Baby clown!" Among the crowd, a woman with a little boy in a stroller and an adorable, little girl about five years old eagerly summoned me. As I approached, it suddenly hit me: *I know that face.*

I know that face! I had seen that face in a photo somewhere recently. The city said that 200,000 people were attending the parade! This woman was the one person I shouldn't run into.

My daughter had just started dating a young man she met at a college party. As fate would have it, he was born and raised in our hometown. Although they had attended different schools, they had many mutual friends. I had seen a handful of photos and now I realized that the woman at the parade was the boyfriend's mom!

My mischievous mind instinctively concocted a caper. I intently pressed my fingers to my forehead and with concentrated squinting (like any good mind reader), I said, "Do you have a son?"

She replied, "Yes!"

I pretended to struggle with my intuition as she waited with bated breath. "I see a new girl in his life."

"Yes!" she exclaimed.

"I get a K for her name."

At this point, the woman's eyes widened and her jaw dropped as she stared in disbelief at the psychic clown. I could no longer contain myself and finally confessed my crime, admitting that I was the girl's mom. We began hysterically laughing as she threw her arms around me and asked to take cell-phone photos, making faces as we all posed with my giant baby bottle and pacifier.

When I returned home, tired but proud of my accomplishments, my husband stared at me with an impish smirk. "You better call your daughter." Unbeknownst to me, she happened to call home that afternoon, asking where I was. Upon hearing I was at the parade, she begged him, "Dad, please stop her!" Finding out I had been taking clown classes mortified her, and the realization her friends would find out her mother was a clown was unequivocally embarrassing. But it was too late. By this point, the Thanksgiving Parade was long over, and her boyfriend's mom had already proudly posted the photos all over the Internet. Gasp.

Fast forward thirteen years, and my daughter married that wonderful, young man and started a family. His mother also attended clown training and joined me in the annual Thanksgiving Parade. I foresee that our grandchildren's lives will undoubtedly be colored with magic, love, and laughter.

—Barbara Espinosa Occhino—

31

The Escape Artist

In the world of mules, there are no rules.
~Odgen Nash

It was another telephone call in the middle of the night. They were always from one of our unamused neighbors, stating, "Jack, your mule is down here in our yard again."

Dad would be standing in the kitchen wearing his pajamas and we'd hear him say, "Uh-huh... okay... again, I'm sorry. I'll be right down."

He always hung up the phone, shook his head, and asked himself, "How does she keep doing this?"

It was always the same old routine. Dad would roust us four oldest boys out of bed and we'd hop into Dad's pickup and go on a moonlight mule round-up.

Getting Shadow back home was never a problem. Upon arriving at our neighbor's, Dad knew how to lure Shadow within his grasp. Was it with a carrot? An apple? Sugar cubes? Nope. Shadow loved one thing: my dad's cigar smoke.

So, Dad would use a lighted cigar to lure Shadow close enough to grab her halter. Then, once Dad had a firm grip, he would put the cigar in Shadow's mouth, and she would actually smoke it.

The moonlight mule roundup ended with Dad driving back home and one of his boys — usually Jerry — being tasked with walking Shadow back.

The next day, my dad always conducted the same inspection: He checked the barbed wire fence all the way around Shadow's domain. And that fence was always perfectly intact — no holes, no low spots, no nothing — so Shadow wasn't squeezing out there.

Secondly, our pond formed a physical barrier on the front of Shadow's three acres. Dad and we boys had intentionally built a white, wooden fence down into the pond on both sides. That pond was a good ten feet deep, so Shadow wasn't wading around the fence to escape.

Again, Dad would scratch his head, asking himself, "How does she keep getting out?"

Then came that fateful Sunday afternoon when my dad was relaxing with his cane pole, fishing in our pond. He was sitting in front of the white, wooden fence with a cold bottle of Blatz, watching his bobber.

Suddenly — SPLASH!

Dad looked to his left, and he couldn't believe his eyes.

There was Shadow, in broad daylight, swimming around the white fence! Upon wading ashore on the side of freedom, Shadow promptly bolted... most likely to one of our neighbors' yards.

Dad simply shook his head, arose, and walked into the house... to await the inevitable phone call.

I'll bet that our family had the only swimming mule in the entire state of Ohio that also smoked cigars.

— John Scanlan —

32

Breakfast with Raphael

Sister to sister we will always be,
a couple of nuts off the family tree.
~Author Unknown

"The chicken is wearing a diaper." The fact that the bird was standing on the dining table and pecking at a bowl of Cheerios also concerned me, although I neglected to mention it.

"What? We're having breakfast," my sister Natalie responded as if I were the oddball in the room before slurping another spoonful of cereal from her bowl.

Now would seem like the proper time to mention that my sister lives on a farm, but she doesn't. Nor does she live in the country. Not even the suburbs. Natalie's home is the small apartment located above the DIY jewelry shop she started two years earlier. And her roommate is a fluffy chicken with an attitude problem.

"I'm not eating breakfast with a chicken."

"Come on. Raphael is a sweetie. She already loves you. Go ahead and give her a hug."

Raphael stopped pecking her Cheerios long enough to lift her head and glare at me. Not to be shown up by a chicken, I glared right back. I started to think that I had won the stare-off battle until Raphael rocked her rump, and an appetite-suppressing splat sounded in her diaper.

"Aww, did you go poopy?" Natalie cooed as if talking to a baby.

With an eyeroll, I grabbed the box of cereal and stomped back to my temporary, makeshift room — all while ignoring the continual baby talk coming from my sister as she changed Raphael's diaper.

I had looked everywhere possible before moving in here. My sister and I had grown apart over the years, though, and this was the first time I had seen her for longer than an hour. The fact that she owned a jewelry store and had a pet chicken had been news to me.

I was doing my best to make do with this last resort arrangement after leaving my husband and the office we both had worked at for ten years. I was broke, homeless, and without a job. Goodbye, designer wear; hello, thrift store. And hello, Raphael.

My sister had offered me a job in her shop, but I had declined. I went off to look for jobs that day, but it was tough. We were in the middle of the 2008 recession. I returned to my sister's apartment that evening with a stack of resumes in my hand, and my feet dragging.

"How did it go?" Natalie called over her shoulder — the one not occupied by Raphael.

"I don't want to talk about it."

"Look, the offer still stands...."

"I don't want to work with you!" I suddenly shouted, sending Raphael into a flurry of flapping feathers. "I don't want to make crappy jewelry! I don't want to eat breakfast next to a pooping chicken! I don't want to be here!" I threw my purse and the resumes onto the floor. "I miss my nice apartment and designer furniture. I miss my upscale breakfasts and luxury lifestyle. But Erik cheated on me, so now I'm stuck here with an attitude-infested chicken who thinks anything that's mine is hers to scratch."

I fell onto the futon and wept into the palms of my hands.

In that quiet, comforting voice from back when we were kids, Natalie asked, "Do you want to hug Raphael?"

Wiping the tears out of my eyes enough to be able to see the fluffy bird standing five inches from my face, I nodded my head and sniffled, "Yes."

— Katrin Babb —

Buckets of Love

*I'm a big fan of dreams. Unfortunately, dreams are our
first casualty in life — people seem to give them up,
quicker than anything, for a "reality."*
~Kevin Costner

"Kevin Costner and his band are coming to Kansas City," my sister Amy told me. She knew I was the movie star's biggest fan. She also knew that seeing him in person was an unfulfilled item on my bucket list.

"He has a band?" I asked.

"They're playing at Knuckleheads. It's an old biker bar that has concerts now."

I called my daughter Becky who knows how to buy concert tickets on the Internet. "Kevin Costner's band is coming to Knuckleheads," I said.

"He has a band?" she asked.

"Yes. Will you buy tickets for me?"

The last time I'd bought tickets for anything was before home computers. I stood in line outdoors on a freezing January day for Neil Diamond tickets. Tickets for every other concert I attended came from friends who were selling theirs.

I had recently tried to use my phone to order tickets for a Willie Nelson concert in Columbia, Missouri, two hours from my Kansas City home. After entering my seat selection and debit-card number, and just before I hit BUY NOW, I discovered that the concert was in Columbia, Maryland, not Columbia, Missouri. The print on my phone screen was a little small. I had mistaken the D in the abbreviation MD for an O, as in MO. Relieved that I hadn't dropped several hundred dollars for nothing, I vowed not to try that again.

Becky agreed. She said she and her boyfriend, Marc, would go with me and my husband, Ken.

I called my friend Deborah. "Kevin Costner and his band are coming to Kansas City, and I'm going!"

"He has a band?" Deborah asked.

Deborah knew all about my bucket list.

My bucket list really says, "Ride in a limousine with Kevin Costner." I added it because of a romantic scene in the back of a limousine in *No Way Out*.

"Maybe you can ride in a limousine to go see him."

We laughed.

The week before the concert, Becky and I were discussing the details of how we'd travel to the concert.

"Whose car should we take?" she asked.

"A limo." I laughed. We agreed to take her car.

After our conversation, and without my knowing, Becky visited the website for Showtime Limo. Her name obviously popped up on the limo company's phone.

"Hello, Becky," the man who answered the phone said. "This is James. We used to work together. Are you calling me or Showtime?"

"I'm calling Showtime," she said.

"I own Showtime now."

Becky explained about my bucket list. "I'm thinking about renting a limo around 5:00 P.M. to go there."

"We're completely booked," James said. "But I have one driver who isn't busy until 6:30. I'll comp you the limo."

Sold!

Becky didn't stop there. She called her ex-husband, Chad, who graduated from film school. He found the movie online and lifted a still shot of Kevin Costner in the limo scene. Becky took the picture to a banner company and ordered a life-size version that would fit in the limo's back seat. When it was ready, she asked Ken to drive to

Gladstone, Missouri, thirty miles away, after work to pick it up.

Ken wasn't jealous of Kevin Costner, Becky told me later. "He said, 'I've had her for fifty-three years. He can have her for five minutes.'"

We agreed to meet at Marc's favorite bar and ride together to the concert. Ken and I arrived first. When Becky and Marc arrived, Becky pulled me off the bar stool. "Close your eyes."

She led me out the door into the parking lot. "Open them."

A uniformed chauffeur held open the door to a black stretch limousine.

"I can't believe it!" I felt like I was soaring in a hot-air balloon.

She pulled me to the car door. "Look inside."

Kevin was stretched across the back seat, wearing a U.S. Naval officer's dress uniform. He faced where I would sit, with his arm stretched out.

"I can't believe you did this!" I screamed. "It's the closest I'll ever come." I hopped in and faced the actor. Becky took a photo.

We parked at the concert, and Becky left the limo to ask the venue manager if Kevin would come sit in the limo. I took a deep breath. The thought of him actually sitting next to me was too much. I looked at Marc. "I need another drink."

He poured some Jameson from the limo bar.

Becky returned. "Kevin declined."

I went limp — not from disappointment. From relief.

Inside Knuckleheads, we found seats at a table with a reserved sign on it. Becky moved the sign from the table to the seat of a chair, and we sat. About twenty minutes later, two security men walked up. "You'll have to move. We have you on videotape moving the reserved sign."

Becky pulled me out of my chair. "Come with me."

Luckily, Becky had also saved two stools that were a little less desirable next to the area where the sound man was pushing buttons and pulling levers. A couple was sitting there.

"Those are my seats," Becky said.

The man shrugged.

Becky explained that the night was for her mother's bucket list. "You had to move my stuff to sit here."

He stayed where he was.

"How 'bout I trade you balcony seats?"

The balcony had comfortable chairs overlooking the mosh pit with a good view of the stage. The man agreed, and Becky left to get special balcony wristbands.

As the couple was leaving, the man whispered in my ear, "Your daughter really loves you."

I smiled. "I know."

We settled in with two members of our group sitting and two standing. The concert began. I had looked up lyrics to many of the band's songs so I would recognize them, but on the first song I could barely hear the words. As Kevin introduced the next song, I turned to Becky. "What's he saying?"

Becky walked over to the sound booth. "We can't hear the lead singer," she said. "Can you adjust the volume on his mic?"

The man rolled his eyes. "If I turn up the vocals, people might find out Kevin Costner can't sing."

I didn't care. All I wanted was to see Kevin in person, and there he was! The night was hot, and so was Kevin. I gazed at him right there in the flesh. He looked exactly like he looks in the movies. It was so much fun.

I texted the photo of Kevin and me to friends and family. It was good enough to fool quite a few of them.

"Is this for real?" my friend Deborah texted back.

"I am in a limo," I wrote.

"You are so good at manifesting."

Others wrote, "Amazing!" Or, "Wow!"

Not surprisingly, a few, including my sister Amy, replied, "Photoshop?"

"Not Photoshop," I said.

During the next week, I showed the photo to anyone who would look. The reactions were mixed, always accompanied by laughter.

My favorite response came from my friend Jean in my tai chi class. She looked at the photo, cocked her head, and smiled. "Is that Warren Beatty?"

— Mary-Lane Kamberg —

34

Ruffled Feathers

If you want something said, ask a man. If you want
something done, ask a woman.
~Margaret Thatcher

For my first seven years of life, our large family lived on a cul-de-sac in Seattle. Our house lay on the outskirts of Sea-Tac International Airport. While our street was in a quiet area, no one would have described it as a "country setting." But, alas, Momma was raised in deep East Texas, and she missed the bucolic lifestyle associated with the rural South.

Mom planted a garden. She acquired a pair of ducks named Chuck and Polly. She tended a large blackberry patch, a grape arbor, and three or four apple trees near the back of our property. She lined our yard with strawberry beds, and she even maintained a compost pile.

None of these endeavors quenched her thirst for the country life. I suppose in my mother's mind, the next logical step was to add chickens to the mix. So, she bought some hatching eggs and set up a temporary pen in our converted garage. I recall the air of suspense as we waited for the inevitable. Finally, the eggs hatched, and a couple dozen fluffy, yellow chicks happily chirped around the room.

Mom somehow managed to convince Dad to fence in one corner of our back yard with a small hen house. She bought a banty rooster and placed her brood of chicks out in the pen when they were old enough. I look back now, and this picture of my early childhood seems a bit surreal. Since we were in the direct path of the airport, we had planes flying overhead most of the day. Down below, my mother had carved out a miniature "farm" complete with a crowing rooster who shared his thoughts early in the morning and any other time he pleased.

Before long, the chicks grew into laying hens. Each of us five siblings received our chance to collect a few eggs from the nests, but since they were Mom's chickens, she planned to do most of the egg collecting herself.

Unfortunately, things did not go as planned. Mr. Rooster did too good of a job watching over the hens. He decided Momma was not the type of visitor he wanted bothering his fine, feathered ladies. Not to be deterred, she would head out with a bowl of feed. Unfortunately, as soon as she lifted the latch on the gate, the rooster would make horrible squawking noises and flap his wings. Sometimes, he even pecked at her ankles. Mom quickly scattered the feed and left. Frustrated with the rooster's lack of hospitality, she'd return to our house screeching her own set of expletives.

One day, as an experiment, Mom sent Dad to feed the chickens. He sauntered to the back part of the yard and opened the gate to the chicken coop. Mr. Rooster stood erect on the fence post and astutely observed Dad with mild curiosity. Dad fed the chickens without a single problem. The following morning, Mom sent Michael, my teenaged brother. Michael, who favored Mom in height and looks, did not fool Mr. Rooster. Michael loosened the gate, entered, and took his time spreading the feed around the hen yard. Mr. Rooster simply watched the morning activity without so much as a ruffled feather.

Everyone in the house decided that Mr. Rooster just needed time to get used to his surroundings and to Mom. Day in and day out, Mom coped with the cockerel. They would each have their say before Mom finished with her chicken chores. No matter what, Mr. Rooster didn't seem to want to make friends with Mom. In fact, instead of getting better, the morning scuffles appeared to be getting worse. Mr. Rooster no longer squawked from a distance. He had surpassed the occasional running at her to terrorize her ankles. Now, Mr. Rooster had gotten brave!

One morning after breakfast, Mom headed out with new determination in her eyes. She tucked the bowl of feed under her arm and snatched up a fly swatter on her way out the door. Dad, Michael, and the rest of us four kids dashed to the glass patio door to watch the showdown. We all knew that when Mom pulled out the fly swatter, someone was in serious trouble. This time, however, we youngsters got to be part of the audience rather than part of the show. From my place in the window, I could see Mom marching across the yard with a bead on the chicken coop. She still wore her nubby, chenille bathrobe and house slippers, and had her hair pinned up in curlers.

Mom approached the gate to the coop with the kind of resolve that only a mother who has had enough can exhibit. Suddenly, I felt quite sorry for that mean old bird. Mom opened the gate and entered the chicken yard. Mr. Rooster arrogantly peered down from his perch on one of the fence posts. Mom reached in her bowl for some grain, flicked her wrist, and spread it judiciously along the ground. So far, so good. Mr. Rooster watched from a distance but nothing more.

Then, Mom made a rookie mistake. She let down her guard and turned her back on Mr. Rooster as she continued to toss the grain. In that moment, Mr. Rooster made ready for combat — his strategy, ambush. That wretched fowl moved in for the kill. He leaped from his perch, furiously flapping his wings, and aimed straight at Mom's full head of curlers!

For several excruciating minutes, my family held our breath as dust, feathers, curlers, and hairpins flew in all directions. Mr. Rooster would attack, and Mom would swing her fly swatter. Mr. Rooster retreated, repositioned, and headed back for more. Mom had little time to catch her breath before flailing her arms once more to fend off that crazy bird. A couple of times, she managed to get in a good whack. She knocked the rooster onto the hard, dirt-packed ground. He'd shake his head, waggle his wattle, and go back for more! Across the chicken yard they went, back and forth, 'round and 'round. We watched from our safe spot in the kitchen doorway. I suspect the hens were also gathered in their own window to watch those two battling it out.

Finally, out of breath and out of feed, Mom lumbered back to the house. Her robe slouched open. Her slippers were smudged with dirt. The curlers were barely hanging on to one side of her head. The other side had curlers missing completely. Tufts of black hair stuck straight out. In her hand, she still grasped the fly swatter. One look at the chicken coop proved that Mr. Rooster hadn't fared much better. Feathers were scattered everywhere!

Strangely enough, Mom didn't have a single problem with Mr. Rooster after that day. Apparently, Mom had showed him who was boss, and Mr. Rooster was willing to concede.

— Holly D. Yount —

35

How to Catch a Tomato Thief

Vegetable puns make me feel good
from my head tomatoes.
~Author Unknown

My parents are meticulous gardeners of their large country property, cultivating every inch to grow award-winning flowers and fruit and vegetables of many varieties.

One summer morning, my dad noticed that someone had gotten into his tomato patch and taken one small, round bite out of many of his almost-ripe tomatoes.

"Someone is eating my tomatoes, and I am going to find out who!" After a bit of research, he discovered that raccoons were the culprits and spotted one sitting high in the maple tree in front of their house.

"Ah-ha! I've got you now!" he shouted at the raccoon. "No more tomatoes for you. I'll be watching!"

The raccoon, seemingly unaware he was in trouble, stayed in the tree. He was still there the next day, which concerned my mom.

"There must be something wrong with that raccoon. Shouldn't he have climbed down by now?"

"Well, he's afraid of me, of course!" my dad said.

"I doubt that. I'll call animal control. They'll know how to get him down."

The animal-control inspector arrived promptly, ready to take action.

He took out his binoculars to investigate the raccoon at the top of the tall maple and discovered that his leg was stuck in a trap.

The inspector was infuriated. "A trap?! That is an illegal animal trap! This is now a crime scene! Who put that trap up in the tree?" He glared suspiciously at my dad.

"It wasn't me, that's for sure. How could I get a trap way up in that tree?"

"Well, then, he must have gotten his leg stuck in the trap and climbed into the tree. The trap wound around the branch and got stuck," the inspector surmised. "And since we are dealing with a crime here, it is out of my jurisdiction. We need to call the police department." He pulled out his phone.

Two police officers drove into the laneway in their cruiser and sprang out of their vehicle, ready to take charge of the situation.

They stood and studied the predicament, agreeing that the raccoon was certainly stuck in the tree.

"I have an idea!" One officer pulled out his rifle. "I'll shoot the lock on the trap, which will open up and set the raccoon free. Then, he can just climb down."

"Oh no you don't!" his fellow officer argued. "Your aim isn't *that* good. Besides, think of the explaining and all the paperwork we'll have to do if your gun goes off!"

The animal-control agent and the two policemen shook their heads.

"This is a problem beyond our capabilities. We'll need to call in the fire department."

The large fire truck pulled up to the front of the house, and three firemen in full gear hopped out.

Cars were starting to stop along the road with people wondering what was going on. A small crowd assembled under the tree with phones out, capturing pictures and videos of the raccoon and all the commotion.

My parents stood on their front porch surveying the action. They hadn't had so much excitement on their property in years. "Maybe I should get out the barbecue and sell hot dogs!" my dad suggested.

The animal-control officer, the two policemen and three firemen stood under the tree, puzzling over the situation.

"How about we use the fire-truck ladder?"

"No, it won't reach between all those tree branches."

"And we need animal control in full gear to go up and grab him. He could be dangerous. Don't raccoons bite?"

"I've got it!" one of the firemen shouted. "We just got a new, super-powered water hose. We can shoot him out of the tree with water!"

"Stand back, everyone!" They motioned the crowd to move away, pulled out their new fire hose, and hooked it up.

The firemen held the hose and directed the water up toward the raccoon. The water blasted out of the hose directly onto the tree branch where the raccoon sat. It cracked the branch and it fell, taking the raccoon along with it. They both landed on the ground with a thump.

The impact of his fall had bent the trap, so the raccoon could pull his leg right out of the trap. With a shake of his behind, he got up and instantly ran straight toward my dad's prized tomato patch.

Everyone in the group cheered as my dad chased after that raccoon, trying to save what was left of his tomatoes.

The next day, my dad decided that he really didn't like tomatoes all that much. He put all his efforts toward his sunflower patch.

But all that excitement must have been too much for the raccoon. They never saw him again.

—Lori Zenker—

Chapter 5

Dad Did What?

Mom and the Lawn Tractor

Insanity runs in my family. It practically gallops.
~Cary Grant

Mom and Dad came from a tough generation. Only the worst injury or illness was worthy of an emergency-room visit. And calling for an ambulance? Forget it. Those calls were reserved for life-threatening accidents and near-fatal shootings, and Mom and Dad had never been involved in either.

Their reluctance to seek emergency care continued even as they celebrated their seventy-something birthdays. "Son, come get your daddy and take him to the blamed hospital," my mother said in a frustrated tone over the phone one day. "He's cut his blamed finger off with that blamed table saw of his."

In the background, I could hear my dad saying that if he could get the bleeding stopped, he would go to his doctor in the morning. As they both insisted I not call 911, I frantically drove the twenty miles to their house and was greeted in the driveway by my mother and father, him holding a towel tightly around his hand as my mother insisted that he "show your son what you did to your blamed finger." The use of "blamed" as an adjective was the extent of my mother's cussing except on special occasions, one of which will soon occur in this story. Thankfully, he kept the blamed towel in place, and I was spared the horror of seeing what remained of his blamed finger.

I drove him to the emergency room where a physician announced that the remainder of the mangled finger, cut diagonally from the tip down to almost the second knuckle, would have to be amputated. My father, who had remained calm in spite of the trauma to the rest of us, became belligerent at hearing this. With a battle cry of, "I was born with it, I'll die with it!" my father made the doctor patch it up as best he could with assorted stitches and gauze dressing, the medical equivalent of repairing a busted car taillight with duct tape and cellophane.

The next morning, he called his family doctor who knew another doctor who, in the end, somehow saved what was left of the mangled finger, which Dad displayed with pride for the rest of his life. It wasn't pretty, but it was his.

A few years before the finger mangling, on a sunny June day, Dad had made a run to the gardening shop while my mom stayed in the backyard garden engaged in her favorite summer pastime: killing ants. Mom had a lifelong running battle with ants.

This scene was repeated many times in their backyard garden: While Mom and Dad tended their tomatoes, Mom would spot a wayward ant, follow it to the colony, and then pour enough toxic chemicals into the nest to not only kill all the ants in the colony but probably any insect within a ten-yard radius.

That day, Mom had been tracking an ant and was on the verge of locating the colony when she tripped and fell. She went down hard and, as often happens with elderly parents, broke her hip. There she lay, taunted by the very ants that, seconds before, she had sought to murder. With her now helpless on the ground, I consider it a miracle that the ants didn't drag her into their colony for revenge.

When my dad returned thirty minutes later, he was greeted with Mom's cries for help from the back yard. Coming to my mother's aid, he did what many of his generation did when dealing with the injured: He tried to help her stand up to walk it off. Although I'm pretty sure that most of her resulting loud declarations were prefaced with "blamed," on this occasion she came up with words that would make dogs whimper and houseplants die.

Having determined that her standing up and walking was not an option, Dad called a neighbor, Bob, to help him pick up Mom from the ground. Dad's plan was to put her in his own impromptu version of an ambulance — a metal lawn cart pulled behind his pride and joy: a bright green lawn tractor. My dad may not have known first aid, but he did know lawn tractors. Although the cart had no suspension, it did have a layer of loose hay in it from his last project. That, along with a couple of old pillows he threw in, helped to cushion my mother. Dad always looked out for Mom's comfort.

With a great deal of effort, my dad and the friend (who was also in his seventies) attempted to pick Mom up to put her into the cart. This produced loud screams of pain and howls of anguish, interspersed by uncharacteristic creative language and outright threats from my mother.

"Maybe we should call an ambulance," Bob said.

"No," Dad said, and Mom moaned in unison.

"Try it again after I get my blamed breath," Mom said.

With Bob on one end and Dad on the other, they started a three count, "One. Two. Thr…"

"OH !&%^#!! BLAMED !!%^#!!" Mom screamed. According to Bob, who related the details that were too delicate to be shared with me later by my overprotective parents, the words screamed by my mother would have made Satan blush. But this time they successfully got her in the cart. Dad revved up the tractor and popped the clutch, the only way the engine wouldn't stall. It was the only time Mom ever threatened to kill my dad. Dad stopped. Mom screamed.

The demonic howls brought another neighbor over, and then another. The wisest of the gathering crowd mercifully dialed 911.

I'm convinced that had 911 not been called, my dad would've pulled Mom the three miles to their doctor's office with the lawn tractor. There he would have asked at the desk if it would be possible for his wife to be "worked in." Luckily, it didn't come to that.

Within minutes, a fire truck and two police cars arrived, followed by an ambulance. The sirens and flashing lights quickly attracted most of the people on their street, who stood in a throng on the corner and whispered among themselves. I suspect many of the whispers were about what kind of man puts his injured wife in a lawn cart and what kind of neighbor helps him do that. The paramedics carefully removed Mom from the cart while Mom screamed. As they loaded her in the ambulance for the trip to the hospital, one paramedic asked why they hadn't called 911 to begin with, saving time and agony.

Mom stopped her screams and curses long enough to reply, "We don't like to cause a blamed scene."

— Butch Holcombe —

37

The Criminal and The Accomplice

*I cannot think of any need in childhood as strong
as the need for a father's protection.*
~Sigmund Freud

The year was 1960. I had recently turned sixteen and received my driver's license. I wasn't all that familiar with the traffic rules and regulations on the city streets of Tulsa, so when Dad asked me to drive him to pick up a bag of charcoal, I was more than ready to take the wheel and get some practice.

We had only gone a few blocks when we came to a four-way intersection with lights. I needed to turn left, and after making sure it was safe, I proceeded to do so. Almost immediately, a policeman on a motorcycle pulled me over.

"What's wrong?" I asked the officer as he approached my rolled-down window. "I wasn't speeding."

"No, ma'am, you weren't speeding, but you turned left after 4:30, and that's not allowed at that intersection."

I glanced at my watch. It read 4:35.

Of course, Dad was more than upset because I was being ticketed for such a minor infraction. No need to repeat the conversation Dad had with the policeman. But suffice it to say, Dad was lucky to not be ticketed for what may have been perceived as a major infraction.

I gave the officer my license and registration. He finished writing out the ticket and handed it and everything else back to me. "How much is the fine?" I asked.

He politely remarked, "Twenty dollars. Have a nice day."

"Thank you," I replied, not sure of what else to say. The policeman pulled around us and headed down the street.

"Dad, I'm sorry, so very sorry."

"Hush now. Don't worry."

"I'll pay the fine. I didn't realize…"

"Hush now," Dad said again as he pointed down the street. "Follow that cop!"

"Huh? Why?"

"Just follow!"

We tailed the policeman for about a mile until he stopped at a convenience store, got off his motorcycle, and went inside.

"Pull over there, next to the cop's cycle," Dad said.

"Huh? Why? Are you getting charcoal here?"

"No, I'm getting something else."

Dad hopped from the car and looked around, appearing to surveil the parking lot. I saw no one coming out or going inside the store, but I did see Dad amble over to the motorcycle and grab something anchored over the back fender. He concealed it inside his jacket and then hopped back inside the car. "Go!" he yelled. "Drive!"

"What? Drive where?"

"That way," he yelled, pointing to a street. "I got the cop's ticket book!"

"You got what? Why did…"

"Just go!"

I didn't say another word. I knew from experience when it was best to keep my mouth shut.

Driving a few more miles, we came to a bridge spanning the Arkansas River. As I began to cross, Dad said, "Pull over there and stop in the breakdown lane!"

"Why? We aren't…"

"Just pull over and stop."

I did so while Dad looked around at the cars on the bridge. It was rush hour, and although the traffic was heavy, no one paid any attention to us. Dad got out of the car and stood momentarily on the breakdown lane. He had the ticket book in his hand. And then, with a mighty side-arm heave, he threw that book over the bridge railing! Its pages fluttered in the breeze like a wounded bird and fell into the flowing water below. Dad hurried back inside the car, tore up the ticket I had been given, and said, "Now guess who's gonna pay?"

"Oh, my gosh, Dad! What did you do? What did you do? We're goin' to jail! I'm gonna be…" I was rambling but couldn't stop. Here I was, a newly licensed driver, and now I was gonna be arrested, fingerprinted, and stuck behind bars for no telling how many years.

"Hush now! Don't worry. Just drive!"

We were never caught—the criminal and the accomplice. Of course, what we did was wrong. If I could, I would apologize to that policeman who, after all, was only doing his job. Once his superiors learned that his ticket book, maybe containing a copy of several tickets written for several days, was gone, did they demote him? Put him on desk duty for a few weeks? School crossing guard for a month or so? I sincerely hope not.

By the way, I never got another ticket. I'm not sure about Dad, though.

—Jeannie Rogers—

P.S. After writing this story and musing over it for a while, my guilty conscience kicked in, and I realized that another apology was in order. So, I sent a $100 check to the mayor's office in the City of Tulsa, along with a copy of this story, trusting that the money will cover not only my fine but the fine of a few others whose evidence of a ticket sleeps in the riverbed! It's never too late to do the right thing.

38

Spinner Night

Dad, I have a secret. You're the best parent.
Please don't tell Mom.
~Author Unknown

As my wife worked a late shift, my three small children looked at me expectantly. "What's for dinner?" one of them said.

The last time I had made dinner was when I made Spam and ramen in college. Now, I had three mouths to feed — ages two, six and nine — but I was crucially short on ideas. Like a deer in headlights, I searched for a possible answer.

"Where's the Twister game?"

"Not Twister," Abby, my oldest, scolded. "Dinner."

I walked to the closet, pulled out the game, and tested the spinner. Then I slid a couple of sheets of paper between the plastic arrow and the cardboard base and sketched out four quadrants. I looked at the kids. "Who wants chocolate?"

Alex, my youngest, screamed in delight.

Abby crossed her arms. "Dad, Mom wouldn't let that happen."

"Mom's not here."

I wrote in the upper right quadrant: chocolate.

Aiden, my middle child, asked, "Dad, what are you doing?"

"You'll see in a second." I pointed at the second area. "How about ice cream?"

Alex started dancing around in a circle.

"When we get four options written on the spinner, we'll spin to see what we do for dinner tonight."

My youngest said, "Dress up like superheroes."

"Absolutely!" I wrote superheroes, with no idea how that would turn into a dinner idea, hoping the dial would land somewhere else.

They debated the final section for a few seconds and then collectively decided on pizza. If they had suggested "Run around at the mall," I would have written it down.

I smoothed out the paper, tested the spinner, and then set it in the middle of the table. We gathered around the hallowed spinner, and I held up my hands. "We are gonna spin it once, and whatever we land on, that's what we'll do tonight."

Abby shook her head. "I don't think this is a good idea."

"It's okay, honey. Your mom will understand."

Alex yelled, "I wanna spin it."

"Great. Go for it."

The spinner ended on a line.

Aiden tried to take over. I intervened before the obligatory fight ensued. Alex's second try sent the little, plastic arrow flying around and around until it landed on… chocolate.

Everyone squealed, "Hurray! Chocolate." Including me. I still had no idea what we were going to do.

Abby squinted at me. "But what are we gonna do?"

"Hop in the car."

We took the normal fifteen minutes to find shoes and jackets and manage the car seats. Then, we were off to the grocery store.

Pushing the cart, I announced, "Everybody, find two things with chocolate. We'll buy them and take them home for dinner." They took off running. I hollered from behind, "Stay together."

Abby grabbed Hershey syrup and a giant chocolate bar.

Alex picked up a bundt cake and bag of Kisses.

Aiden wielded chocolate-covered cookies and a bag of M&M's.

I picked up a half-gallon of chocolate milk and chocolate chips.

The cashier looked at the cart and then stared at me over the top of her glasses. I was about to say, "It's spinner night," but knowing that wouldn't go well, I simply shrugged.

We piled back into the car full of anticipation. Back at the house, we unloaded the loot on the counter.

"First, let's set the table."

The kids grabbed plates, forks, knives, spoons, and cups, and then sat in their normal seats. The only thing missing was their mother—and a proper meal.

"Abby, can you thank the Lord for dinner?"

I opened all the packages and doled out every type of chocolate on their plates. Then I set out the Hershey syrup for them to cover anything they wanted.

"Dear God, thank you for this chocolate and bring Mom home soon."

Fifteen minutes later, with plates empty and bellies starting to ache, we made our way into the living room to play games.

As I wiped the brown happiness off Aiden's face, he said, "My tummy doesn't feel so good."

"Would you like something else to eat?"

"Yes, please."

I put on a movie and quietly gave each of them toast and string cheese. Before long, it was time to brush teeth and head to bed. As I tucked them in, Abby asked, "Can we do this again tomorrow?"

"Sorry, guys. We're only gonna do this when Mom has to work late."

Aiden rubbed his belly. "I hope she works late tomorrow."

The following week, she was scheduled on the late shift again.

Abby asked, "What's for dinner?"

I grabbed the Twister box.

They shouted, "Spinner night!"

— Andy DeWitt —

39

Picker Dad

The rate at which a person can mature is directly
proportional to the embarrassment he can tolerate.
~Douglas Engelbart

When we're children, especially teenagers, our parents constantly embarrass us. One of my dad's habits was the worst! He loved to pick up items he spotted on the side of the road and bring them home. If he saw something that looked like a tool (pliers, screwdriver, hammer), he'd slow the car, pull over to the curb, and run back to retrieve whatever it was. If one of his children was in the car with him, sometimes he'd drive onto the road's shoulder, and ask us to reach down and retrieve whatever he spied. It was so embarrassing!

Over the years, Dad met with some success in his roadside picking. His favorite story on that subject was the time he found a pair of men's blue jeans. He searched through the pockets to look for the owner's identification but found nothing until he put his hand in one of the back pockets. It held a twenty-dollar bill! Of course, he was delighted. But the best part? The jeans were like new, and, after he got home and my mom washed them, he tried them on. They fit. He was so proud of himself.

My brother DeWayne tells of a time when our mom and dad were driving a rental car to the airport to catch a flight. Dad spied a battered toolbox on the side of the road. Despite Mom's protests, he pulled onto the shoulder and gathered everything he could hold. As usual, there was no way to identify the owner who'd lost the treasures.

Delighted with his find, he'd scored pliers, screwdrivers, sockets, and wrenches. But now that he had them, where could he store them? He couldn't keep them in the rental car he was about to return, but he also couldn't bear to leave them for someone else to pick up. He and Mom had a flight to catch! His solution? Stow them all in my mom's carry-on train case/make-up bag.

The adventure didn't end there, however. When he got to the airport, turned in the rental car, and headed through the security checkpoint, things got interesting. Surrounded by TSA agents, he somehow explained the presence of those random tools among my mom's lipstick and mascara, and convinced them to let him board the plane. I can just imagine Mom's mortification.

My nephew Brandon remembers a time when Dad stopped in the middle of a busy intersection in a sketchy area of Dallas. He hopped out of the car, bent down, and picked up small sheets of paper. It was cash! Drivers all around him shouted and honked their horns in anger, but when he waved back and showed the money, they applauded and gave him thumbs-ups. I'm sure my dad gave Brandon a share of the loot.

Perhaps as a result of that incident, Brandon admits that he loves picking up roadside treasures, too. He says, "Heck, half the furniture in my house is stuff that rich people left at the curb with their garbage."

The roadside-scavenging gene evidently infected earlier generations of males in my family, too. My brother fondly remembers our Pap-Paw taking him on "bottle snatching" adventures. They'd pick up glass Coke bottles, take them home, clean them, and redeem the three-cents-per-bottle deposit fee. Then they'd use the money to buy minnows and go fishing!

One time, however, Dad wasn't so lucky. On a Friday evening, we were driving from Oak Cliff, Texas, to Lake Texoma for a weekend at our cabin. The headlights of Dad's car reflected something on the road's shoulder, and he hit the brakes.

"Those look like new tires! They still have the wrappings on them!"

In spite of my mom's protests, Dad pulled into the weeds on the roadside, pushed his door open, and ran back down the shoulder to claim his treasure. As he tore off the shiny, plastic covering from one of the tires, he realized they had no tread left on them at all. They were bald! Three boys scrambled off into the field, howling with laughter, obviously delighted with the success of their prank.

When Dad made it back to the car, he shook his head and laughed. "Those boys sure got me!"

Did that setback stop my dad from roadside picking? Not at all. I actually think it made him more determined than ever to stop for every "perfectly good" item he spotted. After all, there was that wad of cash, and don't forget the blue jeans....

—Sandra R. Nachlinger—

40

The Day the Waterbed Wouldn't Die

The key to being an awesome dad is aging
without maturing.
~Author Unknown

Mom was an interior decorator with masses of magazines. She was filled with more ideas than money or space would allow. She thought that a den would be so nice. "I'll change Karen's bedroom to a den," she said. So, while Dad was at sea, she did just that. From that day on, I shared my room with my little sister.

"Let's change this kitchen," she said just before a long October weekend. Dad was on the ocean somewhere. We emptied the room in preparation for painting the latest trendy colour. We celebrated Thanksgiving eating pizza as we sat upon the kitchen floor.

Waterbeds were a trend Mom saw in a magazine. "The water will support your aching body," she said to the now retired seaman.

Compromise was the best approach when Mom had one of her ideas. Besides, it probably wouldn't be long before another change would be proposed. Dad agreed. Their limited budget was stretched to purchase the waterbed.

My parents soon discovered that sleeping on a giant water balloon was fraught with danger. Dad lay in bed ready for a good night's sleep as Mom joined him, sending a giant wave of water to Dad's side of the bed. He was thrown two feet in the air, blankets and pillows flying about him. He landed with a thud on the wave, now a hump of water. Mom's every tiny movement created an instant wave of motion. Dad would wake up wondering, "Which ship is this?"

Night after night, Dad dreamt of ships and water. Then one night, he woke up feeling cold and damp.

"What have you done?" he asked none too politely.

Mom screamed, "Me? What have you done?"

The bed was cold and wet, very wet. The waterbed had sprung a leak.

Repairing a heavy, water-filled balloon while it was leaking water was no small feat. Dad was an engineer, and he mastered the art of repairing the leaks. His methods were top-secret, and we were sworn to secrecy.

After years of seasickness at night and leak repairs in the mornings Dad finally put his foot down.

"It's time to get a new bed. The waterbed has to go," Dad said.

"But I love this bed," said Mom.

"The dreams of ships have to end."

So, the hunt began for a new mattress. Mom and Dad visited every store in town that sold beds. They lay down together on each mattress, and Dad would insist Mom move about. He wanted a bed that didn't send him flying into the air with Mom's shifting. They tested and tested. The salespeople would roll their eyes when they saw my parents enter the store and say, "What's with these two? Are they never going to buy?"

Then, one day, it was as if the heavens opened, and the angels sang. There was the perfect mattress, named "Bed of Roses." And, for Dad, it *was* a "bed of roses." It was like lying on a soft, pillowy cloud. And no matter how much Mom moved, Dad didn't feel it. He was in heaven. The waterbed was relegated to the back yard and a ceremony was planned.

It was one of those days in early spring when the air is still crisp and the grass has not yet turned into a beautiful green carpet. The invitations had been sent for the family to gather in the back yard. Today was the day we would send the waterbed to its final resting place.

Dad attached the garden hose to the outdoor tap and to the waterbed. Then he waited.

He had long anticipated this day. He had never liked that bed. He had spent more than twenty years being tossed about in a bunk on a ship traversing the Atlantic Ocean. Dad had no true rest with the constant pitch and yaw of the sea.

Dad was more than ready. "Let's get this show on the road. It's time for this waterbed to die!"

We all thought the waterbed would burst. We waited as it grew larger and larger. We were ready for it to pop. But it didn't even spring a leak!

My nephew jumped on it like a trampoline. The water swished, but still no leaks and no pop. It just got hard as a rock.

"This waterbed will not die!" he said.

"Let's encourage it," said Dad as he brought a knife and stabbed the waterbed.

"Let me. Let me!" shouted my nephew. Dad helped him get started. The waterbed had a tough skin, and it took strength to stab a hole. Tiny streams of water escaped from the holes created by the stabs — not the waterfall we were hoping for.

We all had our turn at stabbing. As the water trickled out, the waterbed became softer, so my nephew stabbed again and again. A time or two, we thought it might burst. My nephew jumped with glee. My mom, sister and I stood back to avoid the anticipated soaking. Dad stood still, unable to move. His face was filled with disbelief and disappointment. The waterbed — his source of recurring dreams of the sea and sleepless nights — was depriving him of any satisfaction.

The day wore on. We all got tired except my nephew, who just kept jumping on the waterbed. Eventually, we wandered off. The water slowly leaked out. My dad folded up the emptied waterbed and put it in the truck with a great sigh. He drove it to its final resting place at the dump.

The waterbed had won the battle. The memory of that day has been etched into all our minds. Decades later, we still smile when we think about the day the waterbed wouldn't die.

—Deborah E. Martin—

41

Fun with a Capital F

Even though you're growing up,
you should never stop having fun.
~Nina Dobrev

I was visiting my parents with our teenage kids for the weekend while my husband worked out of town. *Mmm,* I thought as I rolled out of the guest bed. "Bacon."

I could hear voices downstairs, so I pulled on my lightweight knit joggers and a T-shirt, and then headed toward our family gathering spot: the kitchen.

My mom was busy pouring cups of coffee while slicing up oranges and apples for a fruit tray.

"Good morning!" She smiled as she handed me a steaming mug. "The cream and sugar are already on the table."

Dad was stirring up his special pancake batter. He was grinning from ear to ear; after all, he was the Pancake King. The apron, spatula, and squeeze bottles helped him show off his culinary prowess to anyone lucky enough to see him in action.

Pancake making was his idea of fun with a capital F.

Then again, Dad had a way of turning everything into some sort of a game, and fun was the goal. When we were kids, the goal was to stack firewood the fastest. A simple car wash could easily turn into a huge water fight, and our tree swing eventually became a contraption that resembled a human catapult.

Why did I think this day would be any different?

"An airplane? Coming right up!" He loved getting special requests. "A hippo riding a skateboard? No problem."

Dad had mastered the art of creating pancake layers to make detailed pictures with batter. Not that he was ready to become a YouTube sensation or host a PBS special, but I have to give him credit for his artistry.

If one of the kids had a football game coming up, he would create a jersey with their number on it. If there was a dance competition, he could make dance shoes by carefully squeezing thin lines onto the hot, well-oiled griddle. After it began to sizzle, he would add more batter to cover the top. When the whole pancake was just right, he would flip it, exposing the drawing he had made.

That morning, Dad had a new idea. A more fun idea! Sure, pancakes were still on the menu, but he wouldn't be making them. Next to the griddle were two bowls with slips of paper folded in half.

"So," he stifled a chuckle, "everyone has to take a slip of paper from the first bowl to see where you are in line to use the griddle. The second bowl is full of different items you have to create with your pancake batter."

The kids thought it sounded like fun. I moaned.

Really, can't we just eat breakfast like a normal family?

"You have to make the item you pick," Dad said as he warmed up the syrup. "That is what makes this so fun!"

Yeah, so fun. Actually, a bowl of cereal sounded fun right about then.

This was going to take a while. Our oldest son drew number one, and the paper from the second bowl was a Jeep.

"Not too bad," Dad said as he coached him to make the wheels first. "Just take your time."

I watched as Nathan added the body of the vehicle and finally flipped it over.

Soon, several others completed their tasks — a kangaroo, a turtle with a Santa hat, a butterfly — and then it was my turn. I was one of the last ones to go and had yet to pick my item.

I reluctantly reached into the bowl and drew out a slip of paper. I opened it and… WHAT? Richard Simmons!

How in the world was I going to make a "Sweatin' to the Oldies" guru with pancake batter? More to the point, why would I want to?

"I think I will stick with coffee and bacon for breakfast," I said as I handed the batter bowl to the next person in line.

Almost a year later, I was having lunch with a small group of friends. We were chatting about our families, and I mentioned the "create-a-pancake event."

A friend whose dad had passed away a few years earlier paused and then quietly said, "I wish my dad was here so he could ask me to make a Richard Simmons pancake."

Ouch.

The next morning, I put on my apron, pulled out the bowls, whisk, flour, baking powder, and the rest of the ingredients I needed, and then went to work.

My first attempt looked like a fly after hitting a windshield. In the trash it went. The second one was a little better. Still, I tossed it.

"I am going to need more batter," I told our dog, whose tail was wagging at the thought of getting a sample of the scrapped attempts.

Finally, I paused and thought of the words Dad had told our kids when he was passing on his pancake skills.

"Take your time."

Slowly, I made the stripes on the short shorts, then the slouchy socks that screamed '80s and the curly hair.

I posed the iconic figure with one arm up and the other at an angle pointing down as if he had just auditioned for *Saturday Night Fever*.

As the thin details began to sizzle, I added another layer and waited. When the edges started to bubble, I knew it was time.

Carefully, I flipped my Richard Simmons pancake over. I could almost hear him tell me that I wasn't a loser if I just believed in myself.

I took a photo and sent it to my dad.

"A little late, but here it is!" I could almost hear him chuckle when I pushed the Send button.

Even though it took about an hour out of my morning, and the kitchen was a mess, it was fun with a capital F, just like my dad.

— Marci Seither —

42

The Vacation That Never Was

Blessed is he who expects nothing,
for he shall never be disappointed.
~Alexander Pope

received the news with mixed feelings. Dad was coming to London. He would be here for three days. "A sort of vacation." A sort of vacation? What did that mean? Wasn't a vacation a vacation? What did "sort of" have to do with it? I shrugged. Whatever it was, it would be nice to see my father.

Or would it?

I groaned.

A flutter of panic beat across my chest. I looked around. I was panting. Why was I panting? Was I sweating, too? What was wrong with me? I took a deep breath. I had to get this to stop. It was only my father, after all. It wasn't the president of the world coming.

I let out a long breath. Dad... Dad was a judge. And I was a student. I was schooling in London in the hope that I too, one day, would become a judge, after first becoming a lawyer. It was a hope. But it wasn't *my* hope. It was my father's hope. And it wasn't a hope I liked. I didn't like it at all. No, not one bit.

Was that why I was in a panic?

What did being a judge one day have to do with being in a panic?

I breathed in, breathed out, breathed in... I was calming down.

My father and I had never been close. My father was not close to any of his children. He was not a close kind of guy. Guy? I chuckled. You couldn't use that word for my father. He was a man. A judge. A distinguished judge. He was certainly not a guy.

I stared at nothing, making a deliberate effort to breathe slowly.

He'd asked if I was on vacation. From his calculations, he expected that I would be on vacation, and he wanted us to vacation together. I chuckled. Vacation together for three days? Three whole days? This was preposterous! Three days? What would we talk about? What on earth would we ever find to discuss?

My heart was beating fast. The panic was coming again. No, it wasn't coming; it was there. It was there again. Why? Why was it like this for me? Was it like this for others? Was it like this for my siblings? Perhaps it was. But was it like this for others not in my family? I didn't think the answer was yes. It would be yes for children who were abused by their fathers. But mine never did such a thing. Such a thing was far from him. My father was a gentleman, a true gentleman.

Then why did I feel this way? Why was I… yes, scared? I was afraid of my father. I had to face it. Scared was the word. My father was a gentleman, but he was a gentleman whom I was scared of, whom *we* were scared of, we the children.

We had never spoken about it, but I realized now that we were afraid of him. He was a judge, a stern judge, who convicted the guilty and sent them to jail. Was that why we were afraid of him? We were not the guilty, were we? Were we guilty of anything? We were just children who did what children did, except we tried to be good children, to be good all the time, to please our father the judge, the stern judge who had never sported a smile.

I paced my room. Would it have been the same if I had heard him laugh once, just once? I shook my head. I didn't think so. I stared at the wall, seeing nothing. Would it have been the same if I had seen him smile once, just once? I shook my head. I was sure it wouldn't.

I halted in my tracks, thinking deeply. Surely, there must have been times when he smiled at my mother and laughed. I could remember Mum laughing once when she was with him. I wasn't in the room, so

I couldn't see if he was laughing, too. Maybe he was laughing, but his voice didn't carry out of the room. Surely, he must have at least smiled. Would my mother have been laughing so loud without him showing any sign of amusement? Surely, he must have smiled!

I resumed pacing. It would have been nice to have seen him smile. How did his smile look? I paused to look at myself in the mirror. Did it look like mine? People said I wasn't much given to smiling. Had I inherited that from him? I didn't like it. I tugged at my cheeks and tried to pull out a smile. I had to learn to smile more. I didn't want to be like my father.

I certainly didn't want to be a judge. I had never met a happy judge. Maybe there were happy judges, but I had never met one, certainly not a happy-looking one, and certainly not among my father's colleagues.

No, I would never be a judge. Never! I looked around the room. It would dash my father's hopes, yes, but I had to think of myself. I wanted to be happy, needed to be happy, needed not to be stern and never smiling, never laughing. I took a step and continued to pace, and then I quickened my pace as a thought occurred to me. If I didn't want my father to be suddenly disappointed at my decision, shouldn't I at least start hinting to him now that I wasn't going to step into his shoes and become a judge?

Shouldn't that form the core of our conversation during our so-called vacation together?

I blinked. I no longer had to worry. Instead of not having anything to discuss, there would now be lots. I could give him my reasons, and there would be a thousand or more. Ten thousand reasons, indeed, why I couldn't become a judge. But I would leave out the no-smiling and no-laughing bit. That would be cutting things too close.

I chuckled. Yes, I would tell him my interests, which he knew nothing about. I would tell him my passions, tell him my dreams.

I would talk and talk and talk...

Talk until the cows came home.

I sighed. It was a sigh of joy. I sat down on my bed. I couldn't wait for Dad to come. Couldn't wait! I smiled, glancing at the mirror.

It was a grand smile. Grander than Grand Central.

The next day, I received a telegram cancelling. Dad was no longer coming.

— Peter Bana —

43

Living in the Dark with Dad

*Children really can brighten up a house
because they never turn the lights off.*
~Ralph Bus

When Dad heard that I was engaged, the first thing he did was congratulate me and my fiancé. The second thing he did was give my fiancé a printout about saving electricity.

Born during the Great Depression, the frugality of my dad's generation has taken, for him, the form of obsessive worrying about wasting electricity. Light switches needed to be in the off position at all times unless a person was actually in that room — and not just in the room but doing something that absolutely required light.

During parties, our friends and relatives often tripped over the rug in the dark while trying to find their way to the bathroom in the hallway. It could turn into a battle for control, with my mother and all four of us kids wanting the lights on, and Dad preferring to live in the equivalent of an underground cave. As we'd go from room to room, playing or cleaning or visiting with friends, he would follow on tiptoe behind us, turning off each light the second we left a room.

When I used to sneak down the stairs at night for a glass of water as a child, I would find Dad huddled in the corner of the kitchen, straining his eyes to read a book below the solitary nightlight bulb plugged in next to the toaster.

When I was twelve, my next-door neighbor hired me to take care of her dog for the weekend. She left a careful set of instructions, including that I ought to turn her front porch light on each night and turn it off each morning. When she came over to pay me the twenty dollars I'd earned, I was red-faced and ashamed to confess that I had forgotten to turn off the porch light one of the days I'd been in charge.

"You can take the cost for the electricity out of my pay," I told her earnestly.

I was genuinely confused when she laughed, and I was shocked when she told me that leaving a light bulb on for an entire day would have cost eighteen cents or less. That was an eye-opening event. Dad had made it sound as though our family couldn't make ends meet if we accidentally left on one light. From that time on, I rebelled.

While other teens fought with their parents for car privileges, new cell phones, and permission to go to parties, my own fights with Dad were about being allowed to leave on the lights in more than one room at a time. But he never budged.

When I graduated college and still lived at home, my then-boyfriend used to spend weekend nights in our guest room. Imagine his shock the first weekend when his door creaked open as he lay in bed reading and a thin arm reached through the crack — only to flip down his light switch and plunge the room into darkness. Of course, I had to reassure him that the creepy, ghostly arm belonged to Dad, who had assumed my boyfriend must be asleep. Dad couldn't tolerate the light being on for no reason, let alone all night. Privacy was valued far less than electricity in our house.

With his penchant for keeping off the lights, you would think that he'd be a fan of natural light, but no — at least not during the winter, when open curtains or shades could let in a draft of cold air and trigger the heat to turn on. Goodness only knows how much electricity that would waste.

When I finally got married and moved out, my husband surprised me with a grand, romantic gesture. The first night I came home from work after the honeymoon, every single light in the house was on—even in the closets!

—Teresa Murphy—

44

My Kooky Father

He that is of a merry heart has a continual feast.
~Proverbs 15:15

Walter was kicking his legs and banging his fists on the floor, saying, "I want those cookies! I want those cookies!"

"Walter, get up!" Mom hissed.

My sister Janet and I were laughing so hard. We couldn't help it. No, it wasn't our toddler brother having a temper tantrum right there on the floor of the grocery store. We didn't have a toddler brother. It was our father. My perfectly sane father was doing what he loved to do: make his children laugh with the added bonus that he embarrassed his wife just a bit.

We had gone in the grocery store to pick up something—whatever it was has been long forgotten. We went down the cookie aisle, and Daddy picked up a package of cookies and said, "I want to get these."

Mom said, "We don't need those."

I am sure my father checked to see that there were no customers in the aisle, and then he got down on the floor and had his "temper tantrum." Truth is, my dad would do just about anything—usually when we didn't expect it—to see his children laugh. I affectionately call him "my kooky father" because of all the silly things he did while I was growing up.

He would hide Hershey Kisses around the living room and dining room for us kids and then tell us if we were "hot" or "cold" when we went looking for them, which could get pretty dramatic. All the laughing was just as much fun as finding and eating the chocolates.

Sometimes, Daddy and I would go in the kitchen and make a treat for Mom. She was not allowed in the kitchen while we made some surprise from scratch. He would call out — so Mom could hear — various silly ingredients that didn't go into our treat, including Shakespeare's "eye of newt and toe of frog."

One time Mom and I drove to the store to pick up some Easter egg–dyeing supplies and when we got back, through the darkness we saw my father dressed in his white long underwear, with a big wad of cotton attached to his butt, bunny ears, and my Easter basket. He was on his hands and knees, hopping around the back yard.

A lot of the funny and special things Daddy did were for his children. But there was one instance that was mainly for the wife he adored. Mom hadn't been to Newfoundland, where she was born, since she married and moved away twenty-five years before. Daddy planned a surprise visit back to celebrate their anniversary. I don't remember all the logistics, but the ones I remember were impressive.

We had planned a vacation to Montreal to visit Mom's sister Vi and Vi's husband Jim. That's all Mom knew about, but Aunt Vi and Uncle Jim knew about Daddy's surprise. The morning we were to leave for Newfoundland, Mom and Aunt Vi were cleaning up after breakfast when the phone rang. It was an old friend of Mom's and Aunt Vi's calling from St. John's, Newfoundland. She said she was traveling and had a layover at the Montreal airport. Could they meet her there for a chat for a couple of hours?

Everyone said what a good idea this was — everyone but Mom was in on the surprise. While Mom and Aunt Vi washed the dishes, Daddy and Uncle Jim snuck the suitcases into the trunk of the car. When we arrived at the airport, Mom, Aunt Vi, Janet, and I were dropped off while the men parked the car, checked in the luggage, and got our tickets. (This was 1970, so I think perhaps not everyone needed to check in in-person.)

When we all met up again, Daddy realized we were far away from the gate where the plane would be boarding, so he thought he was going to have to tell Mom. Then, there was an announcement about a flight leaving for St. John's — our flight — and Mom said, "Oh, let's go look. Maybe there will be someone we know getting on." Sure, Mom!

When we got to the gate, Daddy began to walk toward the area where only passengers could go. Mom said, "Walter, get out of there! You can't go in there!" With a grin, Daddy kept walking. The people boarding the plane — including a few nuns — were very amused. Daddy pulled the tickets out of his pocket and said, "We're going." I have a photo of Mom and Daddy sitting on the plane. Daddy is looking smug as if he's thinking, *I pulled it off!* Mom is looking stunned as if thinking, *Am I really going back home?*

And that's my kooky daddy. It was so much fun growing up not knowing what crazy thing he was going to do next!

— Kat Mincz —

Chapter
6

Not So Grave

I Wouldn't Be Caught Dead in That

Never underestimate the power
of a good outfit on a bad day.
~Author Unknown

I was blessed with parents who genuinely loved one another, but they were true opposites. My father was punctual, practical, serious, and always on task. He was the pillar of the family. He used logic and common sense to make decisions and never strayed from the norm. My mother was late for everything, original, eccentric, playful, and silly. She found the humor and joy in everything she did. She never followed the rules. Her behavior made others laugh but usually got a disapproving eye roll from my dad. She was social and fun, and she marched to the beat of her own drum — and I mean that literally.

My father was like clockwork. Predictable. He served in the Navy and had the qualities of a soldier. He wanted a clean house and disliked pillows and blankets in the living room as we lounged to watch our one television. He came home from work at the same time every day. He kept the lawnmower busy, and the hedges were constantly trimmed. He had the lushest, greenest grass in the neighborhood. He waxed his car religiously. He polished and spit-shined his dress shoes for church while he whistled. These were things we could always count on.

My mother was the wild card. She would run into the drugstore to buy a birthday card and stay in the store forty minutes while my dad sat outside in the car. Eventually, he'd turn off the engine and roll down the window to chain-smoke cigarettes while he waited. Sometimes, he would tell us to go in and find her. She would usually be found in an aisle of the store offering comfort to a young mom who was upset about a sick child or a woman who just lost her husband and needed an ear. My mother was oblivious that the carload of family awaited her. She was doing what she felt was the right thing to do… at that moment.

At weddings, she would "kick up her heels," as she called it. My father would call it something else. She always loved to dance and clown around. She would grab a centerpiece of flowers from the table and put them on her head. She made herself laugh harder than everyone. Her sisters and nieces all took pleasure in her unpredictable antics.

My mom rode a bike all over town. She never got a driver's license, so her bike was her key to freedom. Everyone in town knew her as the lady on the bike. She waved at everyone who beeped at her. She became a regular sight to those who spotted her on her daily rides. She rode to church, to run errands, and to visit elderly shut-ins, bringing them hot coffee and donuts.

She regularly stopped and picked up banana peels she would see discarded on the side of the road and tucked them in her pocket. She always feared someone would slip and fall. One day, she spotted a silky blue necktie on the side of the road. It looked fine to her, and she put it in her pocket. She had it dry-cleaned and presented it to my dad. He asked her why she had bought him a tie.

"I didn't buy it. I was riding down the street, and it was lying on the side of the road. I had it dry-cleaned. It's a really nice tie," she said.

Dad was not having it. He would never enjoy wearing a tie she had found on the dirty roadside. "I would never be caught dead in that tie," he said dismissively.

One time she saw a man wearing no coat on a cold day. She ran into a nearby store and bought him a coat — not just any coat but a $180 ski jacket.

When I was grown, I came over to their house to show off my new puppy. I wanted to take a photo with the puppy and my parents. My mother raised her finger to signal for me to wait a minute before snapping the photo. It was early January. She ran to the front door and grabbed a half-dead Christmas wreath that was still hanging on a hook. She put her head through the wreath, which had dead needles on half of it. A big, red-velvet bow hung in her face. She said, "Now I am ready! Take the picture!" She cackled and laughed, knowing how Dad would react.

My father was not pleased. "Are you kidding me?" he said. She then insisted that she sit on his lap for the photo. As she laughed hysterically, his eyes rolled back in his head. That picture, to this day, is my favorite. I finally saw that she was trying to take his rigid edges and make them imperfect, to create a place of spontaneity where he could play in her perpetual sandbox. I could see that he secretly enjoyed her antics.

Years later, when my dad passed away, we all went to the funeral home. He looked at peace and so dignified in his suit and tie. My mother asked us if we recognized the tie. It was the one she had found on the side of the road years earlier. She said, "Well, he said he wouldn't be caught dead in that tie, so I had the last laugh." By the time the funeral had ended, everyone who attended had heard about the tie and got a good chuckle during a sad time. That was my mother!

— Blanche Carroll —

Ashes, Ashes

Life every man holds dear, but the dear man holds
honor far more precious than life.
~William Shakespeare

Not long after I buried the ashes of my parents under a magnolia tree, per their wishes, my aunt Sandy called me with a surprise. She announced that the headstones she had ordered for Mom and Dad were ready. She knew they would prefer to be buried in their home state of New York, so she asked me to send their cremains to the cemetery where there was a family plot with plenty of space (for me, too, she added). She gave me the address.

As the only child, I'd often discussed their final wishes with Mom and Dad. They had told me about a particular spot in their yard in Illinois that they wanted to be their final resting place, and I had honored those instructions.

Out of respect, I was unwilling to start over with burials elsewhere. New York? They had last lived in the Empire State before World War II broke out. Why would it be considered their home state in the 1990s?

Days went by, and my aunt called to check on my progress. I assured her I was working on it.

Actually, I was grieving, worrying, cussing, and desperately trying to figure out a solution to please everybody. I searched for urns and noticed that many were simple metal tins, nothing elaborate. I bought two decorative cookie tins at a thrift shop. I was staying at my late parents' house, and there was no computer. Using Mom's manual typewriter, I created labels with their names and the required dates.

I headed to a pet store, where I bought two bags of sparkling white aquarium stones. I researched the average weight of human cremains and filled the cookie tins appropriately. I boxed them up neatly before going to the post office.

After I mailed the package to the cemetery, all was sunny with Aunt Sandy. She could move forward with her plans.

However, cemetery officials in the Great State of New York seemed rather suspicious of my activities and asked me for certified copies of my parents' death certificates. I complied with the paperwork but never offered any explanation about the contents of those cookie tins.

— Roberta Beach Jacobson —

The Last Laugh

*Laughter elicited from a prank informs the offender
that their actions are unacceptable.*
~Kilroy J. Oldster, Dead Toad Scrolls

A t Grandma's funeral over ten years ago, I told a funny story that made the crowd laugh out loud. A relative approached me at the luncheon afterward. "I wasn't sure I was at the right funeral until you told that story about Pern. She was such a character!" he said.

Grandma Pern baked cookies, grew beautiful flowers, and crocheted blankets for her grandchildren, like so many grandmothers do. She played cards with a group of friends and enjoyed going to church, but Grandma Pern was also a force to be reckoned with. She was outspoken, feisty, and swore like a sailor. She complained in writing to every government official this side of the Mississippi when she had an idea for improvement or felt like she had been wronged.

Years ago, Grandma received a phone call from a stranger. The person on the other end of the phone explained that Pern had won a prize, but she would need to send in some money in order to receive her winnings. Grandma immediately smelled a rat but played along.

"Oh, really?" Grandma asked. "How lucky can I be? I'd be happy to do whatever you need!"

After a few minutes on the phone, Grandma Pern started asking more questions. She asked for the name of the caller as well as a phone number. She also asked where to send her payment. The scammer on the other end of the phone gave her some information and said Grandma would be receiving a phone call the next day. A FedEx employee would come to her house to collect the money.

"That sounds fantastic," Grandma said.

Then she called the chief of police in her rural Iowa town with a population of 1,618.

"I'm getting scammed," she yelled into the phone. "I've been chatting with someone who wants to steal my money. I've got enough information to string them up!"

Grandma Pern was irate when the police chief told her there was nothing he could do. He said she just needed to ignore these hoodlums who were trying to take advantage of an elderly person. Then he added calmly, "We have more pressing issues to take care of in this town, Pern."

Grandma wasn't happy with this response and let him know. She decided to take matters into her own hands.

The next day, she got another call from the schemers, who told her to write out a check for several thousand dollars. Late in the afternoon, a FedEx employee would be stopping by her house to pick up the check, they said.

"That sounds great," Grandma said. "I'll be waiting with the money."

True to their word, the FedEx employee arrived. Grandma opened the door.

"We're here for a pickup," the employee explained. "Whatever we're picking up is to be sent priority overnight."

Grandma hadn't written out a check, but she had questions.

"Do I have to pay anything?" Grandma asked.

"No, it will be billed to the party that requested the pickup," the employee answered.

"How are the costs determined?" Grandma asked.

"It's all based on weight," the employee said. "The heavier an item, the more expensive it is. But don't worry, you won't have to pay for anything," the FedEx employee explained.

"Just a minute," Grandma said. Then she disappeared into her spare bedroom, which was filled with a bunch of junk she rarely used.

She appeared with a big stack of magazines she had been keeping for years, as well as the heaviest item she could find that she didn't need: an old JCPenney catalog, the kind everyone looked at years ago when making a Christmas list.

"Can I send all this stuff?" Grandma asked.

"Sure, you can," the employee said. "I'll just need to get a big box."

As the employee packed items into the box, Grandma walked into her kitchen and tore a piece of paper from a notebook.

She wrote in big letters: "Go to hell!" and signed her name at the bottom.

"I just have this note to put inside," Grandma said sweetly, with a big smile. "I really appreciate your help."

As the FedEx truck drove away, Grandma said she felt an incredible amount of joy.

Then she walked into her kitchen, found her notebook, and began writing a letter to her state senator about the situation. After all, she needed someone to take action!

As was often the case, Grandma Pern got the last laugh. She never heard from the scammers again.

— Tyann Sheldon Rouw —

48

First Funeral

*Laugh, my friend, for laughter ignites a fire within
the pit of your belly and awakens your being.*
~Stella McCartney

I didn't attend my first funeral until I was twenty years old. Call me fortunate or call me strange, but my parents didn't take me to any funerals when I was a child. And when I became a teenager, no such occasions arose.

But then my great-great-aunt passed away after an extended illness. My mother gave me the details of the wake, as we call the visitation service in my native New Orleans. I was working until early evening, so we planned to meet at the funeral home. My mother would escort me through my first experience of a formal farewell to a loved one.

I approached the two-story funeral home in the faint light of dusk. The shadowed columns and carvings reminded me of a house I had seen in a horror movie. I wondered if the building might have been used as a movie set some time in the past. The usually busy street seemed oddly deserted as I followed the sidewalk to the entry. Did my steps falter as I approached the concrete stairway out front? I don't remember, but I remember a definite feeling of eeriness.

Once inside, the aroma of flowers overpowered me. My ever-sensitive sinuses began to fill, and I started sniffling in an effort to breathe. People I didn't recognize surrounded me. As I scanned the dimly lit entry hall of the building, I realized there were several visitations going on, and my family wasn't the only one in attendance. The hunt was on for the right parlor.

I walked from parlor entry to parlor entry until I found my aunt's family name posted. Familiar voices reached me through the doorway. I stepped through into a room ringed with upholstered chairs and dark wood occasional tables.

"Did you sign the visitors' book?" my mother asked when she approached me through the crowd. Through allergy-induced sniffles, I assured her I had. She took my arm to direct me to the inner parlor where my aunt reposed. I spotted many familiar faces. Our progress toward the casket was slowed by hugs and kisses along the way.

At last, the crowd seemed to part like a scene in a movie, and I could see the casket and the prie-dieu before it. Candles stood at either end of the casket, and a floral blanket covered part of it. The lines of floral tributes that began in the other room extended into a horseshoe shape with the coffin at its base. I took a deep, sniffly breath before walking forward.

"Are you okay?" my mother asked. "Do you need to sit down?"

"No, I'm fine," I lied and kept walking. I looked around the room at the aunts, uncles and cousins gathered there, and then I shifted my glance back to the casket.

All I could see of my aunt from that distance was her nose. Her hawk-like, Mediterranean nose protruded above the side of the casket. And every single one of my relatives, including my mother, had the same nose. All I could see were noses everywhere I looked!

My own nose was taunting me with tickling sniffles. Good grief, did I have the same nose? I'd always felt my father's Irish heritage had gentled my nose shape, but was I kidding myself?

I fought the laughter threatening to escape me at that moment. My head told me I should be solemn and sad in the presence of my beloved aunt's corpse. My heart kept saying, "Noses, noses, they've all got noses," like some children's nursery rhyme gone berserk. My shoulders shook as I fought the crazy urge to giggle.

"Are you sure you're okay?" my mother whispered to me. "I know this is new for you."

I didn't say anything, just nodded and headed to the little kneeling bench. As I knelt there, I prayed for help in containing my inappropriate laughter. The last thing I wanted to do was upset my family members by laughing at my aunt's nose.

When I felt I had gained control of my laughter, I rose from the prie-dieu and turned back to the room full of noses. A few more hugs, and I was free to leave the room.

Mama and I went outside and were enveloped by the steamy New Orleans night. We walked to the parking lot to head home.

"What happened in there? Are you sure you're okay?" she wanted to know. "You looked like you were choking on something."

"In a way," I told her. "I was choking back laughter. All I could notice were the noses on everybody once I saw Auntie's protruding from the casket. I didn't want to burst out laughing about it, but all the noses were the same big, old beaks."

I looked at Mama, and she looked at me. We both started laughing and laughed all the way to our cars. Auntie's legacy to me was the laughter she gave me that night. She was transformed from the stern and slightly frightening elderly leader of the family to a source of delight. I've never forgotten my first funeral and the last laugh Auntie gave me.

— Mary Beth Magee —

49

Tea Mug Memorial

I've been embarrassing myself since about birth.
~Phil Lester

I t is hard to express the pain of losing my favorite tea mug — a mug that has stood by my side for at least a decade. Always faithful, always ready to carry that precious amber liquid that brings me health and comfort on a daily basis. No matter how much pressure it was under, no matter how hot things got, it never let me down.

Yesterday, I let my mug down. I had just made a delicious batch of my special tea, and I put my mug on the back of the truck while I put some stuff in the back seat.

That's when it happened. I forgot my trusty mug was sitting precariously on the edge of my truck, and I started to back out of my driveway. I am sure now that it was calling to me, but in my hurry, I did not hear its cries of fear!

I backed out, put the car in Drive, and drove away from my house. Only a few yards down the road, I realized that my mug was not in the cupholder! In a split second, I realized what I had done, and I frantically looked in the rearview mirror.

In horror, I saw my mug lying on the pavement. There was now a car behind me, so I quickly pulled around the block and came back out onto my street. My nerves were on edge as a car in front of me drove straight toward my mug! With a sigh of relief, I saw the responsible driver straddle the mug with his car.

But my sigh of relief turned into a sob as I pulled up to my house and saw my mug's lifeblood leaking out onto the pavement. A car had callously run over it while I was circling the block.

My mug's head was crushed, and so was my heart. His life force was gone…

I walked up to my trusty friend and just stared at it. I couldn't believe what had happened. Why?! Why did this have to happen to me?

I documented the scene of the crime, put his limp body on my porch, and went to my destination with great sadness.

What may have hurt almost as much as losing my trusted friend was that none of my boys would come to the curbside memorial service that I tried to have for it when I got home. I asked them nicely. I begged them to be there for their father in his hour of need.

I started with my youngest. "Chase, would you come out to the curb for just a few minutes?"

"Dad, this isn't about your mug, is it?"

"It might be."

He kept saying things like, "Dad, are you serious? It is just a mug!"

Just a mug… JUST A MUG! He knows better than to say that to me. He knows that my mug and I were inseparable. How could I have failed my boys in not teaching them to have empathy for the older generation?

Then I went to Connor, the son who wants to be a senior pastor. The one who will have to comfort people and entire families in their grief sometime in the future. I poked my head into his room.

"Connor, would you come outside with me for a few moments?"

"Dad, I am not going outside with you to have a memorial service for your tea mug."

"But, Connor, you don't understand…"

"Dad, you are a child."

"No, Connor, you are my child, and you should be there for your elderly parent in his time of need."

He just kept laughing and shaking his head. I tried to say something else, but he pointed at the door and said, "GET OUT!" I knew he wasn't being disrespectful. He was just quoting from one of his favorite social-media videos.

I then went to my firstborn son, my namesake: Caleb Michael Powers. I asked him if he would be willing to come outside and have a few moments of silence with me around my makeshift memorial.

"You have got to be kidding, Dad! I love you, but I am not going to go to the memorial service for your tea mug."

"Please, Caleb? You know how much this means to me."

My son then grabbed his phone and started to record me while narrating to his friends about what his dad was trying to get him to do.

I think he shared it on his Snap Face or Chat Book. I couldn't believe that the fruit of my loins was mocking his dad on social media.

I hung my head in sorrow and slowly walked upstairs. I had gathered some sticks from my back yard and made a cross memorial that I tied together with string. I made the solemn walk out to the curb and tried to stick the cross in the ground as near to the spot of the accident as I could.

The ground was frozen. I had to go back in and get a knife to cut through the frozen tundra to allow my memorial marker to stand tall and strong. I planted it into the cold, unfeeling ground and stood there… all alone. I paid my respects and then went back into the house.

At my darkest hour, two young ladies who are like daughters to me came through for me. Maddie Ginter responded to Caleb's mockery of me on Snap Face. She said, "Caleb, you have to understand how hard this is for your dad. Let him go through the grieving process. It is okay for him to have a memorial. Tell him I stand with him in solidarity, but I will not be attending, mostly because I am home right now, and I want to *stay* home. But please just let your father grieve."

About an hour later, there was a knock at my door. It was Miki Ginter. When Caleb's video was making the rounds on Chat Book, she was in the library at her college studying. It was Finals Week. She had a ton of exams to study for, but she left the library immediately to help her aging youth pastor in his time of sorrow. She slowly walked downstairs to where I was expressing my grief by writing this true account on my computer. She had genuine concern in her eyes. She gave me a big hug and two very thoughtful and caring things for my memorial.

Here was someone who understood. She has probably consumed more of this special tea than anyone not named Michael T. Powers!

Finally, I had children who cared. Two precious "daughters" who earned the right to be in our family because there is some kind of squatter's law that says they eventually can own our house if they spend thousands of hours in it during a calendar year.

When I informed my family that I was thinking of taking the remains up north and burying them at my favorite campsite the next time we went camping, my wife said, "There is no way we are keeping that broken mug until the summer. It has to be so full of germs after all these years. You need to get rid of that thing!"

Sigh…

You may think this is all way over the top. You would be wrong. My tea mug was like family to me. For at least ten years of my life, this mug stood by me and fit perfectly in my hand. Who knows, those germs may have even kept me healthy by building up my immune system!

And so here ends my time of trial. I knew this day was coming. I knew he wouldn't last forever. I have tried to find another tea mug just like it over the years, but to no avail. The brand name has been worn off for so long that there is no hope for me to be able to find the exact mug again.

Thank you, tea mug. Thank you for the amazing beverages you brought to my mouth over the years. You will be sorely missed.

— Michael T. Powers —

A Woman Never Tells Her Age

*How old would you be if you
didn't know how old you was?*
~Satchel Paige

"A woman who tells her age will tell anything." It was my mother's favorite adage. It was the creed that her mother, her sister, her two aunts, and even her grandmother also lived by. No one knew anyone's true age!

I'm sixty-nine, and I will admit it! However, I am certain that as I tell you this, my mother must be "rolling over in her grave," as the old saying goes. Mom would be horrified that I announced my real age, much less wrote about it.

I didn't know Mom's true age until I was in my twenties and accidentally found her passport. She thought she had hidden it safely in the bottom drawer of her dresser with her lace nightgowns and lingerie that were too good to wear. As I was soon to be married, she wanted me to have one of her pretty lace nightgowns, and that is when I discovered the truth.

Mom never even told her husband, my father, the correct year of her birth. She was afraid that he would find out that he had married an "older woman," as she was three years older than he was.

Grandma stretched the truth of her age to the limit. I will never forget going with her to the doctor, and Grandma making herself ten years younger when the nurse asked the year of her birth. I stared at Grandma with my mouth open. When I regained my speech, I said to her, "You were not ten years old when you gave birth to my mother!"

"Shush!" was her stern reply.

I feel sorry for any future relatives trying to sort out the genealogy of my mother's side of the family. It won't help any of them to look at the gravestones. My mother had the wrong year carved on my grandmother's monument. She made Grandma not ten years younger, but a few years. However, I will continue to keep Grandma's secret and won't tell you her correct age when she died. I don't want to cause an earthquake in the cemetery.

— Suzanne Alexander —

51

Appreciation for My Skier-in-Law

What you do is your history.
What you set in motion is your legacy.
~Leonard Sweet

'm not the most magnificent physical specimen on the beach, so most people wouldn't look at me and say, "There goes a guy who is into water sports." But I *am* into them — not because I love them but because I have no choice.

The reason? I married into a water-skiing family.

When my wife Barb was six years old, her father Jim taught her to ski in the brackish waters of Florida's Banana River between Merritt Island and Cape Canaveral. On loan from Boeing, her dad worked at the Cape in the early 1960s. It was during the formative years of our country's space program, a time when it seemed that even the sky was no longer the limit for human achievement.

It was the perfect era and the perfect environment for learning water sports. Jim bought a boat and a house on a canal that ran through the middle of a tranquil Cocoa Beach neighborhood, bringing the ski run literally to his family's back door. He was so enthusiastic about the activity that he built a special present for his kids — a wooden dock from which Barb and her sisters could hop into his boat anytime they were so inclined.

They did it nearly daily, and by the time she was eleven, Barb's father made sure she had graduated from kiddie skis to a single slalom, jetting across the boat's wake and eventually spraying water to an altitude twice her height. Her dad also taught her fortitude, since salt water often brings encounters with threatening sea creatures, and memories of multiple stings from Atlantic jellyfish have haunted her dreams.

When my wife's family moved to Washington State, they brought their affection for skiing with them, making pilgrimages every summer to the Columbia River and its ski-friendly setting.

That's when I entered the picture. About the time Barb and I began dating seriously, she invited me on her family's vacation with the question, "Have you ever water skied?"

"Lots of times," I answered.

"On one ski?" she inquired.

"Well, no," I confessed. "But I'm pretty good on two."

She grimaced. "In our family," she scolded, "we all ski on one. And we all do it well. And with my dad driving the boat, that's what he'll expect." With that, I realized if there was any hope of actually marrying this woman, an education in single-plank skiing was in my future.

Along with that came an education in Pacific Northwest water temperatures. Whereas my previous experience had been in the shallow lakes of Texas, most of Washington's waterways originated from recent snowmelt, and I quickly learned that goosebumps were a routine byproduct of water sports there. And with Barb's father around, I also learned not to complain about them.

I'll never forget my first try behind the boat with Jim at the throttle. Floating in the water while grasping the rope, awkwardly bobbing up and down in the icy drink, I was determined to impress him. Finally gaining my balance and my will, I yelled, "Hit it!" signaling Jim to accelerate.

In my imagination, I had pictured this moment, effortlessly rising on top of the wake and amazing my future father-in-law with my perfect form and acute coordination. Instead, the boat lurched forward, and the rope flew out of my hands, leaving me feeling flustered and uncoordinated. And cold.

Jim circled the boat around, and I grabbed the rope for another try. Unfortunately, the second verse was the same as the first — the boat sped off, taking the ski rope, but not me, with it. A third and fourth repetition saw the same results. On my next try, I finally struggled to a standing position, teetered and flailed for a few seconds, and then went down in a spectacular wipeout. Barb decided to put me out of my misery with the words, "Okay, my turn!" Then, following her immediate and stunning display of ski expertise, we returned to the dock with her father, like me, silent all the way.

Despite my clumsiness, I eventually passed the one-ski test (and got Jim's reluctant but genuine blessing). Over the next thirty-plus years, Barb and I continued our family's summer water-skiing tradition in Eastern Washington, though not even a wet suit could cure my near hypothermia. And I never found a remedy for my off-balance awkwardness. Our kids have fared better, not only successfully skimming across the water individually, but a few times skiing in pairs or even three at once. On one memorable occasion, Barb, along with two siblings and two cousins, proved their prowess by executing a Cypress Gardens-worthy, one-boat-five-skier pattern to the applause of our growing family of water-sports enthusiasts. My father-in-law took the role of chief cheerleader.

It was a solemn summer when Jim passed away; losing the patriarch and founder of our family ski tradition was a blow to us all. But the tradition lived on. The torch passed to my brother-in-law, who, every summer, continued to pull dozens of our siblings, cousins, kids and grandkids over the chilly Columbia. No doubt Jim would have been proud to see multiple generations continuing the tradition that he began.

Feeling nostalgic recently, Barb and I returned to Cocoa Beach and took a drive through the neighborhood where her father had settled his family a half-century earlier. Pulling up in front of their former address, we were dismayed to find a new home under construction on the site. We located the owners and told them who we were. They were kind enough to give us a tour of the property, explaining that a hurricane had leveled the previous house that Barb's father had bought.

We walked around the building site to the backyard canal, reminiscing about Barb's childhood ski exploits. Nearing the water's edge, we suddenly halted, staring down in disbelief. Though a hurricane had destroyed Barb's old house, there in front of us, fully intact, was the wooden dock her dad had constructed with his own hands years earlier. The storm may have toppled an entire home, but it couldn't destroy the gift from a tenacious father to his kids, just as it couldn't shatter the timeless memory of his devotion to see them excel.

Like the footings of that dock, his devotion had been driven deep, and like its weathered-but-solid deck boards, the results of his devotion endured.

Even for his clumsy son-in-law.

— Nick Walker —

Family Fun

52

Who's Fooling Whom?

I smile because you're my family. I laugh because
there's nothing you can do about it!
~Author Unknown

If you can't have fun with your kids, what's the point? Like the time when my husband was working in the evening, and I needed to run out to get some groceries. At twelve years old, my oldest could watch his siblings while I popped out. I told them I wouldn't be long and headed downstairs to the basement door that led to the garage.

An hour later, with the garage door closed behind me and struggling with heavy bags, I walked to the basement door. It was locked. With a sigh and a groan, I put down the groceries and knocked hard a few times. No answer. The kids were likely upstairs watching television. Now, I had to walk around and enter through the front door.

Groaning again, I picked up the groceries and made my way to the tool bench for the garage remote control. As I reached for it, I saw a Halloween mask my husband had brought home a few days earlier. One of my daughters had seen the face mask and did not like it. It was of an old man with long, white hair. It was pretty scary. The plan was to wear it for Halloween when my husband took the kids trick-or-treating. I picked it up.

Leaving the groceries behind, I put on the mask, opened the garage door, and made my way up the steps to the solid wood door. Our front door had an old-fashioned knocker on it, and the knock was sharp and very loud. You could hear that knocker no matter where you were in the house — or the neighbourhood, for that matter. *A sneaky approach is a far better idea,* I thought as I reached into the pocket of my leather jacket for my house keys.

The key slid quietly into the lock and turned. As I stepped into the foyer, the television was blaring from the living room. Normally open, the door to the living room was closed. With my hand gripping the doorknob, I wondered if something had spooked my children. Then, with a flourish, I opened the door and took a large step onto the carpet.

I stood still and silent in my black suede ankle boots, my black jacket and a pretty scary mask. Squinting through the holes of the mask, with a small smile upon my hidden lips, I watched the chaos begin. It started as one child turned to see who was in the room. Suddenly, there was screaming and clutching of the closest sibling, and one used her arms and legs spider-fashion to manoeuver backwards from the couch. It was too much. I quickly removed the mask and asked, "So, who thought it would be a good idea to lock the basement door on Mom?"

* * *

The prior year, my two eldest, who were around ten and eleven at the time, walked into the kitchen with nail polish. "We're going to paint Dad's toenails for April Fools' Day." The pair had been tossing around ideas as to what would be a good joke to play on Dad. Painting toenails was a great choice as it didn't involve water falling from the top of the kitchen door onto an unsuspecting father.

I watched as they snuck across the carpeted floor to the foot of the bed where my husband's feet stuck out from beneath the covers. Soon enough, the job was done. I walked the children to the school bus and returned home to make our morning coffee and wake my husband.

The bedroom door was ajar when I poked in my head. "I've made coffee. It's on the counter." Then I stood in the hallway and watched as he swung his feet to the floor, with his back to me, and slowly sat up. He stretched his arms and then slumped over the edge of the bed to stare at the floor. Suddenly, his shoulders straightened, and I stifled a snicker as his head lowered to get a closer look.

"Cher!" he called to me, not knowing I was still in the hallway.

"Yep," I answered from the door.

He stood up and spun around, with a startled expression on his face. "My toes!"

Laughing, I made my way to the kitchen.

***

Now my five-year-old skipped into the kitchen with a smile on her face and excitement in her voice. She said, "I want to play an April Fools' joke on Dad, but I need your help." I put down whatever I was doing and turned to her with a smile of my own. My sweet, innocent little one had a glimmer in her eyes.

With my elbows on the countertop and head resting on my hands, I leaned forward and asked my five-year-old daughter, "What do you need my help with?"

"I was going to ask Matthew, but he said he can't open the wine bottle."

"The wine bottle?" I stood up. "What will you do with the wine?"

"I want to put it in the juice container." She was very excited now. She continued, "Dad has juice every morning, and he doesn't like wine. It will be a great April Fools' joke."

I could see flaws in this idea. Even though the container and the lid weren't see-through, he would see and smell the wine before he drank it, but I didn't want to discourage her. I went along with it and opened a bottle of wine, poured it in the jug and let her put it in the fridge. Then I wished her good luck, woke my husband and left for work.

I came home later, and grabbed a glass from the cupboard and the juice container from the fridge. I hesitated as my husband walked into the room, remembering the April Fools' prank involving the orange juice.

"How was your day?" I asked, still holding the juice container mid-pour.

"Do you know that little girl of ours played a prank on me?"

"Why do you think I haven't poured the juice yet?" I smiled. "So, she got you?"

"It's juice. I poured the wine back into the bottle. Yes, she got me good." He shook his head and pulled out a chair to sit on.

"What a mess. I took a huge gulp and practically choked! Wine went all over the kitchen counter, all the way to the table and on the floor."

"I didn't think it would fool you," I said. I crossed my arms, leaned against the fridge and chuckled.

"Why didn't you think it would work?"

"Well, I figured once you poured it into a glass, you would see and smell that it wasn't fruit punch or juice," I said matter-of-factly.

Suddenly, a little voice beside the kitchen door said, "He doesn't drink juice in a glass, Mom. He drinks his juice from the container."

"WHAT?"

— Cheryl-Anne Iacobellis —

53

Chicken Soup for the Soul

Life's a Game

Money can't buy happiness, but it can buy
board games, and that's enough.
~Author Unknown

I used to think I had three moms. Now, I know that sounds kind of strange, but it's true. You see, my mom was a triplet. They all looked the same, sounded the same, and had the same wacky sense of humor. And all three were larger-than-life and more than a little crazy, but in a good way... most of the time.

Known as the famous — or should I say infamous — Mars triplets, these girls put fun on the front burner.

They grew up playing pranks on everyone they knew — teachers, friends, even my grandparents — because no one could tell them apart. And then, to finally differentiate themselves, the day they turned eighteen, Auntie Betty dyed her hair bright red, Auntie Norma dyed hers platinum blond, and my mom, Margaret, the sensible one (ha ha) remained au naturel, the lone brunette. They kept it that way their whole lives, and they called each other Big Red, Old Yeller, and Rin Tin Tin. Seriously, that's how they signed every birthday and Christmas card.

They were always up for a party, game or impromptu jam session. My dad was a musician who played jazz saxophone and my uncle Peter, Norma's husband, played the bass, so there was always music at our house.

My mom also wrote an Erma Bombeck-esque memoir about her life called *I Married an Idiot*. Funny title, huh? The very first line of the book actually revealed it was a self-deprecating joke on herself — that my *dad* was the one who married the crazy idiot.

She wrote that they had the same breakfast every morning for twenty-five years: a piece of toast and a fight. And, sometimes, no toast. After breakfast my dad would drive off to work, and she'd stand on the front porch shaking her fist and saying, "And don't come back 'til you love me!"

But, in reality, they really did adore each other.

My mom was not a domestic goddess, not even close. But she was an amazing golfer, joke teller, and whiz at games, especially crossword puzzles. She sometimes lost track of time and did crosswords all day long. At 5:00 P.M., she would just "spray a little Pledge behind her ears" so when my dad got home from work, he'd think she'd been doing housework all day!

Whenever she got out the vacuum cleaner, my brother and I would say, "Who's coming over?"

My mom and her sisters and family grew up in Brantford, Ontario. She used to say that, until "that darn Wayne Gretzky came along," she was one of the most famous people from Branford.

We used to have huge family Christmases. We almost always hosted Christmas at our house, and every year there was a big celebration with all the cousins, aunts and uncles. After a huge turkey dinner with all the fixings — still my favorite meal to prepare and eat — there was always a big talent show where everybody, even the kids, had to do something. They literally made us get up and perform, and they wouldn't take no for an answer!

My cousin Beckie and I would usually act out the nativity scene. (It was always a fight over who would be Mary and who would be Joseph.) And I'm not proud to say that I usually won… because it was my house!

We'd safety-pin long white bath towels onto our nightgowns to create old-fashioned robes, swaddle one of my dolls or one extremely docile cat named Sunday into a makeshift manger, and sing a very pious version of "Silent Night."

Hilarious, I'm sure, but come on… it was my start in show biz!

I went on to become an actress, producer and singer-songwriter, and those talent shows were my humble beginnings.

(It also just occurred to me as I am writing this that Beckie and I have always signed our birthday and holiday cards to each other through the years, "To Mary, Love Joseph." The triplets' tradition continues.)

Then, after the talent show, we always had a rousing game with everyone participating. It was a homemade, pen-and-paper game played with categories and letters that our family called "Guggenheim."

I loved the game part of our Christmases, even though, as a child, I remember feeling that I could never win that game... never. I was the youngest of all the cousins, and the parents would never give the kids any help.

I come from a very competitive family.

But, one summer, I was invited to my best friend Karen's cottage, and her family taught me another parlor game they called The Dictionary Game. You had to make up phony definitions to weird words and guess the real definitions. Now, finally, here was a game I could win!

For some reason, I was really good at making up funny or plausible definitions, and I guess I had enough of a wordsmith background from my mom, the writer, that I could often figure out the word origins, too.

So, I came home from the cottage, and suddenly I was the twelve-year-old who taught my family a brand-new game they loved — a game I could actually win once in a while, which was so thrilling to me! And The Dictionary Game ultimately became the inspiration for my board game, Balderdash, which I ended up creating in the mid-1980s. Balderdash became a runaway hit in North America and around the world and has made so many special memories for other families. Really, I never get tired of hearing how people play it every Christmas or every summer at their cottage. Some family member always writes the most outrageous definitions, and they all laugh until they cry.

My parents always encouraged me to follow my dreams and do what I love. It's the best gift they could have given me, and I hope I'm passing it on to my kids, too. I'm so grateful for my life, my wacky family, my parents, my brother, all my cousins... and my unorthodox but memorable childhood. I was raised by two extremely creative, talented, kind, fun, fun-loving and, most of all, loving parents. They really did love me unconditionally, and I think it's been my foundation — the bedrock of knowing I was valued.

For this, I am eternally thankful.

I have a family of my own now: a wonderful husband, son and daughter. We love to play games together, too, especially when we all collapse into fits of laughter. And when we do, I always feel like my mom and dad are looking down, smiling and laughing right along with us.

— Laura Robinson —

54

Kept Under Wraps

I think most people have that crazy uncle
they sit at Thanksgiving dinner with.
~Alan Colmes

Our family has been intrigued by a mystery for many, many years. It all started one Christmas Eve when Uncle Jack arrived just in time for dinner. He stomped the snow off his shoes as he balanced a pile of presents in his arms. We all helped him set the gifts under the tree. "There's more..." he told us, heading back to his car. We formed an assembly line as boxes were handed along.

The tower of gifts soon grew beside the tree. It was quite impressive but for a peculiar reason. Uncle Jack had brought a total of seventeen presents, all wrapped in the same gold paper with large black diamonds. It was quite a contrast to the other gifts under the tree, which were wrapped in pretty holiday paper.

The children didn't care. They were much more interested in the contents and tore into the packages with gusto. We were soon stuffing trash bags with the discarded wrappings.

The wrapping paper appeared again on our father's birthday. We thought nothing of it until it appeared at eleven more birthday parties. We figured Uncle Jack had gotten a good deal on it. Ugly as it was, it was probably on clearance. The paper then appeared on a large gift at a baby shower. Again, it contrasted sharply with the pink and blue pile. "It's the thought that counts," we reminded each other.

On Thanksgiving, three bottles of wine sat on the kitchen counter, each wearing the wrapping paper and a purple bow. We began to wonder if he had purchased the paper by the yard straight from the factory.

When Christmas Eve rolled around again, we took bets before Uncle Jack's arrival. Half of us had to pay up when he walked in with a black diamond-studded gift under each arm. Again, we formed the assembly line, giggling and elbowing each other. This time, we took photos, posing next to the gaudy tower.

The crazy paper has shown up at every event since. We have so many questions. Where did he get it? Where does he store it? Is it one giant roll? Or does he have his basement stockpiled with rolls as far as the eye can see?

Some day, I predict, Uncle Jack will walk through the door with a Christmas gift wrapped in snowman paper. And those of us who bet on the long shot will shout, dance and extend a hand for the massive payout.

— Marianne Fosnow —

55

The King of April Fools

I realized my family was funny because
nobody ever wanted to leave our house.
~Anthony Anderson

My father was the King of April Fools, even if it was only self-proclaimed. For as long as I could remember, April Fools' Day was treated like a major holiday in my house. No one else in my class even knew what this day meant, but my family thought about it throughout the month of March. We plotted and planned how we could "get" the rest of the family to forget, for a quick minute, that it was April first. Some of my dad's best pranks included freezing our underwear so we couldn't find any in the morning; putting plastic wrap on the toilet; and, of course, the classic trick of pretending there's an emergency that doesn't actually exist.

Don't be mistaken: My mom, sister and I were also worthy contenders in the running for Queen of April Fools. There were actually two years when my dad was "dethroned," even if it did take the three of us teaming up to pull it off.

The first time started with my mom scheduling him a dentist appointment on April first. The dentist was a family friend and knew that my dad loved April Fools' Day, so he agreed to participate. Mom asked the dentist to tell Dad he needed a root canal. They even scheduled the oral surgery!

Please understand that my dad rarely even had a cavity and was shocked by this news. Dad came home very upset and couldn't believe it. We were all waiting in the kitchen and yelled, "April Fools!" He stood there in utter disbelief, realizing the dentist was in on it. He had to give us the crown until the next year when, of course, he was waiting, guns blazing.

The second time we won the crown wasn't until years later when my sister and I were in high school. That night, we headed upstairs to bed, and Dad thought he had won that year with some silly prank. He settled into his recliner and turned on March Madness. Little did he know, my sister and I weren't in bed but had snuck back downstairs. We had recently bought a second TV for our basement. Both TVs had the same remote control, but my dad didn't know that. We hid behind him in the kitchen and secretly changed the channel. He quickly grabbed the remote and changed it back. He looked at my mom and expressed how weird that was. We waited a couple of minutes and changed the channel again.

Now, he was getting super-agitated. The game was also nearing the end, so he thought the TV was malfunctioning during the most important moment. The channel would suddenly change; he would furiously change it back; we would wait a minute and then change it again, while muffling our giggles. My mom even had to get up because she was trying not to burst into laughter and ruin it. He was finally so upset that he got up… and then saw us crouched behind the kitchen cabinets. We all burst out laughing, realizing we had yet again dethroned the King.

As my sister and I got older and moved out of the house, it became harder for the family to prank each other, but we still managed to occasionally pull it off. While my sister was in college, she actually missed her flight home from spring break, which happened to be on April first. When she tried to tell us, we didn't believe her. It took about a half-hour of her saying, "This is not a prank. I actually missed my flight," until we took her seriously.

A few years after that, my dad was diagnosed with a terminal disease. He was given months to live, but that did not affect our family's humor. That's just how my dad handled things. The months he was given to live turned into years, and we fortunately held onto every moment we spent together during those five years. It might not have been the easiest of times, but it definitely made us all grateful for each and every moment we got to share together.

It wasn't until the last few weeks that he declined rapidly. We spent a lot of time holding his hand, praying that his pain be taken away. As that final week came and went, the nurses and doctors were saying "any minute now," but he kept holding on. I think we were all thinking the same thing, but none of us wanted to say it: *Is he waiting until April Fools' Day? Is this his way to forever be the King of April Fools?* We all made sure to spend the entire day of April first there, thinking it had to happen that day. They say that your hearing is the last to go, so maybe he was lying there laughing at us, knowing he was going to hang on for one more day. The next day, he left this world but not our hearts — and he officially became the King of April Fools forever.

—Jillian Pfennig—

56

The Magical Age of Freedom

An aunt is a safe haven for a child. Someone who will
keep your secrets and is always on your side.
~Sara Sheridan

In my family, eighteen was the magical age of freedom. When I was ten and wanted to get my ears pierced, the answer was "when you're eighteen." When I was twelve and wanted a kitten, the answer was "when you're eighteen and move out, you can get any pet you'd like." When I was sixteen and wanted to stay out past midnight, the answer was "when you're eighteen and have your own place, you can stay out as late as you want."

There were many fights with my parents that would end with me screaming, "I'll be eighteen in 104 weekends, and then you can't tell me what to do anymore!"

It's so ingrained in our family culture that I think it may be intertwined with our DNA. My brother slightly enhanced the "When You're Eighteen Rule" and would tell his daughters, "At eighteen, you can do whatever you want because you will be moving out."

My brother's daughter Katie turned eighteen during her senior year of high school, which invoked rule number two in my family: "It doesn't matter if you're eighteen. As long as you live under my roof, you'll follow my rules." It's like an algebra equation where eighteen equals freedom — unless "you live under my roof." Then, some freedoms are added, but all other rules apply.

Katie and her best friend wanted to come to L.A. for their senior year spring break and crash at my one-bedroom apartment, conveniently located in West L.A., three miles from the beach. I was absolutely thrilled, right up until they arrived and announced that their main purpose in coming to L.A. was to get tattoos. I was in a quandary. Which rule applied? The When You're Eighteen rule or the When You Move Out rule? I defaulted to the When You're Eighteen rule, but I wasn't sure how their moms would feel about them returning from spring break with a permanent souvenir.

I had to make a choice. I could either pretend I didn't know what they were up to and put my head in the sand, or I could take control of the situation. Their plan was to go to Venice Beach and randomly pick a tattoo booth. At least if I participated I could take them to a reputable tattoo parlor and make sure they didn't pick an ugly design or get an infection. I chose to participate, thinking I was the best aunt on the planet.

I drove them to a well-known tattoo parlor on the infamous Melrose Boulevard, where I'd held my previous roommate's hand as she got her tattoo. They each selected a small design to be discreetly put on their feet. Katie was so brave as the needle hammered ink into the top of her foot. She squeezed my hand really tight, but she didn't cry.

The next morning, Katie begged me not to tell her mom. I thought, *Well, she's over eighteen. I'm not going to tattle on her.* I took my black Lab for a two-block sniff-a-thon, and as soon as we walked in the front door, Katie said so quickly that all her words ran together, "My mom wants to talk to you." Of course, in her excitement, she couldn't keep her mouth shut. Katie sheepishly said, "I'm sorry. It just slipped out." I sighed, thinking, *This kid can't even keep her own secrets.* She told her mom that I took them to get tattoos. I called my sister-in-law, Sue, who, rather than saying hello, answered with my full name: Jennifer K. Murphy. Panicked yet holding back laughter, I responded, "Don't you want to hear my side of the story?"

She said, "Yes, Jennifer, I would very much like to hear your side of the story."

Sue was like a sister to me and took on the very difficult job of being the voice of reason during my wild teenage years. We made a pact that I would do the same for her girls. It was okay for me to keep the girls' secrets as long as it wasn't anything serious.

Sue agreed that the When You're Eighteen rule was in effect. She agreed that I was being responsible by making sure the girls went to a safe and clean facility, and got unobtrusive, tasteful tattoos. By the end of the phone call, she agreed that supervising this adventure was the best thing I could've done, and I was, in fact, the best aunt on the planet.

My friends thought this story was hilarious. None of them had grown up with the When You're Eighteen rule. They all hesitated a little bit when leaving their kids with me and never failed to say on the way out the door, "My kids better not have tattoos when I get home."

A few months later, Katie's little sister Elizabeth came to visit me in L.A. She was twelve at the time. The first thing out of her mouth was, "I want to get a tattoo just like my sister." All I had to do was ask her, "Are you eighteen?" She knew the rule. Wanting to keep my place as the cool aunt, I softened the blow by offering her alternative yet exotic choices: a henna tattoo, a belly chain, or a toe ring. She chose a toe ring... and so we bought matching toe rings at Venice Beach.

Fast forward twenty years. All three sisters came to visit me in Phoenix. As adults with busy lives, the only time I get to see the three girls together is at weddings and funerals, so this was a big deal. They were at my place for less than an hour before they said, "Aunt Jenni, we want to get matching sister tattoos. Will you take us?" They had already picked out the tattoo parlor and knew they were getting four-leaf clovers on their wrists. This time, all I had to do was chauffeur them — because they were all way, way over eighteen.

—Jenni Murphy—

57

Winner, Winner, Chili Dinner

Family: our sanity might be debatable,
but our bond is unbreakable.
~Author Unknown

"Let's have a chili cook-off for Mom's birthday party," my sister Ann in Tucson wrote in a group e-mail to the family. Out-of-town family members were coming to Kansas City from San Diego, Los Angeles, Tucson, and Denver to celebrate Mom's ninety-second birthday. The group included Mom's children, grandchildren—and spouses—and six great-grandchildren younger than seven. "We'll each put in five dollars. The winner gets all the money."

I was all over it. My husband Ken makes the best chili ever. I replied to the group: "Ken is going to win."

"I'm not going to win," Ken said.

Ann was going to try a new recipe with cinnamon. My niece Hope in Denver was bringing green chili. My daughter Becky planned bison chili. The others kept their recipes secret.

My San Diego brother, Brock, lobbied for enchiladas. "Neither of us has ever made chili."

"Nope," I wrote. "Chili."

As the date of the party approached, Ken seemed to be feeling the pressure. "The recipe calls for two kinds of beans, but I usually only use one," he said. "What should I do?"

"Definitely two beans," I said. "Why don't you use three? Throw in some garbanzos. They'll add color and texture."

"Garbanzo beans don't belong in chili." He bought some anyway.

I found an old trophy at a garage sale and took it to a trophy shop. I asked them to engrave "I'm Hot" on it. Ken would like that.

Brock wrote again. "Tacos?"

"Chili," I wrote. "And Ken's going to win."

Then I remembered something that might dampen the enthusiasm. "Mom doesn't like chili," I told my in-town sister, Amy.

"That's okay," she said. "I'll pick up chicken or something for her. We can still have the cook-off."

As I wrapped Mom's birthday gift, I thought about the little ones. "They won't like spicy chili," I told Ken.

I wasn't planning to enter the cook-off, but I had a recipe for Chili Blue from Girl Scout camp. Mom had been our leader, and we had cooked it over campfires in the woods. It's a sweet concoction made with ground beef, brown sugar, bacon, and canned pork and beans. I made a batch for the kids. It tasted just like I remembered.

Ken stirred his own chili and shook his head. "I'm not going to win."

I put my arm around him. "Honey, I don't care if you win. I've just been talking trash."

At the party, I placed my pot on the counter with the others. "This is for the little kids," I said. "And Mom might remember it."

Brock had found a recipe that used chunks of steak instead of ground beef. My son-in-law Eric placed dishes of cilantro and sour cream next to his. Amy sprinkled shredded cheddar on hers. We each put in our money and got a poker chip to place in a cup in front of the pot that held our favorite.

The tasting began. Right away, people complained that the Denver green chili was way too hot, and the Tucson cinnamon chili tasted weird. The San Diego chili was tasty, but when I tried Amy's batch, I thought I might vote for it. Becky's bison chili never happened. Her store was out of the ground meat, and she wasn't prepared to hunt her own buffalo.

My Los Angeles niece, Torin, tasted Ken's chili. "Garbanzo beans don't belong in chili," she said. "Otherwise, I might vote for this one."

Ken slumped and glared at me.

I tasted Eric's. I'm a sucker for cilantro. I had to admit it was better than Ken's, so I dropped in my chip. We filled our bowls with our favorites and found places at the table.

After dinner, Amy stood. "Before I announce the winner, I have a confession. I wouldn't have taken the prize money, but I didn't win anyway. I bought my chili at Wendy's."

I laughed amid shouts of "No way!" and "Unfair!"

Then came the big announcement. "And the winner is…"

Ken looked at the floor.

Amy announced my name!

As it turns out, most of our family members are like Mom. They don't like chili. My sweet-tasting concoction that sort of looked like chili won the day. And that's how I became the first — and probably last — Mom's Birthday Chili Cook-off Champion.

The trophy proudly sits on my desk. And it's true: I'm Hot (but my chili isn't).

Chili Blue

Serves one ninety-two-year-old great-grandmother and six great-grandchildren

Ingredients:
3 slices bacon, fried
1 pound ground beef
¾ cup bottled chili sauce
¼ cup loosely packed brown sugar
2 teaspoons prepared mustard
2 (15-ounce) cans pork and beans
Fry the bacon. Cool and crumble. Brown the ground beef in the bacon

drippings. Place beef and bacon in a stew pot or Dutch oven. Stir in the remaining ingredients. Cover and heat over medium heat, stirring occasionally, until heated through.

—Mary-Lane Kamberg—

Freebird

We can judge the heart of a man
by his treatment of animals.
~Immanuel Kant

I never wanted to live in the suburbs, with its cul-de-sacs and rules about what color you can paint your front door. It seemed too easy, too comfortable, too regulated. I was afraid of the person I would become if I lived in suburbia.

But then kids came along, and my husband and I felt the pull to live near family. So, we left South Philadelphia and moved into a suburban community in North Carolina. It's the kind of neighborhood people describe as idyllic, safe, and lovely. And it is. But still, I rolled my eyes at the HOA rules and winced at the chatter in the neighborhood Facebook group.

"There's a black Explorer idling on the corner of Tahoe and Ridgewood. Anyone know what's up?"

"Has anyone else noticed how horrible the new poop bags are in the dispensers on the trail? They rip REALLY easily."

My city self kept a wary eye on the development of my suburban self. Already within a few months, I was driving the nine-tenths of a mile to the grocery store while my bike collected dust in the garage. It seemed only a matter of time until I'd be fretting about a neighbor's crooked mailbox. I needed something to ward off the tentacles of comfortable conformity and decided that backyard chickens should do the trick. My neighbors' yards would have emerald-green grass and patio furniture. Mine would have chicken poop and feathers.

The HOA approved our coop diagram and paint samples, and the city granted us a Limited Agricultural Permit. And, with that, we were authorized to keep chickens, a maximum of six, on our quarter-acre lot.

We bought six hens: one Rhode Island Red; one silver Orpington; a chocolate-brown Marans; a white "frizzle" with feathers that splayed out like she'd stuck her beak in an electrical outlet; and two Silkies, one with lavender-tinted feathers.

One evening, I watched out the window as my husband tried to shoo the birds from the back yard into the coop. Five of them obediently waddled inside. But the lavender Silkie, as if she were riding an invisible elevator, flew straight up into a tree branch ten feet above the coop. I didn't know chickens could fly that high! David dropped the broom and came inside. "She won't make it through the night."

But, the next morning, our neighborhood Facebook page had a post about a chicken on the loose. She'd made it! Over the next few days, there were more posts.

"Chicken sighting on Ontario Ct. today."

"Did Freebird come home?"

"We should have shirts made… Freebird Come Home!"

"FREEBIRD!"

We made several attempts to catch her, but she evaded capture every time. To my surprise, no one complained on Facebook, not even the man whose yard she scratched up right after he'd had it aerated and seeded with organic grass seed.

As the weather grew colder, it seemed the bird couldn't last much longer. But she kept making appearances all through the fall and winter. By late January, two things had become clear:

1) Freebird was not coming home.

2) Freebird was not a chicken.

Somebody did some avian research and informed the rest of us that she (he?) was actually a guinea fowl: "They have a reputation for being the 'bad boys' of the chicken world. Apparently, they can fly up to forty feet and roost in trees. On the positive side, they eat ticks, Japanese beetles and fire ants."

Freebird continued living on the lam for over a year. Still, no one complained, not even about her horrific screech that echoed across the neighborhood lake at dawn and dusk. Instead, the bird achieved celebrity status.

"It finally happened! I got to see Freebird on my morning walk! Life is complete."

"My kids spotted Freebird today. Even looked both ways before crossing the road."

"Smart bird."

"A legend."

Checking the neighborhood Facebook page became part of my morning ritual. Make the coffee. Go out back and feed the chickens that actually were chickens. Go online for the Freebird scuttlebutt.

Then, one spring day, the inevitable happened.

"Dear neighbors, sad news to report. Early Monday morning, Freebird was murdered by a hawk or owl. Thanks to George and Christy on Ontario Court, who cleaned up the carnage. We will dearly miss that silly, loud bird."

Within days, Freebird's obituary had a hundred reactions and comments.

"Fly high forever, my friend."

"FREEBIRD! Sure will be missed."

"This breaks my heart. Freebird was such a great symbol of independence and perseverance."

And my favorite… "We will always remember the 'Live Free or Die' ideal that she touched in many of us."

I'd misjudged my neighbors and underestimated myself. The places we live do not define us, no more than putting a guinea fowl in a chicken coop makes it into a docile hen. I liked knowing I wasn't the only suburbanite hungry for a dash of the wild. Sure, we live in climate-controlled houses with well-stocked refrigerators… for now. But if we had to, we too could make it out there, living off the land. I like to imagine Freebird's escape inspiring subtle acts of defiance in the community — front doors painted without HOA approval, trees cut down on the sly — nothing drastic, just enough to prove suburbia can't quench the freedom and wildness within.

— Karen Langley Martin —

59

Family Reunion Crashers

The only thing sweeter than union is reunion.
~Kathleen McGowan

It was autumn, my favorite time of year in the Ozarks. The trees were beautiful shades of reds, oranges, and yellows. The cool breeze was a welcome relief and a reminder that the holidays were just around the corner. And it was the perfect day to kick off the season by attending the family reunion at War Eagle Park, home to the annual War Eagle Arts and Crafts Festival. Everyone knew where it was; we didn't even need a map to get there.

Although we had never been to the Kimes family reunion before, it sounded like a lot of fun. We would recognize the group because they'd be set up next to the playground so the kids could stretch their legs and get the wiggles out after the drive. There would be lots of extended family members to meet for the first time, photos to take, family stories to swap and, of course, good food. We had been assigned to bring a casserole. It was sure to be worth the two-hour drive to War Eagle Park.

I double-checked our car: four children, camp chairs, diaper bag, car seat for our red-haired baby boy, jackets, and our casserole. It seemed that everything was in order, so we headed out. Two carsick hours later, we arrived. Our children were more than ready to check out the playground. Our daughter was a little nervous because she didn't recognize anyone there, but neither did we.

"Don't worry," I told her. "These people are all related to you.

Those kids over there on the swings and slides are your cousins. Just go have fun, make friends, and we'll call you when it's time to eat." Anxious to be out of the car, the three older children ran toward their new cousins.

I got the baby out of his car seat while my husband grabbed the casserole. Before we got very far, several older women surrounded us — great-aunts. They all shared the same shade of bright red hair as our baby and made a big fuss over the youngest member of the clan. They took turns kissing him and passing him around. He loved the attention. One of them offered to take the casserole from my husband, and they graciously situated us among all his kin, taking pictures of themselves with the baby. What a fun family we had! All these great-aunts seemed delighted to find such a strong family resemblance in the little guy.

But, as we talked, we realized that we didn't recognize any of their names. There was no Barbara there, the one great-aunt who had invited us. As a matter of fact, there wasn't anyone there who had the last name Kimes! Finally, my husband asked, "This is the Kimes family reunion, isn't it?"

The obvious patriarch of the group said, "No, this is the VanOwen family reunion. Your family reunion is at War Eagle Park. This is War Eagle *State* Park. But since you're already here, you might as well stay and eat." How embarrassing!

Since we were expected at the Kimes family reunion, we decided we should go there. We gathered our children and the casserole and got back into the car as our children waved goodbye to their new "cousins."

Thirty minutes later, when we arrived at the other War Eagle Park, we got out of the car, sent our children to the playground to make friends with their new cousins, retrieved our casserole, and took our red-haired baby out of his car seat. By then, we were surrounded by older women with hair the same shade of red as the baby. They whisked away the youngest member of the clan, kissed him and took photos, collected the casserole, and introduced themselves.

We learned something that day. Babies are universally loved, and we could have gone to either family reunion and felt welcomed. Crashing a family reunion was a good way to make friends.

— Lisa Aldridge —

Grand & Great

60

Oh, That Brazilian

*My day goes from one embarrassing
moment to the next.*
~Ted Danson

My mother thought all women should work outside the home and keep a tight eye on income and expenditures. She had a paying job every day of her life, trained more than one of her bosses, and expected each of us girls to pay for our own clothes and transportation the day we got our first paycheck. Beyond that, she was straight out of another century. Modesty and detachment from all things even remotely sexual were expected.

I remember the first time I took my intended husband (second husband, I might point out; I was no blushing ingénue) to visit Mom. We had traveled across three states to see her and let her give Tom the once-over. When we arrived, she greeted us with the appropriate coffee, cake and busy talk I had expected. Mom then said she must apologize, but she was going to have to leave for an hour or two because it was time for her weekly Bible study class, and she could not miss this one as they were starting a new six-week study.

We assured her that her absence would not be a problem and encouraged her to attend. I asked her what the new theme was, and she shared, in a lowered voice, that it was a class on sex and the Lutheran church. I couldn't help laughing at my mother's distress and teased her a bit.

"So, Mom, are you for it or against it?"

She paused only a second and then said, "Well, I'm for the Lutheran church."

This was my mother in a nutshell.

Years later, when Mom had entered the final years of her life and was getting frailer in body and mind, she moved back to our family home in Colorado and began living with my youngest sister and her big, busy family. There, with a better diet and constant human interaction, she thrived. But there was no denying that eight decades had taken their toll. Three things became readily apparent. First, Mom continuously complained of being hard of hearing while picking up any conversation one wished to keep private. Second, the mental filters that make us all civilized people began breaking down. She pretty much said the first thing that came into her mind. And third, Mom could never pass up a chance to deliver a sermon about thrift.

These factors all came into play two days before my niece's wedding.

I was visiting my sister, helping with preparations for the wedding. On the afternoon in question, we were all busy creating a gala family dinner that would include the fiancé's family. All the action was happening in the kitchen, a large room with a sunny breakfast nook that was Mom's hangout.

There she sat, complaining about not being able to hear well enough to join the conversation, drinking her never ending cup of coffee, and nibbling on a sweet roll.

By mid-afternoon, I was getting the last of three pies in the oven when my niece, the bride-to-be, came in after a day at the spa. She was showing off her mani/pedi and talking about how nice the full-body massage was. Her mom then arched her brow and asked, "Did you get what you were talking about?"

My niece blushed a little and said, "Yes, I went ahead and got a Brazilian." Her voice was low. She was including only her mother and me, but we didn't count on Mom's selective ears.

"What's a Brazilian?" was Mom's question.

My niece looked at my sister and my sister looked at me. I am the oldest, and it was clear they expected me to fall on this grenade. Not a single soul in that room wanted to share with Mom the correct definition of a Brazilian wax.

If you are wondering what a Brazilian wax is, do not Google it. Let me simply explain that it refers to removing hair on the bikini area. Thinking fast, I told Mom that her granddaughter had gotten her legs waxed (all successful lies have some element of truth) and that Brazilian referred to the type of wax. I then asked Mom if she wanted more coffee and another sweet roll. Diversion is important.

Mom mumbled something about young people not knowing the value of a dollar and happily accepted more coffee and a pastry.

My sister, a grateful niece and I all thought we had skated by on the whole thing. Like lambs to the slaughter, we turned our unwitting attention to the family dinner.

Later that night, we were well into finishing up the main course, with everyone's sights starting to focus on the pies that sat on the sideboard, when Mom decided it was time for a morality lesson. Taking advantage of a lull in the table talk, Mom said every bride needed to know how to budget her money. For an example of fiscal profligacy, Mom said that her granddaughter had no business wasting money on some special wax called a Brazilian.

Silence and jaws both fell around that packed table.

Mom then trumped her own ace by adding, "I would never waste money on a Brazilian. You wouldn't get me to get some Brazilian. I wouldn't need a Brazilian even if I was getting married." Truer words, by the way, were never spoken.

We laughed until we wept. My niece may have been shedding legitimate tears, but she was also laughing.

All I could do was offer everyone more coffee.

—— Louise Butler ——

61

Ear Potatoes

No man is exempt from saying silly things;
the mischief is to say them deliberately.
~Michel de Montaigne, The Complete Essays

I admired the beautiful, silky robe my grandmother had gotten for me, running my six-year-old fingers over the cool and oh-so-smooth material. It hung in the closet next to two slightly smaller ones for my younger cousins, special for us to wear on nights we had our highly anticipated sleepovers at our grandparents' house. It was adorned with striking, violet-colored roses, and was so beautiful and comfy that I could not wait to get out of the bath and slip it on over my favorite Teenage Mutant Ninja Turtles pajama set. I was just giddy about my amazing after-bath outfit, perfect for watching the musical my grandmother and I had picked out for our sleepover movie night.

"I think the bathtub is just about full." My grandfather peeked his head into the doorway of the guest room as I was unzipping my suitcase to find my pajamas.

"Okay, Grampa!" I exclaimed, and I snatched up my clothes, ready to play with the cool-as-could-be soap crayons my grandparents had for the bathtub. My grandparents always had the coolest toys and knickknacks for us grandchildren.

"Alright, Gwen. Just be sure to clean well behind your ears. You don't want to start growing potatoes behind your ears, now, do you?"

"Potatoes?" I stopped dead in my tracks and turned to look back at my grandfather.

"Yep, potatoes. You know if you have too much dirt behind your ears, potatoes just might sprout and start growing there," my grandfather explained as my eyes widened like saucers.

"But I don't have potatoes behind my ears, Grampa," I ran my fingers along the backs of my ears.

"Ya know, I thought I saw just a couple sprouts starting earlier." My grandfather took a quick peek. "Yep, by golly, right there! Sure enough, I see two little sprouts popping up. You better get in there and scrub them nice and good, Gwen." My eyes remained wide as could be as I nodded rather incredulously since this was the first I had heard of this.

Why have my parents never warned me this could happen? I pondered as I splashed in the tub, scrubbing my ears while I drew plentiful drawings all over the bathtub walls with the soap crayons. I used up nearly an entire bar of soap scrubbing behind my ears that evening, just to be sure I got those little potato sprouts good and cleaned away.

I did not forget this bit of wisdom my grandfather had bestowed upon me for years to come, and I was always very diligent about cleaning behind my ears.

A few years later, I was at another fun-filled sleepover with my grandparents. After I got out of the bath for the evening and finished brushing my teeth, I pulled out the little handheld mirror from one of the drawers in the bathroom and placed it behind each of my ears, looking very astutely for signs of potato sprouts.

"What are you looking at behind your ears, Gwen?" My grandmother came in to pick up my towel and help me finish up before we started our movie. While I checked behind my ears after each and every bath, my grandmother just so happened to catch me in my curious act at this particular sleepover.

"Looking for potato sprouts," I told her very matter-of-factly.

"Potato sprouts?"

"Yeah, Grampa told me all about it. If I get too much dirt behind my ears and don't clean them well, potatoes will start sprouting and growing there."

"Oh, your grandfather, Gwen. I am going to have to have a little chat with him. He was just pulling your chain, princess."

"What?" I looked very seriously at my grandmother now.

"Oh, honey. Your ears are perfectly clean, but even if there is a little dirt back there, you cannot grow potatoes behind your ears," she informed me. I processed this new information for a little bit, scowling at the revelation that I had been played.

"Do the other cousins know about this?" I questioned.

"You know, honey, I do not know. But we will be sure to warn them." She winked at me as a smile crept up on my face, and I could not help but laugh about my gullibility.

"Oh, Grampa." I shook my head and had a good, long laugh with my grandmother.

My grandfather kept up this story for us cousins for years to come. Now that I had all the correct information on this particular scenario, I always made sure to pull any younger cousins, friends, or visitors aside if I heard my grandfather telling his infamous ear-potato story because I sure did not want any others to spend as much time as I did worrying about the potential growth of potatoes behind their ears.

— Gwen Cooper —

62

A Sweet Bon Voyage

Dementia care — it's not rocket science;
it's heart science.
~Gail Weatherill, RN

few weeks after moving my family from Pennsylvania to Indiana, I got a phone call. I'd been busy settling in, getting my children signed up for new sports and hobbies, and discovering our new town — which all came to a halt when I learned I'd become an emergency caretaker for my grandmother with Alzheimer's with just two days to prepare. My mother and sister were driving my grandmother to Indiana and temporarily moving her a mile away from me at my mother's house.

With her there, it was just my mother, sister, and me trying to navigate Alzheimer's. We had no time to do research on how to handle it. We didn't know the best ways and tricks to settle down someone who didn't recognize her family, in a brand-new, strange place, and was very anxious and afraid.

When I arrived at my mom's house on the first day with two kids in tow, I walked in on my grandmother, mother, and sister crying. My mom tried to get my grandmother comfortable, explaining that she was her daughter, and we were family. In my grandmother's mind, however, she was currently in her twenties, and she was terrified that my mother, in her mid-fifties, could be her daughter. We needed a way to calm everyone down. Since this was during the pandemic, we had no idea when we could get her professional care. It was overwhelming and scary. How were we going to get through this?

Late that night, when my mom and sister went to sleep after their twelve-hour drive, I stayed up with my grandmother. Every time she came out of her room, she was in a different time period of her life. I had to adapt quickly each time — figure out how old she thought she was, where she thought she was, and who I was. Sometimes, she was a young teenager needing to call her dad. Other times, she was a young mother of three and needed to look in on her kids. In one moment, she was only newly dating my grandfather, and the next she thought my grandfather was with their kids. If I didn't recognize where she was in her timeline right away, she'd get anxious, so I had to ask just the right questions.

One time, she told me how nice this cruise ship was. It had a beautiful pool outside the window, the kitchen was big and always had someone ready with snacks, and her room was lovely. My grandmother loved to travel her whole life, and cruises were her favorite. She loved to go into the lobby and chat with new people.

It was then I started putting together the pieces of an idea. We'd go along with what she already thought was happening. I'd be a cook on the ship, up late in case anyone got hungry and the one to make everyone breakfast in the mornings. My younger brothers were the cleanup crew, quickly doing dishes and taking out the trash, as she liked everything tidy. My mom was the cruise director, and my sister was an assistant helper.

No longer did we try to tell her we were family. She loved to talk to us like a brand-new person each time she saw us, so that's what we became. She was no longer Grandma; she was Janet. And we always approached her by saying, "How can we help you? Do you need anything?" in our best customer-service voices. Instantly, she calmed and wasn't so tearfully frightened.

For the next week, we took shifts. My mother and sister spent late mornings and afternoons in charge of entertaining, making sure my grandmother stayed safe, calm, and fed. I would come over just before dinner with my kids to give my mother a reprieve and time out of the house. I slept on the sofa and would get up all night with my grandmother, showing her where the bathroom was, explaining where she was and what everyone was doing, fetching her cups of water, turning on the news, and tucking her back into bed while also doing the same for my children.

In a few days, we had to do more than just keep her "on the cruise ship." A nursing home in the center of our tiny town, on beautiful monastery grounds, was willing to take her. But first, she needed a chest X-ray, physical, and Covid test.

My grandmother hated doctors just as much as she loved vacations. Now, we had to involve others in our idea. My mother quickly filled in the doctor, and he rolled with it, calling himself the cruise ship's medical team. When my grandmother was too scared to get her physical, my mother claimed it was for herself and needed someone to sit with her. Soon, the doctor was taking both of their blood pressures and going down the list. My mother ended up getting a free physical, and it kept my grandmother calm! The nurses enjoyed becoming cruise-ship personnel for a little while.

Once my grandmother passed her tests, the nursing home started the admittance paperwork. They loved the idea of the cruise ship so much that they said they would stick with it. The nursing home would now be a big, beautiful ship, boasting a large restaurant and long hallways full of passenger rooms. The Alzheimer's ward buzzed with news of their new patient. They never had such a fun story to act out before. During a time when cruises were impossible, they couldn't wait to get onboard and pretend to be on a great vacation!

My grandmother loved to pack her bags, so the night before we took her, we all packed together. I brought my overnight bags and put them in the "loading area" of the living room. My mom pulled out suitcases and set them next to mine. Then we invited my grandmother to pack with our help. She loved putting everything together. When she asked where we were going, we said we had booked a brand-new ship that she'd love even better than this one. She couldn't wait to go.

In the morning, we packed the van and made it our "shuttle bus." In Pennsylvania, my grandmother had been terrified to get in that same van. Now that the van was taking her to the cruise ship, she eagerly hopped in. My stepdad John was our bus driver. When we got to the nursing home, she happily greeted the staff who welcomed her on board. As soon as they told her that it was nearly mealtime, she hurried off with them, leaving me to call out a goodbye because she raced off so fast.

The nurses give us weekly updates now, telling us how much my grandmother has relaxed and enjoys her cruise lifestyle. She's not afraid; she isn't anxious; she doesn't cry. We're able to visit her every other week, but we still let her think we're just regular cruise staff. Our family grew even closer working as a team and playing make-believe for our grandmother before wishing her bon voyage on her next journey.

—Jill Keller—

63

Loons

I love technology, and I love new gadgets.
I can no longer figure out how to use
any of them, but I love them.
~Jerry Zucker

I sat on the back patio at my grandparents' house one summer evening and listened as my grandfather recounted memories of a fishing trip he had taken with my great-uncle at Loon Lake in Michigan. "I don't remember how many fish we caught, but all I can remember is the beautiful sounds of the loons on the lake that evening. They echoed through the sunset, and we would just listen to those exquisite birds." My grandfather continued to explain the various calls of the loons to me, and just how peaceful and beautiful it was there at Loon Lake. "You know, I would really like to get a CD of their calls," he said.

"I can find that for you online, Grandpa," I said.

"Really? That would be just dandy." My grandfather smiled at me lovingly, as his eyes twinkled in happiness. "Just dandy indeed."

"Perfect! I will bring it with me next weekend."

It was quite easy to find some digital files online, and by the following weekend I had quite the compilation put together. We sat and listened to the sounds of the loons. I learned the difference between their wail, tremolo, hoot, and yodel. I never knew how versatile one bird could be, and how beautiful all their calls were.

We sat and listened well into the evening, and once it was time for me to go home, I showed my grandfather how to turn the sound files on and off on his computer so he could listen whenever he wanted.

Later that week, I received a phone call from my grandfather asking for some technological help with the loon files.

"Hiya, Gwen."

"Hi, Grampa. Have you been listening to the loons some more?" I inquired, as I could hear their calls distinctly in the background.

"I sure have, but I need your help. I got them turned back on the next day after you left, and now I can't figure out how to turn them off." It was now Thursday, and the day after I had left would have been Sunday. I held back a laugh.

"You mean you have had that on for going on five days now?"

"Yes, indeed," my grandfather chuckled. "I told your grandmother I just love the sounds so much, but I think she is about fit to have me tied now if I don't get them turned off," he acknowledged in seeming defeat.

"So, you have let them play this long under the ploy that you are just enjoying it that much? Even through the night?" I couldn't help it anymore, and I burst out laughing on my end of the phone. "Oh, poor Nanny!" I exclaimed.

I talked him through the steps to get the sound files we had downloaded onto his computer to turn off. The following weekend, I wrote down the steps for him just in case he needed them for future reference and made sure my grandmother knew where to locate these instructions too. For her own sanity.

We have had many laughs over the years about this, and how he and my grandmother had their own trip to Loon Lake without having to leave the house. It still makes me smile to this day, just thinking about the loon sounds resonating throughout their house for nearly five days due to my grandfather's stubbornness.

— Gwen Cooper —

64

Under Where?

I feel like every day of my life is a
funny wardrobe malfunction!
~Nikki Reed

"It's a gorgeous day. Let's get out of here and have some fun," Grannie said to my mother, and then she looked at me. "How about we grab a bite to eat and then spend the afternoon shopping?"

I hopped into the back seat while my mom road shotgun on our drive downtown. After only a few seconds on the road, Grannie grumbled under her breath, noting the low level of the fuel gauge. "We're riding on fumes. We need to gas up," she said with a sigh.

Grannie wheeled the vehicle into the nearest gas station. Knowing my grandmother rarely used credit, my mom flapped a few bills, offering to pay, but Grannie shook her head. Parking beside the pumps, she swung the driver's door open with a groan. In her floral print dress, my short, stout grandmother attempted to exit the vehicle in a ladylike manner but required a bit of a push and a jump. As she straightened up next to the car, she got a strange look on her face.

Although my mother and I had no way of knowing it, the elastic band at the waist of my grandmother's giant, grannie panties had let go. Grannie shuffled toward the back end of the car with wide eyes, trying to keep everything in place.

Pinching her dress at the waist with one hand, Grannie held everything in place as she worked with haste. Then she frowned.

There was no way to remove the gas cap and mate the nozzle to the car without using both hands.

She let go.

So did everything else. Except gravity.

Grannie's face flushed as she stood between the car and the gas pump, with her giant underwear around her ankles. She had no other option now but to finish the task at hand. When the pump clicked off, she rushed to exchange the nozzle for the gas cap, and then shuffled back toward the open driver's door.

Waving at my mother, Grannie yelled out, "I hit a snag, so I'm taking you up on your offer."

"Sure, Mom." My mother dug into her purse again and produced the money for my grandmother, who shook her head.

"No, I need you to pay. Do you mind?"

Before she opened the passenger door, my mother looked back at Grannie, puzzled and a little worried. "What's going on, Mom? Is everything okay?"

With blazing cheeks, Grannie nodded. "It's fine. I'll tell you later. Just hurry!"

Nodding but confused, my mother dashed into the store to pay, and then returned to the car to find Grannie back inside the vehicle and in a rush to go.

"What happened?" My mother's curiosity had peaked as we wheeled back onto the road.

"I lost my shorts," Grannie muttered, unable to hide her embarrassment.

"I beg your pardon?" Mom said. We both gawked at my grandmother in disbelief.

"I know they were old, but I thought they still had some life in them. I guess I was wrong because the elastic let go, and they hit the ground."

Through sputters of laughter, my mother managed to gasp, "What did you do with them?"

"What could I do?" Grannie looked at my mom with a frown and then back at the road. "I kicked them under the car."

My mother and I giggled, and Grannie's face glowed red-hot, but she could see the humor in the situation and started to laugh, too. On the road, heading back to her house, we continued to chuckle about the enormous surprise that awaited the next person to visit the gas pump.

"Well, I guess we really do need to go shopping," my mother teased. "We can't have you going knickerless." Mom got a lot of mileage out of that incident, not only that day but well into the future. There was no living down the gas-station caper and the underwear that went under where?

Visiting my grandmother was always fun, and she never failed to amuse us. I loved how she could laugh at herself and roll with all the craziness that life threw her way. I'm sure the gas-station attendant failed to see the humor in it, but we will never know. Grannie was too embarrassed to visit that gas station again.

—Cate Bronson—

One Step Beyond Frugal

*I think the family is the place where the most ridiculous
and least respectable things in the world go on.*
~Ugo Betti

My grandmother was the sixth child in a line of thirteen girls, no brothers. Her father died before the Great Depression. But my great-grandmother and her thirteen daughters managed to keep their small farm thriving.

My grandmother learned at a very young age how to pinch a penny. DIY wasn't a craft idea back then; it was a way of life. Everything had a purpose and was used, reused and then repurposed — nothing wasted! It was a character trait that stayed with my grandmother throughout her lifetime, creating some very humorous moments, although a few family members may argue her economizing was more embarrassing than humorous.

My grandmother rarely discarded anything and never threw away a piece of clothing. If it couldn't be mended, patched, resized, or handed down, then the cloth was repurposed and used for numerous things, even cleaning rags — nothing wasted. While she was spring cleaning one year, she gave various items to the Goodwill along with a bucket of old scrubbing towels. However, the Goodwill driver politely declined the old towels.

I was twelve at the time and embarrassed by my grandmother trying to give away old rags! She argued with the driver that they were perfectly useful cleaning towels, but he held his ground. Later that day, using her ingenuity, my grandmother unzipped an old, sagging chair cushion and used the worn-out but clean towels for stuffing — nothing wasted!

That wasn't the last time her thrifty behavior embarrassed me. After church on Sundays, we often went out to eat as a family, but the older I got, the more embarrassed I became. For whatever was left on the table, my grandmother would politely request a to-go box. Then she would stuff the container with any uneaten food along with every packet of butter, sugar, salt and pepper still on the table — nothing wasted! One Sunday at a dinner out, she reached for a glass saltshaker to stuff in her large pocketbook. My startled grandfather had to pry the glassware from her fingers.

Although my grandmother had plenty, it was a habit she couldn't break. Even into her golden years, she couldn't let anything go to waste. She still made her own soap, washed and reused plastic bags, used coffee grounds for fertilizer in her garden, and rarely turned on her dryer. On rainy days, she hung the clothing inside, and the living room became a maze for playing hide-and-seek.

My mother called her the queen of frugality, yet she wasn't a hoarder or stingy. She always made sure her neighbors and family had plenty. My grandfather understood my grandmother's unwavering need to economize, and it was appreciated, but the last straw occurred one Sunday afternoon at Weavers Restaurant.

Weavers Restaurant was one of our frequent go-to places after church. That day, because of our larger-than-normal party, we were seated in the very back of the restaurant at a large, round table. I can't recall what I had to eat that day. I only remember the awkward and mortifying episode upon leaving the restaurant, as people stared and whispered.

For all my grandmother's penny-pinching faults, she meant well. That Sunday, she wanted a container to take home an uneaten side dish. She knew the restaurant would discard the left-over food, and she couldn't bear the atrocity of wasting something edible. However, the waitress said it wasn't possible. They only had brown paper bags, and the left-over red beets were swimming in juice. It didn't matter.

My grandmother insisted on the brown paper bag.

I still remember the look on my mother's face as my grandmother dumped the dish of red beets into the brown paper bag, juice and all, and then stuffed the beets in her purse. My grandmother carried a large vinyl brown-and-white pocketbook, big enough for the kitchen sink. She draped the bag over her shoulder and, in her very ladylike fashion, wearing her ankle-length dress, high heels and clip-on earrings, she sashayed through the crowded restaurant with beet juice dribbling from her pocketbook, making a colorful path to the car! The bottom of her white pocketbook was forever red, but — nothing wasted!

— Dana D. Sterner —

Sharing a Lap Dance with Grandma

If you're going to try, go all the way.
Otherwise, don't even start.
~Charles Bukowski, Factotum

The stripper was down to his black boots, a red thong with suspenders, and a matching red fireman's helmet. He pointed directly at me where I was hiding in the shadows. I tried to think of any polite way to avoid the next few minutes but it was too late. He beckoned with one finger, as he gyrated over one of the seated spectators.

That spectator was busy running her fingers up the stripper's bare stomach like a child running up a slide. Once her fingers reached his chest, her palm flattened and slid its way back down to the trail of hair beneath his belly button.

With no other option, I forced one foot in front of the other until I reached the chair next to the woman he was straddling. With my heart pounding nearly as loudly as the music, I sat down next to that spectator — my grandma. *Well,* I thought, *this isn't an experience I ever thought I'd have.*

A couple of weeks earlier, I'd received a phone call from my dad while visiting my friend out of state. Excusing myself, I stepped into the hallway to answer. At first, the conversation went as expected. He asked if I had arrived okay and how I was doing. Then a silence lingered on the line, and I knew there was something he wasn't saying. After a moment, he told me his brother had called him that morning with a request.

My uncle lived out of state and didn't visit regularly. He wouldn't make it to Christmas, but he still got his mom, my grandma, a gift. The problem was it couldn't be wrapped or mailed because "Well, it's a stripper," Dad informed me.

I leaned against the wall, convinced I'd misheard him. "What?" was all I could manage. I didn't know much about my uncle other than he'd divorced his wife, and the adults in my family had decided to keep her instead of him. He moved to California shortly afterward, and I'd rarely seen or heard about him since.

After repeating what he'd told me, Dad added that my uncle thought the idea would be hilarious. His justification for the gift: "What do you get an eighty-year-old woman who has everything? An experience."

The problem was he wanted it to be a surprise, but Grandma and my great-aunt Helen lived together. Without someone else there, the older women wouldn't willingly allow a strange man into their house. So, would I, his nineteen-year-old niece, be there to let the stripper into Grandma's house without her knowing?

Obviously, I said yes.

Skipping ahead to the night of discussion, I walked into Grandma's house with a wad of ones in my purse — compliments of my uncle. Grandma and Aunt Helen knew there would be a surprise that night, but they didn't know what it was.

We ate dinner together, and I attempted to evade their questions while they giddily discussed their excitement. For a little bit, they lost their wrinkles and silver hair, and I could imagine them as gushing schoolgirls.

When the doorbell rang, I set up two chairs side by side in the middle of the open floorplan and instructed them to sit down. As I turned to walk away, Aunt Helen called out, "I know what the surprise is!" while clapping her hands.

"Okay, one more guess," I said and stopped to hear what she had to say.

"A clown!" Aunt Helen bounced in her seat, and Grandma's eyes grew wide in anticipation at the suggestion.

All I could think to say was, "Nope… but hopefully, it'll still make you laugh." While walking toward the door, I knew that if there was a hell, I was surely going there for this.

The stripper was tall and broad. My uncle said to expect a mailman, but a fireman stood before me. After confirming he had the correct address, he handed me an old-school CD player and instructed me to turn on track five once he entered the room.

While the stripper lingered behind the corner, I returned to the two older women, who were still bustling with delight. I rushed to a corner and plugged in the player, got it ready, and hit Play right when the stripper appeared.

"I hear someone needs their fire alarms checked," the stripper announced.

Grandma and Aunt Helen paused and exchanged looks of confusion. "I don't think so," Grandma said with her hands falling to her lap. "My grandson checked them just last week."

The stripper shot me a confused look, and pulsing electronic music played in the awkward silence before I explained that the stripper was not a real fireman; he was a stripper. My heart raced while they considered what I said and slowly came to grasp the situation.

Would they panic or become angry? Would I be in trouble? Should I call Dad? Just when I was about to dial for help, a sly smile crept across Grandma's lips. "Why, yes, Mister Fireman," she swiveled to face the stripper, "I think we do need our fire alarms checked," she crooned.

I stood back in awe as I watched Grandma transform into a woman I'd only ever heard of. She was feisty, flirty, and adventurous. I'd learned whispered stories about this woman, but the woman I knew was a believer in rules and always ready to point out that "funnest" isn't a word—the correct usage is "most fun," she'd inform me. Yet here she was, relaxed down to her soul and tugging on the earlobe of a male stripper in her living room. Most fun, indeed.

Before the night began, I thought Grandma would be put off by the gift. To my surprise, it was my fun-loving great-aunt Helen who became rigid in her chair and uncomfortable in her skin. Within minutes, she excused herself and left to stand behind the kitchen island — a safe distance away but still in full view of the show.

That's when the stripper noticed me in the shadows and beckoned me to take the vacated seat. Upon sitting, the stripper maneuvered and straddled my right and Grandma's left thighs. He pulled my wrist toward him, placing my hand on his chest where Grandma's was before.

Then, turning around, he somehow managed to put both hands on the floor and got his legs positioned on either side of us. Looking over his shoulder, he said, "You can smack it if you want," referring to his rear end on Grandma's lap. My eyes went wide with surprise, but Grandma was quick to respond, "No, but I'll snap it," before pulling the band of his thong and releasing it, causing it to snap back into place.

It's been fifteen years since that night. It was the start of seeing how dynamic Grandma was. She had a wild side to her that I can't help but be inspired by for the rest of my life. She passed away peacefully in early 2020, but this memory will remain with me forever. Besides, who else can say they've shared a lap dance with their grandma?

— Katrina Paulson —

67

Good Girls Get Ice Cream

A grandmother is God's gift to her granddaughters.
~Author Unknown

My mother's signature on all her paintings and each ceramic piece she created was a small, hand-drawn heart. After she died, my daughter Margie took a picture of Mom's little heart on one of her creations and ventured into a tattoo parlor for them to make a transfer. That day, she had the delicate heart inked on her left wrist. My niece did the same. Then my grand-daughter Emily followed suit and got the symbol on her shoulder.

Both Margie and Emily began an insidious campaign touting tattoos while in my presence. Tats were not in my wheelhouse, never had been and never would be. Even though I'm a nurse, I'm a coward when it comes to having things done to me. I didn't get my ears pierced until after eight-year-old Margie got hers done. She sat bravely on the stool at the piercing kiosk at the mall while I looked at earrings until she was done. I couldn't even watch. When we left the shopping center, I took her for an ice-cream cone. On the next trip to the mall, my school-aged daughter held my hand as I got my ears pierced. It turned out there was nothing to it. Afterward, we went for ice cream.

Margie and Emily's campaign for me to get my heart tattoo started years ago. Certainly, it was different from my personal decision to get my ears pierced. Now, I was seventy-eight years old. Finally, I admitted that, copied from an original that my mom had drawn in her own hand, the tattoo would certainly have special meaning. Still, I resisted, and still, they persisted. One day, I weakened and said, "All right, all right, I'll get the tattoo." Margie immediately made the appointment.

Two days later, the three of us were in the car. The tattoo parlor was not at all like I had pictured. It was light, bright, clean, and welcoming. There were many private rooms complete with chairs much like a dentist's office. The artists were warm and friendly.

Margie asked, "Are you nervous?"

The artist placed the transfer over my wrist. "Is this where you want it?"

"Perfect!" I replied. I turned to Margie. "No, I'm not nervous. Should I be?" I turned back to the artist and asked how long it would take.

He said, "Not even a minute."

My granddaughter held out her hand. "Here, Gramma, just squeeze my hand."

"Why will I need to squeeze your hand?"

The artist dipped a sterile needle into black ink. He started his work. I heard buzzing, but I didn't look.

My eyes widened. I reached out to squeeze Emily's hand.

The artist pronounced, "There, you're done!" He placed a sterile bandage over the top of my mother's adorable, hand-drawn heart on my right wrist. I was glad I did it — and equally glad it was over.

Margie proclaimed, "Twenty-two seconds! That's how long it took."

Emily did a little dance, singing, "Grandma's got a tat. Grandma's got a tat!"

"Okay, you two. I was a good girl. Now, take me for ice cream."

— Nancy Emmick Panko —

Chapter
9

Mom Did What?

68

My Mother the Rabbit

*Our family is just one tent away
from a full-blown circus.*
~Author Unknown

In a family of electricians, nurses, and grocery-store managers, I was considered the black sheep when I changed my career path during my senior year of high school. Instead of studying to be a doctor, I was going to double-major in theatre and television production. For four years of college, I wore a crazy-girl crown with pride, performing on stage and creating short films with friends. And I added a few jewels to my crown when I entered a graduate program to study for my Master of Fine Arts degree in theatre at a university 600 miles away.

I'd grown comfortable being the odd duck in my practical family. But during my first year of graduate school, my mom called on a Sunday afternoon, like she had every Sunday since I'd moved away from home. Our conversation started as usual about what we'd done that week. Mom was a registered nurse working for a large hospital. She'd been single for a few years and had been trying to find ways to keep herself busy since my sister, brother and I had moved out.

"I was helping Pam this weekend and met a guy. He's a real clown," Mom said with all seriousness.

Instantly, in my mind, I imagined my mom going out for coffee with a guy dressed up in a full clown outfit, curly red wig, giant shoes and all.

"Pam's brother manages an event center where they were hosting a circus this weekend," Mom continued. "He paid us to clean up trash in the bleachers between shows. I was taking a break, and this clown started talking to me."

I listened intently as Mom described the third-generation Brazilian clown who tours with his parents performing comedy in the circus. It was all he'd ever done and all he knew how to do. As the months passed and my summer break neared, each Sunday phone call included an update about Lucio, the Brazilian clown.

When I told my mom that I wouldn't be coming home for the summer because I'd been cast in the summer theatre acting company, I could almost hear her shrug over the phone.

"That's no problem. I think I'm going to take a leave of absence from the hospital and tour with Lucio."

Up to this point, Mom's relationship with Lucio had been nothing serious I thought, just phone conversations and the occasional joke to a friend about my mom dating a real clown. I never would have imagined that she'd run off and join the circus!

"You kids are out of the house," she explained. "My parents are in good health. If I'm going to do something like this, now seems like the best time."

A month later, I had to pass my crazy-girl crown over to my mom when she packed her bags and hopped a plane to New York City. There she met up with Lucio and the new circus company he'd joined. This one was all Spanish-speaking and was scheduled to tour the U.S. stopping in cities with large populations of Spanish speakers. Lucio was excited to join this particular circus because he'd spent years touring Central and South America and was fluent in Spanish.

Mom was put in the act and given a special role. One of the circus's sponsors was General Mills, and they decided that the Trix Rabbit had to be the ringmaster. The costume consisted of a giant, cartoon-like head and a full-body fur suit. It fit perfectly on my short mom. The producers didn't want anyone too tall wearing the suit because that might frighten small children.

Mom toured with Lucio and his parents, living in their RV like the other performers and traveling all over the country. It was an odd time, hearing reports from Mom on the other performers and her part in the show, which grew to include assisting in the clown routine. Even my fellow graduate students listened wide-eyed when I updated them on her newest adventure.

Finally, her tour schedule landed her in a place I could visit. While Dallas was a long drive from graduate school, one of my classmates was from Dallas and said we could stay at her dad's place. She and I invited a few more friends and loaded up for a road trip.

Beneath the dancing, colorful lights inside the circus tent, my friends and I watched my mom from VIP seats. The crowd applauded her and laughed at the antics she performed with Lucio and his parents. Under the big top, she stepped confidently in a rhinestone-studded costume, her long ponytail wig swishing against her back. And the smile never left her face.

The next summer, Mom was offered another contract with the circus. She'd had a good year not only performing but also becoming part of the circus family. Her nursing skills came in handy on occasion to treat a cut or give advice on an ailment. And because she was one of the only native English speakers in the circus, she took on the role of English tutor for the younger members of the touring families.

After attending a summer workshop, I had a few weeks free and met up with Mom and the circus. While uncommon and challenging in some ways, the appeal of circus life was evident. Waking in the morning with the elephants outside our RV window became the norm. So did joining acrobat practice, tutoring children with homeschool lessons, and helping with face painting during intermission.

Circus life is unlike anything else I've experienced. Everyone was part of their own performance troupe, but, together with the stagehands and musicians, they made one big family. Friends cheered when the acrobats would hold their babies up carefully to sit on the palm of the dads' hands. This taught them balance at a young age, preparing them to be the next generation of performers. On a day we went to the beach in south Texas, other acrobat families were practicing stunts in the safety of the water. They attempted to teach me how to step up and stand on a man's shoulders for a pyramid. I spent more time laughing and falling underwater than actually achieving the task.

We laughed together. We shared food together. We celebrated birthdays and other celebrations together. And as I got on the airplane to fly back for graduate school, I was joyful. Circus life had opened doors to a new world for my mom, one where she was thriving.

Sadly, the circus went under and didn't tour again after that summer. All the performers went on to other circuses. Mom and Lucio parted ways and she went back to nursing. But when meeting new people, I still enjoy saying, "When my mom ran off and joined the circus…" and watch their eyes widen, just like the children watching her prance across the stage in a large rabbit costume.

— Annie Lisenby —

69

A Most Embarrassing Story

*But I learned that there's a certain character that can be
built from embarrassing yourself endlessly.*
~Christian Bale

A synagogue Bingo fundraiser had turned out to be a lucky night for our family. Both my great-aunt Ida and my mother won prizes.

Aunt Ida had won the latest model clock radio. My mom received a rather strange reward: a pink, crocheted, padded clothes hanger.

My great-aunt was holding the box that contained the clock radio as my mother approached. On the front of the box was a picture showing off the prize's spiffy, new design. My mother glanced at it.

"Aunt Ida, you won a great prize," my mom said enthusiastically. "You must be so excited."

My great-aunt replied, "Pearl, I see you won a prize, too."

"Yeah, look at this piece of junk," my mother responded, holding up the crocheted hanger.

Aunt Ida became visibly upset.

"Pearl, I'll have you know I made that," she said.

My mom had messed up. It was an embarrassing moment.

Just how embarrassing a moment it was would come to light several months later when my mom and a group of her friends descended upon

Pittsburgh's WIIC-TV (Channel 11) studios for a locally produced, early afternoon variety show.

The trip had been planned for weeks. It promised to be a very interesting event. There was the lure of getting a behind-the-scenes look at how television worked as well as the possibility of a close-up view of a local or national celebrity.

On previous shows, Andy Williams, Pat Boone, The Mills Brothers, Connie Francis, Richard Chamberlain, Phyllis Diller and Cassius Clay (later Muhammad Ali) were among those who had showed up at the WIIC studios.

About seventy-five women, mostly homemakers, were in the live studio audience the day my mom and her entourage showed up. Everyone had just been seated, and it was only about twenty minutes before airtime when someone affiliated with the program passed out pencil and paper and asked all in attendance to write down their "most embarrassing story."

With the Aunt Ida Bingo debacle still fresh in her mind, this was a moment my mom was well prepared for. She wrote down the events that had transpired several months prior at the synagogue. Pieces of conversation from that night were still firmly embedded in my mom's head:

"Pearl, I see you won a prize, too."

"Yeah, look at this piece of junk."

"Pearl, I'll have you know I made that."

And so, my mom answered the question, and the show began minutes later. She and her friends were enjoying their ladies' day out and being part of the studio audience when, about halfway through the hour-long program, the host asked if "Pearl Hecht could please stand up."

A Channel 11 camera zoomed in on my mom.

"Pearl Hecht, we understand you had a very embarrassing moment that occurred after you won a Bingo game," said the host. "Could you tell us about it?"

With the cameras rolling, my mom spoke into a microphone and retold the Bingo story. The host laughed. The live audience laughed.

My mom's story had been judged the most embarrassing out of all the guests' stories at the WIIC studios that day.

I was a young teenager when this momentous event took place. And I remember my mom being involved in some long phone conversations that night. Friends and neighbors were calling our house. They were abuzz. They had seen my mom on television.

Whether my great-aunt Ida saw the show or if anyone ever told her about it, I don't know.

What I do know is that, unlike at Bingo, no one at WIIC handed my mom a prize for finishing first. That surprised me. It seems she should have won something.

Then, again, considering it was live television, perhaps it was just as well.

— Stephen Hecht —

70

What Mom Knew

*We must learn to regard people less in
the light of what they do or omit to do,
and more in the light of what they suffer.*
~Dietrich Bonhoeffer, Letters and Papers from Prison

I remember a late-afternoon thunderstorm in Texas. Black clouds obliterated the sun, and a flash of lightning was followed by a thunderous boom. I was five years old.

This was about the time I began to notice my mother's odd habits. She handed me what looked like a butcher knife. "Sylvia, go outside and cut the cloud," she said.

I glanced at my abuelito, who was in the kitchen with us. He winked. "Make a big cross in the air," he said, "like this," pantomiming a giant X.

I stepped off the kitchen stoop carrying a knife whose size and weight almost overwhelmed my small body. Somehow, I managed to draw something resembling an X in the air.

Back inside, my mother and her father sipped coffee. A couple of hours later the rain subsided, and the sun shone brightly. "Did I do that?" I asked.

"Yes, of course," my mother said.

Somehow, even at that young age, I knew I had not done anything. I didn't know how to read, but the weatherman on our little, black-and-white television had warned us about the thunderstorm that morning.

I grew up in a neighborhood barrio dissected by Interstate 35 on the south side of San Antonio. It was a modest, safe neighborhood. In the summer months, I heard Casey Kasem's top-forty hits as well as Mexican ballads blasting out of open windows, but I also saw and heard behaviors bordering on superstition.

Many of the people living in our barrio had been born when redlining and housing covenants were the norm. Some of them, like my grandfather and my mother, had little formal schooling. When they left their rural communities, they settled in the parts of the city where they were allowed to live.

My grandfather was born in 1899; his wife Theodora in 1898. When Teddy Roosevelt and his Rough Riders camped out at Roosevelt Park in 1898, my grandparents' families were living just south of the city in Atascosa County. My mother was born in 1928 right before the Great Depression. She went as far as the second grade in Atascosa County. "We had no electricity or running water on the farm," my mother often reminded me.

"When did you move to San Antonio?" I asked her once.

"When America went to war we thought there would be jobs in the city. My mother, your abuelita, passed away soon after. I was thirteen."

"Do you miss her?"

"Yes," she said, adding, "then my sister Maria died two years later."

During this particular thunderstorm, I also remember that my mother covered the mirrors with towels and sheets. And she hated owls; she thought they were bad omens. And if a black cat crossed our path while walking, we had to wait until some other poor soul crossed ahead of us.

There were other idiosyncrasies. If a hearse went by, we stopped and stood by the side of the road with our heads bowed. Whenever we passed a Catholic church, whether on foot, by bus or by car, we made the sign of the cross.

Now, I understand some of her habits were religious, but then there's the time when I came home from school in the first grade to talk about the Three Billy Goats Gruff and the classmate who lost a tooth. "Mami, our teacher told us about the tooth fairy," I said excitedly.

"There's no such thing," she said. "And while we're talking about this, you might as well know the truth: There is no Easter Bunny or Santa Claus for us. It is all make-believe. Now, help me sort and rinse these beans. Today was wash day, and I got behind."

I had already suspected there was no Santa Claus at our house. We normally did not leave out cookies and the one toy just appeared unwrapped, but I was angry that the news was broken to me that day, so I lashed out, "I get so tired of eating beans."

"Too bad," she said.

We had to cook a pot of beans every morning because my mother would be up before dawn rolling out homemade flour tortillas that she would fill with refried beans, diced fried potatoes with eggs or, if we were lucky, a piece of American cheese — my personal favorite. She did this every morning for my father's lunch pail and for breakfast for my siblings and me. My mother did this from the time I entered first grade until I graduated from high school. We never ate cereal or pancakes.

My mother passed away twelve years ago. She had given birth to six children in eight years. I am the eldest. My siblings and I graduated from high school; some of us went to college, and some joined the military. My mother did the best she could with her second-grade education.

Some things have gone by the wayside. I do not cut clouds, cover mirrors, or worry about black cats.

When our children were young, my husband and I left cookies and milk out for Santa and a carrot for the Easter Bunny. I remember my husband going out (sometimes in the snow) to hide eggs before the kids woke up. And we always left a tooth in an envelope for the tooth fairy.

But one thing brings me back to that small San Antonio barrio. Whenever I wash and sort beans, memories of my mother come to mind. The process is therapeutic for me.

I sort and wash pinto beans or black beans, and then I rinse them three times with cold water. I let them sit in the water for a few hours or, if I am in a hurry, I will boil the water, pour it out and refill the pot with fresh, cold water. I bring the pot to a boil again, and then cover and turn the burner to a low simmer for two hours. Right before serving, I add fresh cumin, garlic, and a little salt and pepper. I eat them right out of a bowl, but I also love them on salads instead of croutons.

And guess what? I recently discovered beans are a superfood. Who knew?

—Sylvia Garza Holmes—

71

Hot Dog Day

"Well, that escalated quickly" is our family motto.
~Author Unknown

My eighth-grade teacher, Mr. Holcomb, was at the front of the classroom holding a stack of papers. "On your way out, I'll be handing you a Parent Volunteer Form for Hot Dog Day on Friday," he informed us. Hot Dog Day was a Northwood Junior High tradition held for eighth graders on the last Friday in May. The playground was transformed into a carnival with games, prizes, cotton candy, and, of course, hot dogs.

Unlike most mothers in our neighborhood, mine rarely if ever volunteered for anything. Her days were consumed by luncheons, shopping, tennis games, and salon appointments. Spending the afternoon at Hot Dog Day would require a gap in an already packed schedule. Nonetheless, even with the odds strongly against me, I snatched a form from Mr. Holcomb and walked home determined to turn the tide.

"I need you to be a volunteer for Hot Dog Day on Friday," I mentioned casually when I got home.

"Oh, honey, I can't do Friday. I'll try and help out next time."

"Mom, there will be no next time. I'm graduating in three weeks."

"You're graduating?" she asked with a teasing smile.

"Can't you just say yes? Can't you, for once, be like all the other moms?"

I reached into my notebook and put the form on the kitchen counter. She took a long look at it and gave a sigh. To my utter surprise, she filled it out and sealed the deal with her signature.

Friday finally arrived, and after morning classes, we all rushed out to the playground. The parent volunteers were putting the final touches on the setup, and my mom was in the center of it all. While the other parents were dressed in jeans, tennis shoes, and visors, my mother chose a different fashion statement. She wore perfectly pressed linen capris and fabulous high-heeled sandals with freshly pedicured toes, full make-up, including false eyelashes, and her hair in a long ponytail, courtesy of what was commonly called a fall in those days.

She took her spot at the bun steamer. The first boy in line stopped at my mother's station and held out his plate. As she opened the tin, a gush of steam engulfed her face. She let out a gasp and screech and promptly fainted. She crumpled to the ground dramatically and lay there for what seemed to be an eternity. The toes of her sandals pointed upward, and her false eyelashes were sliding down her face from the moisture. The adults gathered around and cradled her head. They were fanning her with napkins and repeatedly asking if she was okay. When she came to, a group of teachers walked her inside to the nurse's office. I was told she was going to be fine and that my father was coming to pick her up.

I could not believe what had happened. I was humiliated. My mother had become the first parent to ever faint at Hot Dog Day. I felt like I would never be able to show my face at school again, and I quite simply wanted to die.

My best friend Ellen came over and put her arm around me.

"Boy, your mom will do anything to get out of volunteering," she joked.

But was it a joke? I asked myself. My mother always did have a flair for the dramatic, and this would certainly have been a most memorable way to make an early exit. Nah, she couldn't have… or could she?

Hot Dog Day went on, and as much as I thought it wouldn't, so did life.

— Allison Stiefel —

72

Moving In

To describe my mother would be to write about a
hurricane in its perfect power, or the climbing,
falling colors of a rainbow.
~Maya Angelou

y eighty-five-year-old mother's eyebrows rose as she offered that familiar tilt of the head, the one that told me something was up. I tensed my shoulders and clenched my jaw, waiting for whatever was coming next.

I could handle it. She was predictable, though dramatic. I expected her to blurt out her thoughts on the latest political upheaval, analyze the percentage of late-night break-ins on the elderly, or share the senior community news.

Instead, she calmly said, as though she were sharing her dinner menu, "I'm going to downsize and sell my house and nearly everything I own." The breaking news was followed by a matter-of-fact stare.

"Do what?"

She tightened her lips into a slight pucker before she said, "And I'm moving in with you."

Images flashed through my mind of my obstinate, independent mother parading around my home as though she owned the place.

I remained quiet, externally calm. I was the typical pleaser with no desire for conflict, usually waiting until I was completely in the corner before I came out swinging.

I decided her announcement was a momentary delusion, perhaps a reaction of medication. A few days after her announcement, my brother and I enjoyed a few laughs over Mom's ridiculous idea. After all, our mother was too independent to be controlled or placed in a confined space long-term with any of her children. She had made this clear on many occasions when I'd begged to live next door to her. I'd wanted to be close enough to watch over her but not too close, but she'd always refused.

I enjoyed living alone, hearing the quiet, writing and reading and cooking whenever I wanted, even into the late hours of the night. I hated noise. My mother loved radio, television, and phone calls, endless phone calls. We would not make good housemates.

I really panicked when she started having yard sales—not one or two, but yard sales every weekend. Ads in the paper sold off what the yard sales couldn't. I forced myself to confront what was happening, and I begged for some cherished items before they drifted onto someone else's walls or into someone else's cupboards and closets.

Her home went on the market. Still partly in denial, I believed it would take weeks, if not months, for her home to sell. Within a week, there was a buyer.

Her belongings began to show up at my home, sometimes when I was there and even when I wasn't: books, clothes, trinkets, food.

This couldn't be happening.

"I'll be a floater," she said whimsically on one of her trips to my house. "I'll stay with you, then with my brothers in Maine, some of my friends. I'll just float around and enjoy myself." She grinned as though she'd just discovered the perfect lifestyle and had a plan to write the great American memoir about her adventures. "I'll take my cat everywhere with me. I can't bear to leave him behind or give him away." She fluffed at her flaming red hair and tucked an unruly strand behind her ear. "What do you think?"

"No one will want you showing up with your cat."

My answer seemed a shock to her, an absurdity. I could see her wheels turning. After only seconds, she added, "Well, I just won't tell them he's coming. We'll just show up. What can they do?"

Shocked that she was in such a delusional state, I took a deep breath and forced myself to respond by explaining all the reasons why selling, moving in with me, and fearlessly dragging the cat across the country in secrecy were terrible ideas.

Unbothered, she tossed her hand in the air as though discarding my words and simply said, "You're so dramatic. It'll be fine."

Then Mom got Covid. She seemed fine at first but began to get sicker. Her breathing grew raspier with each day, the cough louder each time I spoke with her on the phone. Time was running out, and if she was going to get the monoclonal antibody infusion treatment for Covid-19, it had to be now. I was afraid. She was afraid, but she marched herself down to that clinic and sat in that chair hooked to an IV for two hours and received the antibodies.

In the days before the infusion, and the few days after when I wasn't sure if she would end up in the hospital, I no longer stressed about her floater plan, whether it was right or good or logical. I just wanted my mother to be okay, to survive and not die. We had our differences of opinion, but she was my mother. I loved her desperately and couldn't imagine my life without her. For the first time in sixty years, I was forced to think about losing her, and I didn't like it. She'd always been vibrant and full of energy. Seeing her so sick wasn't easy.

Soon, she was better and arrived at my home with more stuff. Eventually, she had more yard sales, selling more junk than the local antique mall. And, to this day, she remains convinced of her mission to declutter her life so that she can wander the United States and spend time with her friends and the family she has left.

Now, I see things differently. Her moving in with me hadn't been part of the plan — living next to her had been — but she was alive, and I would see her idea as a blessing. I realized I don't have to understand her, just love her while she's here and take every moment I have with her as a gift.

I'm not saying we'll get along perfectly, but my view is much more panoramic and filled with more color than I've ever seen before. We're all different, each of us, and that's okay. I only have one mother, and sometimes she's a little weird, but I'll take that weird anytime and thank the good Lord for creating her that way.

— Lori Carol Maloy —

73

Smacking Up the Family Car

It's my car now, but as soon as it's fixed,
it'll be my daughter's again.
~Jeff Stahler

I had just gotten my license at age nineteen, after five attempts to pass the road test. Then I scratched the whole side of the family car while backing out of my college parking lot. My dad was on a business trip at the time, and my mom was very nervous about telling him what had happened to his cherished car.

My mom suddenly remembered a joke one of her friends had told about a guy having to tell the person whose cat he was watching that the cat was dead. When my dad called that night and asked how everything was, my mom nervously replied, "Not too good."

"What do you mean?" said my dad.

My mom replied, "Susie is pregnant. Oh, and by the way, she also smacked up the car."

There was dead silence on the other end of the phone until my dad finally responded, "Oh, my God, that's terrible!"

My mom, not really thinking that my dad had taken her seriously about the first part, responded, "Oh, Harry, go easy on her. You know she only had her license for two weeks, and her perception is off when it comes to parking in tight spots."

"I'm not worried about that. Do you know who the father is?"

My mom answered, "Oh, I only told you that cock-and-bull story about Susie being pregnant to soften the blow about her smacking up the car!"

My dad was so relieved I wasn't pregnant that he hardly gave a hoot about the car. Thanks, Mom!

— Susan Zwirn —

74

Ernest

You can ask "why" all you want, but it doesn't mean
a damn thing if you're not listening to the answer.
~Author Unknown

One Sunday afternoon, my elderly parents and I were taking a ride in the country. I was driving, Dad rode shotgun, and Mom was in the back seat. We chatted as we drove along, admiring the cornfields and farm animals. Then Dad mentioned that he had been trying in earnest to fix his VCR.

Suddenly, a loud voice came from the back.

"Ernest? Who's Ernest?"

"No, Mom," I replied. "Dad said he was doing something in earnest."

"But who's Ernest?" she asked again.

"There's no one named Ernest. Dad tried in earnest to fix something — like he was serious about it."

A pause.

"Oh. Is he your neighbor?"

"Who, Mom?"

"Ernest."

"No, Mom. Dad just meant that he was seriously trying to fix something."

"Oh."

Another pause. She added, "Does he have any kids?"

"Who, Mom?"

"Ernest."

"Mom, there is NO ERNEST!"

"Oh."

Switching the subject to regain a sense of decorum, I began talking to Dad for a few minutes.

Then I heard a voice from the back, "Did he die?"

"Who, Mom?"

"Ernest."

Just to simplify things, I said, "Yes, Mom, he died."

Then my dad, who was not following any of this, asked, "Who died?"

And, of course, Mom answered proudly, "Ernest!"

Mom and Dad have since passed away. I take solace in the fact that they have now gotten to meet Ernest!

— Patricia Gable —

75

Mom's ChapStick

Joy is the best make-up. But a little lipstick
is a close runner-up.
~Anne Lamott

My mother has always been a very fashionable woman and quite youthful for her age. At seventy, she went ziplining in Hawaii and colored her hair purple because she thought it looked great on Katy Perry. She keeps up on all the current make-up and skin-care trends, always moisturizing and sunscreening to ensure her face stays healthy and glowing. She samples all the latest color palettes on offer at Ulta and department-store cosmetic counters to complete her beauty regimen. Most times, she coordinates her shadows and lipsticks with her outfits, be they turquoise, pink or — her favorite — purple (mainly because then she can also match her hair).

She has a group of ladies who have kept in touch over the years, and although they've pretty much scattered all over Pennsylvania, they try to get together once a month to play Tripoli. Betty was hosting this particular evening, a bitter cold one in December several weeks before Christmas. My mom, bundled in scarf, hat and mittens to protect against the punishing, frigid wind, quickly reached into her handbag for her ChapStick, still one of the best lip moisturizers found at the drugstore for less than three dollars. She smeared it all over her mouth, believing the skin around the lips must be protected against the elements as well.

She was the last to arrive and pulled off her hat to reveal her freshly colored hair, the aforementioned Katy Perry-inspired purple.

"What do you think?" she asked her friends.

Although aware of her unconventional sense of style, this time the ladies didn't react quite the way my mother had hoped. They regarded her with strange expressions on their faces, choosing their words carefully as if afraid of offending my mother with their opinions.

"Is it my color?" my mom prompted.

The other four women glanced at each other uneasily. Kitty spoke up first, her words tentative.

"Well, I guess what really matters is whether or not you like it."

My mom was slightly discouraged by their reactions, but she liked her hair and supposed that was all that mattered. Still, it was a little unnerving the way they all kept shooting her curious glances all night, and she was almost grateful when Betty got up to serve the cheesecake, signaling the end of the evening. She approached my mom with the coffeepot and held it above her mug.

"Can I give you a refill, Suzie?"

My mom looked down at the mug. "Oh, this isn't my cup," she said. "It has a purple lipstick stain."

Betty eyed her peculiarly. "What do you mean? Yes, this is your mug. And that's the shade of your lipstick."

"But I'm not wearing any lipstick," my mother said.

"Suzie," Jeanette chimed in incredulously, "yes, you are. And it's all over your mouth."

My mom got up from the table and went into the powder room to check her reflection in the mirror. Sure enough, she had purple lipstick all over her mouth, the bright tint reaching out to her cheeks and just beneath her nostrils. Apparently, when she'd rummaged around in her purse for her ChapStick, she'd grabbed her new MAC lipstick instead.

After my mom washed the lower half of her face and explained the mix-up to the girls, they all sat around the table and laughed for a good, long time.

"You really had us worried there, Suzie," Jeannette confessed through her giggles. "We're always prepared for a bold statement when it comes to you, but your appearance today left us completely speechless!"

—Rachel Remick—

Chapter
10

In-Laws and Out-Laws

Mary Quite Contrary

*Humans are not proud of their ancestors
and rarely invite them round to dinner.*
~Author Unknown

om, where's the ketchup?" I looked around for the bottle. We were having lunch at my in-laws' house. They ate their big meal at noon, so we were having hamburgers, French fries, green beans and, of course, dessert.

Mary, my mother-in-law, pushed a bowl of plastic packets of ketchup, mustard and mayo over to me.

"Where'd you get these?" I asked.

She laughed. "I get them when we go to McDonald's. They have them out for us to take."

I nodded and opened the ketchup packet, squeezed, and waited. Nothing. I got another one and squeezed. A rubbery, dried-up string of ketchup came out. I wondered how old these were.

She laughed again. "I take some when I get coffee."

"Mom, they're there for your food, not when you only get coffee," my husband, John, explained to his mother in a patient voice like one would use with a toddler.

Defensive, she shot back. "I'm entitled to them. I paid good money for those."

I gave up on the ketchup and ate the hamburger plain. I couldn't face what the mustard or mayo would be like.

A fly buzzed around the house and landed on John's plate. Annoyed, he asked his mom for a flyswatter after lunch.

"It's in the garage. I'll get it," she offered.

"No, I'll do it."

A minute later, John called to me from the garage. "Come look at this."

He held a beat-up bedroom slipper (with pink flowers and fur trim), wrapped with silver duct tape around a broken flyswatter. It was a handle with a shoe on the end of it, ready to demolish bugs.

"What can we do with her? Why won't she buy a new flyswatter? Why does she steal ketchup?" He shook his head.

I agreed. "She believes she's a customer because she bought a coffee. In the pantry, I saw a bowl of sugar packets and creamers."

"Well, at least, she uses those for her coffee," John rationalized.

I sighed. "Except she doesn't use cream or sugar in her coffee."

My mother-in-law, Mary. Should I continue?

She was sweet. Never an unkind word or deed.

But she was thrifty. To the extreme. And it wasn't because she needed the money. John said it was because of the Depression, but they were born after that. They grew up average, no worse off than anyone else. She had a sense of entitlement, and when she approached a salad bar, she took one of everything. After all, she paid for it.

One weekend, John's sister and family visited, and we went out for lunch. We placed our orders at the counter and waited to be called when our food was ready. While we waited for our sandwiches, Mary left the table, and when she returned, she put a bag of potato chips by everyone's plate. When we got our lunches, they each came with a bag of chips. Now we each had two bags of chips.

"Where did you get all these potato chips, Mom?" John asked.

"Oh, from the baskets on the counter. They're there for us to take."

I looked over and saw a large wicker basket filled with chips—for sale.

"No, Mom, they're for sale. You have to buy them." John used his toddler voice again.

She put on her stubborn face. "Then they shouldn't put them out there." Her chin jutted out, and she lowered her eyes. A little embarrassed at being caught, she sipped her coffee and wouldn't look at us. She knew what she was doing.

John gathered the stolen chips and returned them to the basket. He told me later that he spoke with the store manager and mumbled an excuse that his mother gets confused.

Later that day, back at their house, we had a cup of coffee, and she pulled out the sugar packets.

"So, if you don't use sugar in your coffee, what do you do with them?" I asked. I waited for a response, my mind racing.

"I use the sugar when I bake," she explained.

Visions danced in my head of empty sugar packets piled on the kitchen counter, spilling on the floor, torn open to fill a cup of sugar for a cake...

If the doorbell rang, I expected the police coming to pick up my mother-in-law.

Through all this, John's father never commented about her taking things. The funny part — he was a retired cop.

One Saturday, John and I picked up his parents to have a nice lunch and get them out of the house.

Suddenly, as we drove along, a terrible smell filled the car. John looked sideways at me.

I gave a small shrug. It didn't go away; it got worse.

Bang! Bang! His dad hit the inside of the car door with his cane. "Stop the car, stop the car! There's a dead cat in here."

A dead cat?

He kept hitting the car door with the cane until John pulled over into a parking lot.

"There's a dead cat in here, I tell you," his dad insisted.

John and I got out of the car, and Mary got out of the back seat holding her purse.

She looked sheepish. She opened her purse, and the disgusting odor rose from her purse. Then she closed it. It was so bad that we walked away, fanning our hands. My stomach jolted, and I gagged.

John took the purse from her, opened it, and looked inside.

He held the purse as far away as his arm would reach. "Mom, what is all this in here?"

"It's kale."

"Kale?" We looked at her, stupefied.

Not a dead cat but kale, which she had stolen from the salad bar at lunch (last week!) and put in her purse. She didn't open her purse all week, and the kale had liquefied. And, well, you can imagine the mess and smell.

"So, you took kale from the salad bar?" John asked, unbelieving. "Why?"

Mary nodded. "I was going to make soup with it. Make a nice, hot soup."

Hot soup in Florida, in August.

John looked over at me like I had something to do with this.

I held up my hands in surrender. "They line the salad bar with decorative kale. She took it and put it in her purse."

Mary snapped her purse shut. We locked her purse in the trunk of the car and went on our way to lunch.

Did she throw the purse away? Of course not. She rinsed it out, washed it (it was cloth) and put it out in the sun for a few days.

She carried it the next week, all clean, ready to fill with ketchup and sugar packets.

— Sydney Bayne —

77

Concert Catastrophe

My husband treats me like a princess, and this implies
that he has been raised by a person who is a queen.
~Author Unknown

My boyfriend's mother was missing! And it was on my watch. What would my boyfriend say?

Roy and I had only started dating recently. I was still getting acquainted with his mother Martha. What was clear to me from the beginning was how different she and I were. She was artsy and bohemian. She enjoyed gardening, collected copper kettles, and she loved painting and making crafts. Meanwhile, I was all business, from my university education to my corporate job.

On this occasion early in our relationship, Roy had bought us tickets to a concert in which he was singing with his choir. He had to arrive at the concert hall early, so we arranged that I would pick up Martha and take her to the show. Roy had entrusted me with both our tickets since his mother was apt to misplace things. After we took our seats, I handed her a ticket so she would be permitted to re-enter the hall if she needed to leave for any reason during the performance.

The lights went down, and the concert began. The choir sang beautifully. The audience was attentive, applauding enthusiastically after each number. Martha appeared to be enjoying herself, although she seemed rather restless and a bit noisy at times — flipping pages in the program, opening candies with crinkly wrappers, and occasionally loudly "whispering" a comment into my ear. I didn't know her well enough at that stage to feel comfortable shushing her, so I just sat there in quiet embarrassment.

Intermission came as a bit of a relief. We walked out of the hall into the foyer together and then parted ways as she spied some old family friends. I didn't want to intrude, so I wandered off by myself. Truth be told, I was just relieved to have a few moments to myself.

After twenty minutes, the lights in the foyer flicked on and off, and the bells began to chime. The second half of the concert was about to begin. I consulted my ticket and headed back to our seats. The seat beside mine remained empty, and I began to get annoyed. Eventually, the house lights went down, but Martha still hadn't materialized. My irritation changed to concern.

The concert continued, with the choir singing as beautifully as before. But now I was the one who was restless. Where was she? Should I go to the bathroom to see if she was there? Had she gone home unexpectedly because she was ill or didn't want to watch the rest of the show? If she'd left, had a friend given her a lift or had she taken a taxi? What if something had happened to her? And what would Roy think?

Needless to say, the rest of the concert was a blur for me, and I didn't enjoy it one bit with all that worry gnawing away inside me. Nonetheless, I didn't really see an obvious or easy solution to my dilemma, so I sat tight and waited impatiently for the performance to end.

At long last, the show was over. I jumped to my feet, thinking I would try to meet Roy backstage to alert him to the problem of his missing mother. As I walked up the aisle toward the back of the hall, I suddenly spied Martha. There she was, sitting calmly in an entirely different part of the hall from where our assigned seats had been.

She saw me, too. I waited for her to make her way over to me. Upon getting within earshot, she looked at me accusingly and asked, "Where were you?"

— Marina Bee —

78

The Day the Bag Rang

Even the gods love jokes.
~Plato

t was just an ordinary Tuesday. Hot but ordinary. It was only 7:00 A.M., but it was already eighty degrees. Steffany, age two, played with her cereal, and five-month-old Chip kicked his feet and sucked his fist while I made breakfast.

"Steffy, please just eat your cereal." She was making handprints in her oatmeal. Chip stopped midway through his bottle. As I lifted him to burp, I was suddenly showered with spit-up.

After both of us had been cleaned up, I put Chip on the living room floor with his red rattle and went to the kitchen to clean up. Steffy had spread oatmeal on the floor and was making footprints! *Count to ten*, I thought. *She's just precocious.*

Coffee mug in hand, I sat at the table, sweating and feeling sorry for myself because we didn't have air conditioning. I decided to make macaroni-tuna salad for dinner and had just put the water on when I heard Steffy crying. I found her in the bathroom standing in front of the toilet. Her little shorts and training pants were down around her knees, sopping wet.

"Honey, what happened?"

"Me go potty. Me stand just like Daddy, but it went all down my legs." More crying.

"That's okay, punkin'. Let's get you changed." (I bit my bottom lip so I wouldn't burst out laughing.) The phone rang.

"Hello?"

"Hello! Is this Mrs. Bender?"

"Yes?" I replied.

"Mrs. Bender, I'm from New York Telephone's maintenance department."

"Yes," I replied.

"We're working in your neighborhood today, and I'm notifying our customers that we'll be cleaning out the telephone lines with a high-powered blower. You need to put your telephone into a bag to prevent dust from blowing into your house."

"Okay. Thanks for calling."

I will never live down what I did next.

I went straight to the kitchen closet, pulled out a brown paper bag, put the phone into it, and taped it shut! I made the salad and started the laundry. The phone had been in the bag for an hour or so. Each time I walked past it, I checked for escaping dust.

Suddenly, the bag rang! I hated to do it, but I let it ring. The kids and I headed for the park and the cool, shady trees.

Funny, I thought as we walked, *I don't see any telephone trucks.*

I spread out the old, blue, well-worn quilt, and gave Chip a toy and Steffy a book.

I opened my latest travel catalog and read about a twenty-one-day cruise through the South Pacific. I closed my eyes and could almost smell the coconut suntan lotion... "Wait! That's not my lotion... it's Chip!"

I snapped out of my daydream and reached into the diaper bag.

"What the heck?" I wondered as I pulled out Winnie the Pooh.

"Steffy? Where are the diapers?"

She explained, "Winnie wants go to park, too. Winnie no wear diapers, silly Mommy!" I just looked at her. I looked at Winnie the Pooh in my right hand and my trip to Tahiti in my left hand, closed my eyes and counted to ten for the second time that day.

"Where are those telephone trucks?" I wondered again as we strolled home.

With the kids down for their naps, I sat at the table eating a banana, staring at the bag. Curiosity was killing me. I approached the bag and ever-so-gently pulled the tape back just enough to peek inside. No dust. Yet. I went to the basement and sat on the bottom step where it was cool. The phone began its muffled ring again. Taunting me.

I can't, I just can't, I thought, imagining myself picking up the receiver and suddenly being blasted in the face and choking on a high-powered, dust-busted clump of dirty, filthy telephone-line debris! By the tenth ring, I was in agony. It stopped. I vowed to tear that bag to shreds the next time it rang!

It was 3:00, and Charlie would be home soon. Time to get the kids up for juice.

Charlie stomped into the kitchen and angrily demanded, "Where the heck have you been all day? I've been calling and calling!" Both kids started wailing.

That's it! I thought. *I've had it! No more counting to ten!*

I proceeded to tell him about the phone company calling to notify our street that they'd be cleaning out the telephone lines, and it would only take a few hours, and I put the phone in the brown paper bag just like they told me to, and I'd been thrown up on, almost pooped on, had to cut short our time in the park because Winnie the Pooh doesn't wear diapers, and swore that if he said one more word about trying to call me all day, I'd scream! And then I just stood there, hands on my hips, daring him to speak.

He stared at me, wide-eyed. Finally, he spoke slowly.

"You put the phone where?" I pointed to the taped paper bag.

"They told you they were going to do WHAT?"

His voice was getting louder. And then... he started to laugh! He leaned against the table and started slapping it, laughing hysterically.

Wait a minute, I thought. *Was this a joke?*

"Charlie!" I yelled. "If you put someone up to this, I swear..."

His glasses were off now. He was wiping away tears of laughter, trying to compose himself.

"No, it wasn't me... but..."

He started laughing uncontrollably again. I burst into tears.

"C'mon now, it's okay. It's just somebody's practical joke. We'll find out and..." He totally cracked up again! I tore off a paper towel and blew my nose. I wanted to run to the basement and stay there for the rest of my life.

I sniffed. "Why were you calling me?" Charlie wiped away his tears again.

"Well, it's too late now, but Roland [my brother-in-law] called and said he and Jan had two extra gift certificates for dinner tonight at Chez Pierre."

I groaned, picturing coq au vin with crème brûlée for dessert versus macaroni-tuna salad and an ice-cream sandwich.

"Yeah, it would've been nice, but he said he needed to know as soon as possible."

"Why the hurry?" I asked.

"Beats me. He just said to call you right away..."

"Roland!" We blurted his name simultaneously and fell into hysterics.

Later that evening, I put our plan into action and made the call.

"Hey, Roland! It's Pam. How are ya?"

"Great! What's up?" (He was trying to sound normal.)

"Well, Charlie just called." (He was a volunteer fireman, and it was meeting night.) "One of the guys just gave him tickets for this Saturday's exhibition Buffalo Bills game. We know how much you like the Bills." (He LOVED the Bills!) "So, if you and Jan... hello? Roland? Roland?" I hung up and waited.

Not fifteen seconds later, the phone rang.

"Hello? Hello? Sorry, Roland, I can't hear you! You really need to have your phone lines power-cleaned!"

— Pamela Kae Bender —

79

Oops

A daughter-in-law cannot be perfect by herself.
A beautiful mother-in-law helps her be one.
~Author Unknown

"Hi, Connie." My sister-in-law's familiar chipper voice greeted me from the other end of the phone line early one Monday afternoon. "Mom and I just finished baking banana bread, and we'd love to bring you out a warm loaf. Can you have the coffee on in half an hour?"

Since thoughts of my mother-in-law's freshly baked banana bread clouded my sensibilities and rendered me unable to think of an excuse, I replied in my cheeriest voice, "Of course, come on up. I'll be here!"

What was I thinking? I can't let my mother-in-law see the house like this! She's under the impression that I'm perfect.

I had to think fast! There were three options: I could lock the door, hide and hope they'd leave the bread on the doorstep; I could call back and tell them I had forgotten that I had other plans and offer to stop by and pick up my banana bread; or I could attempt to clean the house within thirty minutes.

In a fleeting moment of guilt at the thought of lying to my husband's mother and sister, I chose what seemed like the impossible — clean the house in thirty minutes or less.

Although I never claimed to be the perfect housekeeper, I did take solace in that my relatively new house remained reasonably tidy considering we had five very active kids. The past week, however, had been even busier than usual with running the brood back and forth for extra-curricular activities. As a result, the house took the brunt of neglect.

To add to my quandary, I'd spent the morning sitting on the patio drinking coffee in an effort to recuperate from the hectic weekend of activities. But I told myself, "Where there's a will, there's a way." Then I put my words into action!

I gathered up an armload of the kids' socks, pants, shirts and jackets that were scattered across the living room and family room and gave them a quick toss onto the laundry-room floor, not bothering to take the time to see if they were in need of washing. There would be plenty of time for that later.

After making sure the laundry-room door was pulled tightly closed, I headed for the kitchen to load the breakfast dishes into the dishwasher. Thankfully, I had remembered to unload the dishwasher the night before. Things were looking good, and I still had twenty minutes remaining. I ran around the entire main floor, rapidly picking up trash and discarding it in the garbage.

I quickly swept the entryway and kitchen floors before dragging out the vacuum for a quick sweep over the three carpeted rooms, tossing toys into the toy box as I worked my way across the floor.

Glancing at the clock on my way upstairs to the kids' bedrooms, with a gym bag slung over my shoulder, soccer cleats under my arm, tutu and tights in one hand, a scarf looped around my neck, a baseball cap atop my head, and a stack of books and binders in the opposite arm, I was relieved to find I had five minutes to spare. That gave me just enough time to tidy up the bathroom and run a brush through my hair.

Whew! I did it!

I put on a fresh pot of coffee, and since my guests hadn't yet arrived, I decided to wipe off the chicken eggs I had gathered after taking the kids to the bus stop. It would be a nice gesture to give them some eggs in return for the banana bread.

I was standing at the kitchen sink finishing the last egg when I heard a knock at the door behind me.

"C'mon in," I called out, too tired to physically greet them.

I had to choke down a chuckle when the first words out of my sister-in-law's mouth as she entered the kitchen were, "Wow, your house is immaculate, and you even have time to polish eggs!"

After exchanging hugs and our usual informal greetings, we ventured into the dining room and sat down at the large, wooden table. As I excused myself to go back into the kitchen to get the coffee mugs and put the loaf of delectably fragrant bread on a platter, I heard them whispering that they didn't understand how I did it with five kids. It was about all I could do to keep from confessing, but my selfish pride won!

My mother-in-law sliced the bread while I stepped into the kitchen for some butter and the steaming pot of freshly brewed coffee. I felt such a wonderful sense of satisfaction as we relaxed and devoured the scrumptious, warm, buttered bread. A sheepish smile spread across my face as I relished my accomplishment.

But that smile was short-lived when my oldest son strode through the front door. With a look of shock on his face, he loudly exclaimed, "Man, who cleaned the house?"

My mouth fell open, and I did what any disenchanted mother of a smart-mouthed teenager would do. I shrewdly suggested, "Sit down and have some of Grandma's delicious banana bread, hon!" Then I quickly changed the subject.

—Connie Kaseweter Pullen—

80

Frozen in Time

Laughter has no foreign accent.
~Paul Lowney

He was back! After many months travelling to different countries with his modeling agency, our son Mike had returned from his last placement in China. We were excited to have him home again. After chatting via Skype for so long, I could finally hug him and tell him in person how much he was missed and feed him his favorite meals. This time was a little different, though. It didn't take long to discover he had managed to keep an important secret from us. He'd fallen in love.

His girlfriend was also a model and had worked in the same countries at the same time as he had. Mike's face beamed as he showed us a picture of this tall, beautiful blonde, and we knew he had found the love of his life. Before long, she was on her way to Canada to stay with us for a few months. We could tell it was a serious relationship from the first day we met her.

Her name was Ivona, but Mike called her Ivi. She was sweet, gentle-spirited and lovely. She had grown up in the Czech Republic, but because she was well-travelled, our culture didn't seem to be a difficult adjustment. The biggest hurdle for her was the English language. She had studied it in school, but there were so many unfamiliar idioms, expressions and terms that our conversations were sometimes a bit challenging. She worked hard at it, though, and her vocabulary grew every day.

One day, Ivi decided to venture out into the city alone and chose the mall as her first stop. Parking the car in the crowded lot, she grabbed her purse and headed into the building. There wasn't really anything specific she needed; it was just an adventure.

An announcement was just finishing as she walked through the doors.

Striding into the mall, she immediately sensed something was wrong. Everyone in the mall stood like statues — moms holding children's hands, dads with parcels under their arms, elderly people with walkers, and teenagers in the food court getting lunch. Everyone was just staring, not moving, not speaking. As her eyes darted about the mall, she wondered if they were even breathing!

Weaving back and forth through the frozen people, she couldn't understand what was happening. *Perhaps I am dreaming. Or maybe they are staged mannequins. What if I am going crazy?* she thought.

Looking around at the strange phenomenon, she suddenly felt frightened and decided to get out of there. Drawing her sweater tightly around her body, she wove back between the statues and ran out through the doors. Ivi couldn't get into the car fast enough.

Once home, she was relieved to see that Mike was moving about the kitchen making lunch. Taking a deep breath, she blurted out her traumatic experience.

"Mike, this town is crazy. You wouldn't believe what is going on at the mall. When I went in, all the people were frozen in place — men, women and children. They were all just standing there, looking at nothing. Nobody was talking or moving. It was so scary. I don't want to go back there again!"

"What? I don't understand. Are you sure you weren't imagining it all?" he asked.

"No! It was real!"

Mike scratched his head, and then a grin spread over his face. "What day is this? Is this November eleventh? I know exactly what was happening. In this country, Ivi, on the eleventh hour of the eleventh day of the eleventh month, we stop and remember the soldiers that died in past wars. To honor them, we stand still and quiet for a few moments wherever we are and remember what they have done for their country. We call it Remembrance Day, or in the U.S. it's called Veterans Day. You must have just missed the announcement that it was eleven o'clock, and a time of silence would be observed." He began to chuckle, realizing how strange this must have seemed to her. The more he thought about it, the funnier it became. His chuckles soon turned to gut laughs, and his perplexed girlfriend had no choice but to join in.

Sobering up, Ivi shook her head. "I hope I can figure out all your customs before too long. Maybe you should tell me now if there are other things I need to know. I don't want to have to go through something like that again."

Not long after that crazy day, Mike and Ivi were married and moved into a darling bungalow in town with their two giant Rottweilers. Ivi speaks perfect English now. We are so proud of her, but we still chuckle over her strange introduction to one Canadian custom. As for Ivi, every November eleventh, she thinks of that day when she walked through what she thought to be people frozen in time and smiles a tiny smile.

— Heather Rodin —

Mother(s)-in-Law

I went from resenting my mother-in-law to accepting her,
finally to appreciating her. What appeared to be
her diffidence when I was first married,
I now value as serenity.
~Ayelet Waldman

ivorce. It's a heavy-duty word. But one thing that often goes unconsidered is the loss of a perfectly broken-in mother-in-law. My first MIL lasted ten years. Quiet and demure, she hesitated to give her opinion. But when our first child was born, I was desperate for motherly advice.

"Why does she keep crying? What should I do?"

"Oh, I'm not going to tell you what to do," she said quietly. "I'm not going to be the Interfering MIL."

In retrospect, although frustrating to me, those were the Golden Years. I've since remarried, and I've been adapting to my New MIL for the past twenty years.

Mary is a jovial, warm-hearted woman from Albuquerque. She's 5'10" and wears lots of big, turquoise jewelry and fringed, long leather skirts. Her purses could easily hold a small calf. She's addicted to the Home Shopping Network and vodka. She's always up for a party, although it takes her two hours to "put on her face." The constant sips of vodka act as coasting brakes to her make-up sessions, but she always emerges beautifully put together.

She drove her RV to visit, bringing her four-pound, pedigreed

Apricot Teacup Poodle, Babe.

Mary and I decided we would cook dinner. Moving barefoot slowly through the kitchen in her gaping muumuu, with Babe cradled up against her ample bosom, she drawled, "Honey, where's your garlic press?"

I got nervous. I was raised on Spam, and I like to eat my steaks well done with ketchup on them. A garlic press? I had some garlic powder in the cupboard, but I didn't think it was pressed — unless, of course, it was caked up and dry.

Deflecting the question for a moment seemed like the wisest thing to do.

"Um, if I had one… What would it look like?"

She burst into laughter. "Honey, tomorrow we're a gonna take you shoppin'!"

The back wheel of the RV hit the curb as we left, the pots and pans in the back bouncing off the countertop.

As we entered the mall, she exclaimed, "I need a drink!"

"Okay, there's Orange Julius, Starbucks…"

"I'm telling you, I need a drink! There we go! A Ground Round restaurant."

She waved over the waitress as we entered. "Bring me two margaritas, won't you, darlin'? What do you want, sweetie?"

"Um, coffee, I guess."

An hour later, we walked happily into the Chef's Corner Store. We bought several kitchen implements I didn't recognize and a set of heavy cookware. I struggled with the bulging bag banging against my scrawny leg.

Veering toward a high-end fashion store, she crowed, "I'm also gonna teach you the proper way to crack an egg! But, first, we're gonna get ya some nice clothes. You've got no sense of style; you don't wear enough make-up, and you're too short." She sighed. "We'll just have to work with what we got."

Fortunately, she tired quickly, but she made me sit through a makeover session at the beauty counter. She bought me cleanser, primer, toner, foundation, and several other items in pretty, silver-colored tubes.

"How am I going to have time to do all this?"

"Not a problem. Now, I'm just gonna sit here. You go get the RV." My arms ached carrying the numerous shopping bags as I walked across the hot parking lot.

Unfolding the rear steps, I struggled to stack the bags in the narrow hallway. I wiped the Ultimate Cheek Bronzing Cherry Me Pink blush dripping down my cheeks.

"Good Lord," I muttered. I shoved a few sticky, lint-covered Good & Plentys from her dusty dashboard into my mouth and pulled up to her.

"I'll drive," she announced. "I take this thing to my manicure appointments, to the PX Air Force base to get my groceries, and to the American Legion so's I can have a nap if I need one."

"It's better if I drive. You can relax."

She climbed in, but as soon as we left the parking lot, I started to cough.

Two half-full water bottles were in the cup holder. My eyes watering, I grabbed the bottle nearest me.

Quickly, I took a large swig, and the pungent taste, searing my throat, caused a torrent of coughing.

Mary cackled raucously as I took a sharp turn, her doughy, tanned upper arms flapping in tandem as we bounced.

"That ain't water, honey! Now there's one more thing you're gonna have to learn." She grinned. "I got me a little system. The water bottles with the blue caps are filled with water. Now the ones with the white caps, well, let's just say, that's my Special Water. What I do is tell the grandkids that the water bottles with the white caps have stale water in them, so's they leave them alone."

"What if they decide to help clean out your RV and pour them out?" I wiped the last few tears from my eyes.

"Well, I didn't think of that. But no matter. There's plenty more where that came from."

When we got back to the house, I went to the guest room to put away her bags.

The sudden smell gagged me. Babe was on the queen bed with

a cooling, loosely swirled pile of dog poop rising like a Dairy Queen cone nestled among the decorative pillows.

"Babe! What did you do? Mom? Babe pooped on the bed! How did she even get up there?"

I reached out to snatch Babe off the bed and caught a glimpse of her perfect, white teeth as she snapped at my hand. I jumped back.

Mary came in. "Now, watch out. Babe's a one-woman doggie." She made kissy sounds and scooped her up lovingly.

"Sometimes, I put her on the bed when I'm talking on the phone, and I just forget about her. And then, why, she can't jump down! Course, sometimes, she prefers to use the bathroom rug to do her business."

She smooched Babe. "The little shit! I love her so."

Babe smirked at me over Mary's shoulder as Mary said, "Now you just get this cleaned up, and we won't bother cookin' dinner tonight. All that shoppin' wore me out. Let's just order some Chinese."

"Yes, mother," I replied, narrowing my eyes at Babe.

Two weeks later, Mary was ready to head home. She backed up the RV jerkily off the driveway and into the grass. We yelled at her to stop while Babe watched proudly from her lap.

As she drove past, we saw our basketball hoop and support base snagged on the chrome trim of the RV, rolling and bobbing behind her.

"Wait!" Mark yelled. "WAIT!"

"Bye, bye, sweethearts," she waved merrily. "Y'all take care! Love ya!"

As she turned onto the street, the rear RV wheel, once again, bounced up and over the curb. The basketball hoop wrenched itself loose and flopped, uselessly, onto the newly blooming flowers.

We both started laughing as Babe gazed back at us, her carefully fluffed bangs moving gently in the breeze.

"I can assure you," I smiled at Mark, "I'm never going to break in another mother-in-law."

— Connie L. Gunkel —

82

Stuck

People say that life is the thing, but I prefer reading.
~Logan Pearsall Smith

"**S**tuck? What do you mean that we are stuck? That is not funny, Rey!" As I looked up and saw the look on my dad's face, I realized he was not joking with my mom. We were trapped inside a cave, four adults with seven children. Panic started to set in quickly. How could this happen? How were we going to get out?

I concluded that the new motorhome was cursed. It seemed like one thing after another happened on our trip. Now, we were stuck inside a cave. My uncle had asked the park ranger if the size of the motorhome would be a problem. He stated it would not. However, the additional foot on the newest model was an issue. The cave did not go straight through to the other side. There was a point where it curved, and a giant boulder jutted out about halfway through. A smaller vehicle would have just cleared the turn. Worse yet, it was a highway, so cars were backing up behind us honking their horns.

The park rangers finally came up to investigate. They told my uncle that he was going to have to pull it to one side and pull it through. They hoped that the damage would be minimal. The only other option would be to back it up and head back hundreds of miles out of the way. Either way, the motorhome would be damaged. My uncle asked my aunt what she wanted to do. My aunt did not respond. My uncle asked her again. Still no response. Finally, he shouted, "Get your nose out of that damn book!"

There were horns honking, kids being noisy, and my uncle repeatedly yelling her name. She didn't even acknowledge our presence. She sat in her chair engrossed in her book, clueless to what was transpiring around her.

Frustrated by my aunt's non-response, my uncle decided to hug the left side of the road. Any damage would be to the right side of the motor home. As he pulled around the boulder in the center of the cave, we could hear metal scrape against the rock as well as the sound of breaking glass. It was so loud that we covered our ears. My aunt still had her nose buried in the book. The passenger-side mirror fell off, scratching the window beside her. My aunt never looked up. Once we were free and on the other side, people cheered while honking their horns. She turned the page and just kept reading, unaware of any dilemma.

My uncle pulled off at the first roadside stop. While examining the motorhome, he could see that the molding and passenger-side mirror had been torn off. It could have been worse since the door could have been damaged. It would have made it difficult for us to get in and out. Everyone except for my aunt joined him outside, taking a break from the latest incident to wade through a stream.

Since my aunt was still inside reading her book, my uncle spoke to all of us before we got back in the motor home. In a stern voice, he told each of us not to say a word about what happened to my aunt. He wanted to wait to see when she noticed the damage to the side of the vehicle. None of us said a word.

Several days later, while in Yellowstone National Park, she noticed. On our way back from seeing Old Faithful, my aunt was screaming for my uncle. She had seen the side of the motor home and all the damage. Visibly upset, she grabbed my uncle when she saw him. She screamed in a voice that sounded more like a howl.

"Dick, someone has vandalized the motorhome! The whole side is scratched up, and the mirror has been torn right off!"

The rest of the family just watched while doing our best to keep a straight face so as not to give anything away. Some of us even changed direction, walking to the other side of the motorhome.

My uncle looked back at her and said, "Are you sure? I don't see anything different from when we got out to go into the park. There isn't even any broken glass or tire marks."

Then my uncle smiled. My aunt's eyes grew wide. She was furious. She smacked my uncle on the shoulder while calling him a jerk. He just laughed. As a matter of fact, at that point we all were laughing. My aunt even began to laugh, too.

When we told her how it had happened, she didn't believe it at first. She thought that we had made up the story. To this day, I think that she still believes that someone vandalized the motorhome.

— P.A. Alaniz —

83

Checkpoint

Against the assault of laughter, nothing can stand.
~Mark Twain

"**H**ere," I said when we reached the security check at the airport. "I'll put your purse on the conveyer, and you need to give the attendant your cane before you go through the gate."

I was sending my mother-in-law to Montana for a nice visit with my sister-in-law, her daughter. I deposited Mom's carry-on bag on the conveyer and dropped my car keys in one of the small, plastic bowls placed on the counter for that purpose. Mom was such a sweetheart, but she got confused sometimes, and we all tried to make new things easier for her.

"I'd rather keep my purse," Mom said, clutching the strap that crossed her chest protectively. "What are those bowls for?" she asked the attendant, peering over the counter and into the colorful blue and yellow bowls.

"They're for your keys and change and anything else metal that might set off the alarms," she answered, smiling.

"I'm supposed to put my money in there?" Mom asked. The attendant nodded.

"Why?" Mom asked.

"So the alarms don't go off when you go through the gate." Mom peered in the bowls again and started to ask another question but stopped.

She hesitated but finally pulled her purse strap over her head and hoisted the large, bulging black purse up onto the counter, unsnapped the big flap, and opened the first of several sections. She began piling the contents on the counter next to the purse.

Out came a roll of dollar bills banded together, Kleenex, Band-Aids, keys, fingernail clippers, a brush and comb, face cream, hair spray, a pocket mirror, clipped coupons, notecards, a bag with strips of postage stamps and return address labels, two lipsticks, four eyeglass cases, five hair rollers, seven bottles of medicines whose labels she read out loud before placing them on the counter, several candy bars, an apple, half of a banana, a jar of cold, cooked oatmeal, and two fat wallets. She opened one, unsnapped the change purse, and shook out the coins that bounced and rolled to every corner of the counter. Retrieving the coins, she leaned over to look into the blue bowl that held my keys and then dropped her coins into the yellow bowl. We watched as she unzipped all the little pockets inside the purse and began extracting coins.

"No, no." The attendant stopped her when she finally realized what Mom was doing. She gently put her hand on Mom's arm. "You don't need to do that. You can just put everything back into your purse and put your whole purse on the conveyor."

"But I want my purse," Mom said, pulling it closer to her and farther away from the attendant. Mom eyed her with suspicion and reversed the "emptying" steps, carefully reorganizing everything back into her purse one item at a time, including every coin into its allotted place in her coin-keeper. She zipped her purse shut and, before I could stop her, pulled the strap back over her head, settling the strap protectively like an ammunition belt across her chest. She turned toward the security arches as if the matter was settled.

The attendant turned to me apologetically. "She'll have to put her purse on the conveyor to be scanned in order to enter the concourse," she informed me quietly, glancing at the people waiting in line to get through security who rustled with impatience. For good reason.

"Here, Mom, that purse is heavy. Let me just put it up here for you," I said.

"My purse is just fine where it is. It's not too heavy," she dismissed me.

"But we have to let them scan its contents in order to get through security," I explained.

"Do you mean they want to look at what's in my purse?" she asked. "I don't want anyone snooping in my purse. It's none of their business what I have in my purse!" She clutched her purse tighter.

"It's for everyone's safety. They scan for anything that might be dangerous."

"Like what?" she wanted to know.

"I don't know. Like a bomb or a gun or something," I said.

Mom was righteously indignant. "Do I look like someone who would have a gun in my purse?" she demanded. "Who would think that?" Now her gaze swept the entire security staff to determine who would dare think such a thing about her. She was offended and didn't trust any of them.

"It's okay, really. Everyone must do it. Look, I'm putting my purse up here. They won't open it; they just do an X-ray of what's inside, and the girl sitting right over there just looks at the X-ray as it goes by. Then it comes out the other end, and you can pick it up just as soon as you pass through the security gate." I had visions of wrestling my mother-in-law for possession of her purse. She finally, reluctantly, pulled the strap back over her head. I all but snatched her purse from her and swung it onto the moving belt before she could change her mind. She watched skeptically as it disappeared.

We still had the people scanner to go through. It took three tries, lots of explanations, and much cajoling to finally convince her to relinquish her cane and let me put it on the conveyor. I handed her to the attendant, who guided her through the scanner to the other side. I got through in record time, retrieved the car keys and her cane, shouldered the heavy carry-on, and picked up both purses, carefully handing hers to her.

The gate alarms sounded behind us, and she turned. "What's that alarm? I've never heard that before. What does it mean? Is there a fire?" she asked, almost panic-stricken.

"He probably just forgot to empty all his pockets," I tried to reassure her as she watched another attendant carefully waving a wand over the man's body after he had failed security for the third time.

"Things have changed a lot since the last time I took a plane," she informed me. She clearly did not consider the changes for the better.

"I know," I agreed. "It's too bad, too, but security is getting tighter and tighter for everyone's protection."

Now that we'd finally gotten through the gate, we headed to the departure area. Mom appeared to be deep in thought as we proceeded down the ramp to the gates. Finally, she stopped walking and looked at me quizzically, glancing back down the concourse toward the security gate with a confused expression.

"I still can't figure out what we were supposed to put in the offering bowls," she confided.

— Margaret V. Doran —

84

Pickle Daze

I always said your best palate is your own,
not mine. I'm a guidepost.
~Robert M. Parker, Jr.

t was a cold February day, and we didn't feel like going out or even leaving our seats around the kitchen table. Somehow the conversation turned to pickles, specifically bread and butter pickles, and how my brother-in-law Fred thought B&G pickles were by far the best of breed.

My husband Bill and I were staying the weekend at the home of my sister-in-law Denise and her husband Fred on Long Island — the New York Long Island. My brother-in-law Stephen and his wife Mary were in from Michigan. None of the grown kids were around. It was just us somewhat lazy, cold-averse empty nesters, free to do what we wanted without judgment from the twenty-somethings. The six of us always have a great time together no matter what we're doing.

Bill and I had just stayed at a resort in Pennsylvania that prides itself on its wine list. We had ordered flights of wines each night and written down our tasting notes. I had been very proud of myself for guessing the right Robert Parker wine scores for the three wines each night, deciding that I did indeed have a sophisticated palate. We even took a wine course from the sommelier, complete with more tasting notes.

Anyway, it turned out that Fred's favorite B&G bread and butter pickles were sometimes hard to find so Denise had brought home "inferior" brands over the past few months. They had four brands of bread and butter pickles in the pantry, and we had nothing better to do, so I suggested we test Fred and see if he could really pick out his prized B&G pickles from the four brands.

Denise, being an organized person, set up a blind taste test for the five of us. She gave us each four little piles of pickles on a plate, labeled A, B, C, and D on small pieces of paper. We set up categories to evaluate: color, crunch, cut, taste, and nose (a reference to wine tasting). I was hoping that Fred would get it right. He's a very competitive guy and hates to lose.

And then the tasting began.

Stephen, who has a Ph.D. in physics, and worked as a safety engineer at GM and Ford for decades, took an analytical approach, numerically based. He assigned values to our five criteria. His winner was Pickle C with eleven points and his loser was Pickle D.

Mary used a more narrative approach. She had written comments for each of the four contenders. She found Pickle B to have "good crunch" but a "slightly more vinegary taste." She guessed that the B&G pickles were Pickle C and found they were "not as crunchy" as others and had "an off taste." Mary is super nice, so she said, "I didn't pick a best." I guess she didn't want to insult anyone. But under duress she admitted that she liked Pickle D the most. That was the one her husband liked the least.

Bill, Mr. CEO, cut right to the chase. All he said was "A=5, B=4, C=6, and D=3." He chose Pickle C as the best, just like his brother Stephen.

Denise read my tasting notes aloud next. I characterized Pickle A as too pale a green color, with an awful taste. I said it was "a poor excuse for a pickle," and for its score, being a words person more than a numbers person, I compared it to fine wines and said it was "the Manischewitz of pickles." And I didn't mean just because they are both kosher.

Pickle B had a "traditional color" but a "weird taste with extra spice" and a "weird texture." I said it was like "bad cognac." Pickle C had a nose that was like "swamp odor" and a "weird aftertaste" and I said it was like "Chilean sparkling wine."

My winner was Pickle D, albeit with its own issues regarding color and cut. I said it "was the best example of a bread and butter pickle, but just don't look at it." Its wine equivalent was a Robert Mondavi Cabernet.

And then it was Fred's turn. Fred honed in on his favorite B&G pickles, saying they were Pickle C. But he blew it when we described Pickle D as "Mt. Olive yuck," as we discovered when Denise pulled the dish towel off the four contenders and we learned that Pickle A was Mt. Olive, B was Vlasic, C was indeed B&G, and D was Stop & Shop.

All three men liked B&G best, which made Fred feel good. The women, being cheap dates, liked the Stop & Shop house brand the most.

And I discovered that my palate might not be quite as sophisticated as I thought.

— Amy Newmark —

Family Bonding

85

I Hate You, Limburger Cheese

*At a family reunion, you'll meet every human
to whom you're related. Will you be elated?
That's still to be debated.*
~Author Unknown

Some years ago, we had a family reunion in a park just outside Philadelphia. It was a wonderful thing — four generations came together for the first time in ages. Cousins who hadn't seen each other in twenty years hugged with tears in their eyes. Over a hundred people showed up, and there was plenty of food, fun, and booze for all.

But even Irish people can't just sit around drinking and gabbing all the time; we needed something to do. There were the usual outdoor games, like softball and a horseshoes tournament, but the true highlight was the *Survivor* challenge. My aunt Joan was a devotee of the popular reality show, and she created her own version of it for the reunion.

About twenty of us competed — mostly kids and younger adults, plus a few of the more adventurous forty-somethings. There was a bizarre game that involved running around a cardboard path in the grass, thwacking each other with pool noodles. There was something like tag with water balloons. All were goofy, all were fun, and no one really bothered keeping score or voting anyone out.

Naturally, my aunt saved the greatest challenge for last. She had tested our speed, strength, and endurance; now, it was time to test our courage. And, in true reality-TV style, that meant we had to eat something weird.

"Limburger cheese?" we all cried together. Aunt Joan cackled like the villain in a cheesy horror movie as she brandished a sealed plastic bag. A few well-placed thunderbolts would have fit the moment perfectly.

Our hearts dropped. We had all heard about the legendary stinkiest of stinky cheeses, but none of us had ever seen it before. It didn't look like much—just a fist-sized yellow block pocked with divots—but it was terrifying anyway, like that too-normal neighbor whom you half-suspect is a serial killer. There was an aura of menace about it. But, after coming this far, we weren't going to back down, right?

Wrong.

"Ugh! It smells like sweaty gym socks!" my sister-in-law cried. "No way am I eating that."

She wasn't alone. Nearly every one of the so-called survivors wimped out after just one whiff. Grown-ups, kids, athletes, couch potatoes—quitters, the lot of 'em. But I, of course, have the heart of a champion; I wasn't going to let some dinky block of malodorous dairy come between me and my trophy. I stayed in.

Only one other competitor had the guts to challenge me—my nineteen-year-old cousin, Nancy. We took our places in the middle of the ball field, staring each other down like two boxers waiting for the opening bell. Then Aunt Joan handed us our chunks of cheese, and we popped them into our mouths.

Ugh, it did taste like sweaty gym socks! Not that I've actually eaten sweaty gym socks, but now I don't have to because I know what they taste like. I stuck it out, though. Emboldened by the cheers of the crowd, I chewed, and I chewed, and I chewed some more. I was going to win this thing and take my place as the reunion champion—the ultimate Survivor. I could practically hear "Eye of the Tiger" playing in my head.

But the Limburger wasn't going down without a fight. It had a powerful weapon on its side, and the more I chewed, the more it unleashed its pungent fury. The funky flavor stomped around my mouth, personally insulting every one of my taste buds. The juices oozed down the back of my throat, and the stench slithered up my sinuses and soaked deep into my brain. It was awful. Within moments, the cheers and the ballfield faded away — I was lost in a world of stinky cheese. It felt like a football team had buried me in their laundry cart after practice, and I quickly realized something very important.

If I swallowed this horrible, nasty glop, I was going to hurl.

Yep, underneath the jerseys and jock straps, I could taste the vomit preparing to erupt up my throat, and believe me, that was not a winning combination of flavors. That was where I drew the line. I had outwitted, outplayed, and outlasted nearly everyone, but I was not going to outspew them.

I grabbed a napkin and spat out the remains of my nemesis. Then I gargled, rinsed, and did everything I could to relieve my poor, afflicted taste buds; unfortunately, Limburger lingers. I sighed and consoled myself with the thought that I had given it my best shot, and there's no shame in quitting as long as you try.

Then I heard it — the sound of a champion. A physically ill champion. A few feet away from me, Nancy was bent over, throwing up Limburger chunks into the grass at her feet. The crowd around her scattered out of the way, covering their own mouths. She had done it — she had swallowed the cheese, and she paid the ultimate price for her bravery.

Obviously, she was the winner. Victory belongs to the bold, and Nancy had outdared us all, even yours truly. I tipped my cap to her, and together we hoisted her up on our shoulders (once she had stopped, you know) and carried her around the field, singing "She Is the Champion" with more enthusiasm than tunefulness as she waved her trophy to the crowd.

As we put her down, her dad came over to see what was going on. "Oh, Nancy won, eh?" he said. "Congratulations!" He patted her on the back with a smile. Then he noticed the leftover slab of death gloating on a picnic table. His face lit up. "Ooh! Limburger cheese!" he said. "I haven't had that in years!" And he popped a chunk into his mouth and gobbled it down happily.

Survivors. Some people have the courage to face what scares them; some are just born without fear.

— Steven Stampone —

86

My Family Tree Has Split Ends

Some call it chaos; we call it family.
~Author Unknown

I am the mother of three children. Along with my husband, the five of us have formed a very unusual blended family! My step-daughter and I call us "The Twisted Brady Bunch." Here's how it began: When Adam, my best friend Patty's cousin, separated from his wife, I asked Patty if she would put in a good word for me. My marriage had also ended, and at forty-two I wasn't prepared to give up the hope of being married again. Fast forward two years.

The catalyst was a Memorial Day barbecue organized by Patty and Lea, a friend whose home included a pool and tennis court. On a hike in the redwoods, Adam and I found ourselves walking in lockstep. We talked about our kids. From his first marriage, he had a son my daughter's age and a daughter a few years older. We talked about plants and wildflowers. A tech executive who had worked for Steve Jobs, we bonded over the fact that one of my career highlights was working on an ad campaign for Apple. I had met and been mesmerized by Steve when he gave a presentation at our agency.

Adam was charming in a geeky sort of way. The more we talked, the more I realized that he was just my type: a true Renaissance man. His interests included literature, music, and art. As it turned out, he was also a passionate Francophile and was intrigued and delighted by the fact that my daughter, in an immersive program since she was four, spoke fluent French. He was impressed that I was a top achiever in my corporate sales job and that, not least of all, I was an accomplished home cook. The evidence was a tasty Asian salad of eggplant and noodles that I made especially for the barbecue. Adam was also a serious foodie.

Toward the end of the day, playing hearts with Patty and Lea, Adam surprised me. "Why don't you and Simone (my daughter) come to stay at Martha's Vineyard this summer?" He had already rented a large house for the month of August in Chilmark so that he could spend time with his family who lived in the Boston area. When we parted that evening, he kissed my head. "I hope I'll see you again soon!" Visions of blended-family bliss danced in my head on the drive home. His children were fourteen and eleven — his son only five months younger than my daughter. I couldn't imagine a better situation. Simone would have siblings, and Adam and I would have endless weekends of family fun.

The next week, on our first date, we hit it off over Thai food, talking endlessly about work, our kids, and food and wine. It became clear early on that we were a good match and wanted to be together. After a month, he announced that he wanted to marry me.

Scheduling was brutal. Our custody arrangements were opposite. I had my daughter Tuesday, Thursday, and every other weekend. His ex had his children all weekdays, and he had them every weekend. The first months, we strategized how best to re-organize his schedule so that we could spend time with the kids and time alone. His kids were bereft. They loved their weekends with their dad. It didn't help that their mother had started divorce proceedings, and things were very tense between the two exes.

The problems started to crop up like weeds in cracks. I lived almost an hour away in Berkeley; he and his kids were in Palo Alto. His son thought I was "trying too hard" when I offered to make him breakfast, and his daughter cried hysterically, begging him to leave me. It didn't help that, as soon as Adam got together with me, his ex decided to give it one more try. Although she had dumped him, she now tried to woo him back.

I had my own hurdle to get over. Adam knew that my ex was a woman. He knew that I had had my daughter in the context of a same-sex relationship. He was wonderfully accepting and inclusive. But we had to tell the children, and he had to tell his family. Fortunately, his mother was a feminist and had no trouble with my history. His children had grown up in the Bay Area where same-sex marriages are part of the fabric. The way things turned out was a surprise to both of us. It wasn't my past that was the problem for his children; it was having a stepmother!

The first sign that things were not going as smoothly as we had hoped was on Martha's Vineyard. His son came down with a migraine. According to Adam's report, Joshua couldn't abide having fun while his mother was home alone.

Maybe it was too soon to try to blend the families, we thought. But we couldn't go back. We made more bad decisions! When Adam and I decided — naively — that we would live together in San Francisco, life got very bad. We hoped that his kids would be with us a couple of days a week — with Adam driving them to school. But the traffic in the Bay Area had gotten so bad that the commute made everyone miserable.

Soon, his son refused to come to see us, proclaiming that it was clear that his father's priorities had changed. We had a very rough five years while the kids finished junior high and then high school.

Once the kids went to college and began independent lives, things improved markedly. I was no longer the evil stepmother or the enemy. I was their father's loyal and devoted wife and partner, the woman who brought him joy and comfort.

Fast forward ten years. A family gathering now looks like this: my ex and her partner and daughter, our three kids and their spouses, two grandchildren, and Adam and me. We are all around the table enjoying Adam's excellent cooking and fabulous wine. And when you ask Simone about her family now, she says: "My family tree has split ends."

—Joan Gelfand—

87

Feeling the Love from Twenty-One Cousins

Cousins are those rare people who ask how we are
and then wait to hear the answer.
~Ed Cunningham

O ur family has a long history of shenanigans. Over the years, there were feuds, grudges, rivalries, and recurring conflict. Despite this, there was always an undercurrent of love and loyalty among my parents' combined twelve siblings. I grew up wondering if that intense combination of devotion and discord was a part of the American immigrant experience.

My father was the first to arrive to the United States in the 1970s through a college scholarship. He sponsored many of his siblings for U.S. citizenship soon after. With so many aunts and uncles came a lot of offspring. I had twenty-one cousins, and many of us shared a distinctly ethnic last name.

Although we did not all live in the same state, we remained connected while growing up. We'd see each other during summer breaks, and at weddings, graduations, and other family events. My cousins and I looked alike, and that brought instant camaraderie at our gatherings.

When I began to think of a family of my own, I loved the idea of a big family and decided to have four children with my husband. As adults, my cousins doted on my children, and two of them agreed to become godparents. Having cousins was a blessing in my life.

One evening, several months after being diagnosed with a serious illness, I was taking a slow walk with my children around our neighborhood. They were at my side, ready to catch my arm in case I might collapse after a grueling ten-hour surgery earlier that week.

I was exhausted and anxious. However, these walks were encouraged by my doctor to support the healing process. Our small party eventually wandered by the community mailboxes. We rarely received snail mail, but I decided to check on a whim and was surprised to find a letter there addressed to me.

> *Dear Cousin,*
>
> *Cancer is at the very least a ridiculous inconvenience. Not great news, but not the end of the world either. Being positive is a good thing… but I personally found it annoying to hear that. Feel all of your feelings. You're entitled. When I was seven years old, my mother had a radical mastectomy and was given six months to live. She said, "Buzz off, cancer. I have children to raise." She lived for another fifteen years until we were settled, in college, and had steady beaus. Please send me your phone number. I'll be on call for you anytime, all the time. I know you must feel frightened. It's natural.*
>
> *We can have a good cry topped off with absolutely everything all at once and some laughter. This, too, shall pass. I love you. I will pray for you, real hard. I'm not religious. However, I have always known in my core that the universe has a power or powers that are greater than all of us.*
>
> *Sending the biggest hug, love, healing and no judgment. Do you need anything?*
>
> *And when Greyhound opens up a reliable route between us, perhaps I can sneak away for some good ol' cousin time, or I can take care of the littles so that you and hubby can have a night off. I'll teach them how to play dominoes, drink mojitos, smoke cigars, and fix a 1950s Chevy.*

This unexpected note from my much older cousin came as a bit of a shock that evening. I had not heard from her in several years and wasn't certain until that point whether she was aware that I was sick. Her words made me laugh out loud and provided new insight into our family's medical history.

Inside the envelope she had also included a check with a generous donation that she had collected from all twenty-one of our cousins. A Post-it Note was attached to the check.

From a distance there is only so much we can do, but we wanted to come together and show you how much you mean to us, even though it might not have always been obvious, spoken, or shown. We love you and are sending loving energy your way, every day. Love, your cousins

As I absorbed these messages, my four children witnessed their speechless mother, overwhelmed with tears and gratitude, and watched as I was lifted up in that moment by my family.

We were all scattered across the country. Until that point, my health journey had been relatively private. It was my cousin's words, inked in blue pen on a piece of yellow lined paper from a legal pad, that offered instant reassurance. Holding the letter, I felt my family willing me to get better, carry on, and get to the other side of my illness. During a crisis, the power of our cousin bond was undeniable to me. Now, I could truly begin healing.

— Sky Khan —

88

Mom the Magic Dragon

We're all a little weird... And when we find someone
whose weirdness is compatible with ours, we join
up with them and fall into mutually satisfying
weirdness — and call it love.
~Robert Fulghum

Once I'd married her dad, Kaitlin, age eight, asked what she should call me since I had officially become her mom. I sat down with her and her older brothers, Justin (sixteen) and Logan (thirteen), and told them they could call me whatever they felt comfortable with — Mom, Victoria, or V. All had been addressing me as Victoria for the past two years, so that felt pretty normal, but it didn't take into account the life-altering commitment we'd just made to one another.

I wanted my title to reflect my relationship to them in front of others. Kaitlin excitedly started chanting, "Mom, Mom, Mom." However, Justin and Logan felt that if they addressed me as Mom, they would be disrespecting their real mother, who had passed away. My new husband just wanted everyone to love each other and didn't care about labels. So, it was decided. I would be Mom to Kaitlin and Victoria to the boys.

The following day, Kaitlin reversed her decision and said that it would be best if she called me Victoria, like her brothers do. "Most people have moms, but not everyone has a Victoria."

My chest tightened just a bit. "Ah, I see. Well, okay. If that's what you want to do." I could hear the higher-than-usual pitch of my own voice.

Kaitlin, always the empath—even at eight and despite her autism—took my hand and kissed it. "Don't be sad; I love you just like you're my real mom."

"Oh, yeah, I know. And you know how much I love you." She then skipped off to her room. I suspected her brothers had had a conversation with her after our initial discussion.

Later, I called the boys to the kitchen table and had a little pow-wow of my own. I asked if they had persuaded Kaitlin to call me by my first name.

With head bent, Logan tipped his chair back, refusing to make eye contact. His silence confirmed my suspicion.

Justin took a different approach. He grabbed last night's leftover chopsticks and began drumming a tune by The White Stripes on our dining table. "Yeah, maybe. What's the big deal? That is your name, isn't it?" Always the jokester, he asked if I would prefer, "Big Shrek Mommy? Or Puff the Magic Dragon?"

"No, I just wanted her to be able to make the choice that felt right for her, without any familial pressure." I didn't want her to feel bad about accepting me as a mom—title and all.

I pointed out that they both had memories of their mother. "You guys remember her voice and her laugh, and the way she made you pose for endless pictures."

I made a sweeping gesture with my outstretched arm around the room. "Do you know how many scrapbooks, with your smiling faces, we have in this house? No? Any guesses?"

Both shrugged.

"We have seventy-eight scrapbooks, not including the ones in the attic. They are filled with mostly your photos, and I bet you can conjure up memories for most of them. You remember her as your Cub Scout leader. You know her love of kites, s'mores, and German folk songs.

"Kaitlin has none of that. She was too young when your mother passed away. She has no mental file from which she can pull a memory of her mom. If you two believe that she really wants to call me Victoria, then I'll let the issue pass. But if you think she'd like me to be Mom to her, I ask you to give her that gift."

The next thing I knew, Kaitlin had decided that she should call me Mom, and her brothers were okay with it. I smiled. I realized that these two beautiful boys, who were newly mine, were mature beyond their years, and their love for their sister outweighed their fear of disloyalty to their mother.

Seven years into the marriage, my sons still do not address me as Mom, but they do refer to me as Mom when they're with their friends. I'll take it.

I remember one time when Justin introduced me to one of his friends as his mother-in-law. I laughed and explained that unless he was married to my daughter, I couldn't be his mother-in-law. He said, "Yes, you can. You married my dad, which means you became my mother in the eyes of the law." His friend laughed and said, "Dude, I don't think it works like that."

"Technically, I am your stepmother, although I dislike that term." When Martin and I merged our families, I didn't want to use the term "step" as in stepmom or stepsister. To me, it felt like the title implied an outsider trying to get in. It's like you're a step away from the inner circle. We are a blended family with two girls (I brought my young-adult daughter, Ari, to the marriage) and two boys. They are each other's siblings regardless of genetics. I love them all.

Justin said he was still going to say that I was his mother-in-law because that just made more sense. I remember laughing, shaking my head. "You know, you can always call me Big Shrek Mommy or Mom the Magic Dragon."

His friend laughed again, "You know that's probably what he's going to call you from now on."

I nodded as they left to go play video games. Barely out of the room, Justin called over his shoulder, "I love ya, Shreky."

"I love you too, Justin."

— Victoria Lorrekovich-Miller —

89

The Box

The happiest moments of my life have been
the few which I have passed at home
in the bosom of my family.
~Thomas Jefferson

Every Christmas, we get "The Box" from my uncle, who owns a local sporting-goods store. He supplies uniforms to the sports teams and does T-shirt printing for parties. Every Christmas, instead of presents, he sends us the rejects from his shop.

One year, we got knit caps that sported a company's misspelled name. It was "Lovie's Mower Service" instead of "Louie's Mower Service."

Another year, we got a birthday-party T-shirt for a woman's ninety-sixth birthday when it was supposed to be her ninety-seventh birthday. And another time we all got green football socks that weren't exactly the right color for the football team that had ordered them.

You never know what you're going to get out of The Box, so we play a game with it on Christmas Eve. My father takes out one item at a time, and each of us has the chance to take it or not. It goes around the whole circle, and if someone wants it, they take it. If no one wants it, it goes in the pile to charity.

We have had a million laughs over the years, with family-reunion shirts, baseball pants, and different minor-league baseball teams' attire with colorful names. The Box never disappoints.

I'm not sure what we will do if my uncle runs out of things to send us! It's a beloved, if a bit wacky, Christmas tradition.

— Darcy Daniels —

90

Worst Gift Wins

What soap is to the body, laughter is to the soul.
~Yiddish proverb

y ninety-three-year-old stepmother is fabulous, but she is a terrible gift-giver. It became obvious after my dad passed away that he was the gift buyer of the family, always finding just the right thing for each of us. We all love her, so we never complain. In fact, we've made it a competition. We actually hope to get the worst gift because that means we win.

We used to open our gifts from her with a little fear and trepidation. But since it's become a competition, there is also now a little hope that the gift is really awful, just not too embarrassing.

One Christmas, my sports-obsessed boys got fairy dolls. My fifty-something sister got a CD of *High School Musical 2* when she requested a U2 CD. My husband was the proud recipient of old-man jeans, the ones in the bright blue denim with the crease down the front of the legs.

One year, my brother-in-law was the frontrunner to win the worst gift award. He was given a lovely sport coat. For a moment, we all thought someone else gave it to him. But then my stepmother explained the gift. She bought it at her church's rummage sale, so it was a used sport coat. All right, that's not so bad. But then she said it had belonged to a man from her church who had died, and his wife had sent it to the rummage sale. It doesn't end there. She said that my brother-in-law looked really good in it. In fact, better than the last time she saw it on the man from church because he was wearing it in the casket. At least, there was a dry-cleaning ticket in the pocket.

Well, we thought my poor brother-in-law would be the all-time winner of the worst gift, never to be topped. But then it was my turn.

I opened my gift and came face-to-face with a strange-looking, little doll. It was a weird gift for an adult who doesn't collect dolls, but I was sure there was a story behind it. Oh, there was. My stepmother got all excited as I lifted this rather ugly doll from the box and showed my family. She said, "I bought you that doll because it looks just like you. As soon as I saw it, I thought, 'My Lord, that's Lisa!'" My children were unsuccessfully stifling snickers. My husband, sister, and brother-in-law leaned in to get a better look and not miss a word of what would come next. She continued, "It has curly brown hair." Okay, but in my mind the resemblance ended there. She went on, "And one eye is smaller than the other, and she has an overbite and a double chin. And if you notice, her arms are disproportionately short for her body." My sister, brother-in-law, and husband were barely holding it together, and my kids were knee-slapping laughing out loud.

"And you think it looks like me?" Maybe I had misunderstood what she said.

"Yes, just like you. That's why I bought her. The likeness is uncanny," she said proudly. And there it was — my forever win of the worst gift ever.

— Lisa J. Radcliff —

91

Cooking Lessons

Most turkeys taste better the day after;
my mother's tasted better the day before.
~Rita Rudner

'm going to pick up the kids from their mom's house," my brand-new husband, Mike, said as he grabbed his keys. We'd just gotten back from a glorious, romantic honeymoon the day before, and now real life as a blended family was starting. Mike and I had each brought two children into the marriage; they ranged in age from five to twelve. I had full custody of my children, and Mike split custody evenly with his ex-wife. In the year we'd dated, the kids had always gotten along well, and I had high hopes that our blending process would go smoothly.

When Mike returned home with the kids, his twelve-year-old son, Jason, put a plastic container in the fridge.

"What's that, Bud?" I asked him.

"Oh, my mom made her famous meatloaf while we were with her, and she knows how much Dad likes it, so she sent some back for him."

"Your mom's meatloaf is famous?"

Jason nodded. "Yeah. It's one of the best things she makes. Whenever company comes for dinner, that's what she fixes. Plus, it's Dad's favorite."

I tried to keep a neutral expression on my face. "That was nice of her."

"Yeah, my mom is super nice. You'll like her a lot."

"I'm sure I will, honey."

The minute Jason left the kitchen, I turned to Mike and said, "You're not eating that meatloaf."

His mouth dropped open. "Why not?"

"Your ex-wife made you your favorite meal—on the day after you got back from your honeymoon with your new wife. Don't you think that's a little strange?"

He shrugged. "Not really. I mean, she didn't make the meatloaf specifically for me. She made it for the kids. She just saved some for me."

"Well, I don't like it. I feel like she's trying to compete with me for your attention."

"Babe, she and I have been divorced for three years. I don't think she's trying to woo me back with meatloaf. She sent the meatloaf home with Jason instead of throwing it out. There's nothing more to this than not wanting to waste food."

I sighed. "I guess you're right. I'm being silly."

"It's cute that you're jealous, but you have no reason to be."

I hugged him and tried to put the leftover meatloaf out of my mind.

But a week later, Jason brought another plastic container back from his mom's house. "She made her famous turkey tetrazzini," he said. "She saved some for Dad."

I smiled, hoping Jason couldn't tell it was fake. "That was nice of her. It's wonderful that your mom is such a great cook."

"She's a terrific cook. It's one of my dad's favorite things about her."

I cringed, noticing his use of the present tense. *He's only twelve years old,* I reminded myself. *He doesn't mean anything by it.*

Days later, Jason brought yet another plastic container from his mom's. "It's her famous stuffed chicken breasts," he said.

"Those are famous, too?"

Jason nodded. "They're delicious. My dad thinks so, too."

That night after the kids went to bed, I told Mike that the little food deliveries were really making me uncomfortable. "She literally sent her famous breasts for you to enjoy."

Mike rolled his eyes. "Chicken breasts, honey. Chicken."

"I don't care. I don't like that she's doing this."

"Babe, I promise you that she doesn't want me back. If we say anything about it, it will send the wrong message to the kids. We don't want to make waves this early in the blending process."

My shoulders slumped. "I don't want the kids to think I'm not going to get along with their mom. I just don't like her sending you food to remind you of 'the good old days' when you were married to her."

"Honey, we got divorced for a reason. My good days are with you now. No matter how much food she sends back with the kids, I'm happy to be with you."

Was I being silly? Was I making too much of this? I decided that, for the good of the kids, I would just ignore it.

And I tried. I really did. But when Jason walked in with a plastic container filled with her famous whatever and a Post-it note on top with reheating instructions — and the words, "Love you, Sweetie" — I demanded that Mike put a stop to it.

He called his ex-wife and explained that she needed to stop sending food home with Jason. "I think it's inappropriate," he said.

"It's inappropriate that I'm feeding our son?" she asked.

"The food is for Jason?"

She laughed. "Of course. Who else would it be for?"

"Well, we thought… never mind." He hung up and looked at me triumphantly. "See, I told you there was nothing to worry about."

He was pretty surprised when I burst into tears.

"Do you know what this means?" I said between sobs. "It means Jason has been lying about his mom making the food for you. He's trying to get you guys back together. This is terrible. We're never going to blend like a real family."

Mike rubbed my back. "He'll get used to everything. It'll be okay."

The following week, Jason brought home a container of his mom's famous tuna-noodle casserole. "It's amazing," he told me. "Another of Dad's favorites."

Mike walked into the room. "I hate tuna, and your mom knows that. She didn't send that for me." He looked Jason right in the eye. "She didn't send the meatloaf or the other food for me either."

Jason's face fell. "How did you find out?"

"Your mom and I still talk to each other. Why did you tell us something that wasn't true?"

He shrugged. "I don't know."

"Bud, I know this is a hard transition for you, but your mom and I aren't going to get back together. I'm married to Wendy now, and she and her kids are part of our family."

"I know that. I like Wendy, and I like having two more siblings."

"Then why did you lie?"

He sighed. "I didn't know if Wendy was a good cook or not. I thought if she knew that my mom is an awesome cook, she might try a little harder to make stuff I like."

Mike and I exchanged a look, and I could tell he was trying not to laugh. "That was really sneaky, and you owe Wendy an apology," he said.

"I'm sorry I lied," Jason said. "I'm sure I'll like whatever dinners you make."

I patted his shoulder. "I forgive you, and I've got news for you. In this house, dinner will be a team effort. I even have matching aprons for everyone."

Mike grinned. "They're pink."

As Jason ran from the kitchen — and the fictional pink aprons — Mike and I high-fived. We'd survived our first blended-family drama.

Now, we had to survive teaching four kids how to cook.

— Wendy Jones —

92

The Gift of a Towel

The highlight of my childhood was making my brother
laugh so hard that food came out his nose.
~Author Unknown

My heart was heavy the night of December twenty-third as I readied my home for our family's annual Christmas Eve luncheon. I'd just learned that my ninety-three-year-old former mother-in-law had taken a hard fall and been rushed to the hospital. As a result, she and her younger son would be unable to attend our party. I'd also just learned that our two grandchildren were spending Christmas Eve with their mother instead of our son. With our oldest and youngest family members missing, how would the party ever seem as festive as usual?

As I busied myself with myriad holiday preparations, my eldest son, Henry, bounded into the room.

"Hey, Mom," he called brightly, "do you have a shirt box? A really big one?"

"I've got some in the cellar," I replied absently. "I'm not sure how big they are."

"I need it for Josh's gift. For a towel," he added happily as he raced downstairs.

Preoccupied, I didn't ask the question that immediately sprang to my mind: "You're giving your brother a towel?"

I'd been privy to the gift exchanges between my three now thirty-something sons for decades, so I was well-versed in their standard choices: video games, DVDs, Magic cards, hiking gear, wine or beer. But towels? Never! Consumed by my own thoughts, however, I didn't pursue the matter and promptly forgot all about it.

At noon the next day, a spirited group of nine people, ages thirty-two through eighty-six, gathered for food, games, and a gift exchange. We traditionally open gifts round-robin-style, so all eyes zero in on the person unwrapping at any given moment.

When the gift-giving began, Henry called out excitedly, "Josh, you've got to open my present first!"

As eighteen adult eyeballs awaited the big reveal, Josh opened a large shirt box and pulled out a neatly folded white towel — or, rather, a mostly white towel peppered with a bunch of curious black lines.

As eight puzzled adults and one beaming brother intently studied the gift, Josh stood up and released the towel to its full length. The air filled with startled gasps and then surprised silence as jaws dropped and eyebrows hiked skyward. For a split second, Josh looked as bewildered as the rest of us. Then, abruptly, he burst out laughing and shot his brother an appreciative thumbs-up!

Instantly, the silence shattered as giggling guests scrambled madly for their cell phones to document the unique gift. For there before us — boldly sketched with a wide-tipped black marker on a king-sized white towel — was a frontal outline of a naked man, artistically rendered save for a few comical distortions: biceps bigger than Popeye's, stubby legs and painfully flat feet (clearly, Henry had run out of space), and a few other hilariously drawn features.

Obviously enjoying the gift's significance, Henry and Josh chuckled merrily, oblivious to everyone else's confusion. But when my thirty-something niece quipped loudly, "Gee, Aunt Wendy, are your Christmases always like this?" Henry suddenly saw the gift as the rest of us were seeing it. In a flash, exhilaration turned to dismay.

"Oh, no — wait!" he cried, mortified. "You don't understand!"

Desperate to put his gift in its proper context, Henry explained that he and Josh had recently been discussing their personal pet peeves. Apparently, Josh — a self-professed germaphobe — had good-naturedly mentioned his chief showering complaint.

"Josh told me," Henry began, "that when he uses the same bath towel two days in a row to be ecological, he never really knows on Day 2 which part of the towel was used on which part of the body on Day 1. As a result, he worries that he'll end up drying his face with a section of the towel that was used on a more… uh… unsavory part of the body the day before."

By this time, poor Henry practically had to shout to be heard above the roar of laughter. But as his tale unfolded, my heart swelled with pride and affection as I pictured these two young men kicking back with a brew, discussing life's petty annoyances. In truth, there's nothing I love more than watching my boys interact with one another. Despite the increasing complexity of their lives, with each passing year their capacity for lighthearted joking with one another only grows greater, their bonds ever stronger.

After bringing everyone up to speed, Henry ended triumphantly, "So, you see, guys, my gift solves Josh's problem perfectly! As long as he dries each part of his body with the corresponding section of the towel, he'll never have to worry about that again."

As the room buzzed with conversation and good-natured razzing, I grabbed my camera and captured the merriment on each guest's face as a priceless gift between two brothers became a precious gift of fun and fellowship for our entire family.

In the years since, whenever I scroll through those Christmas Eve photos, I relive the wonder of what turned out to be our most playful, relaxed holiday ever. Despite my initial sadness, my spirits soared when a creative and quirky gift reminded me that, despite life's endless curveballs, love and laughter will always brighten a room and bring about amazing new memories. In fact, I wouldn't be surprised if one day — at some future festive family gathering — someone pipes up with, "Hey, remember the Christmas towel?"

And, just like that, another room will explode with laughter.

— Wendy Hobday Haugh —

93

My Wife's Ex-Husband

Friendship... is born at the moment when one man
says to another "What! You, too?"
~C.S. Lewis

The two most influential men in my life were my dad, who taught me how to be a father, and my wife's ex-husband Joe, who taught me how to be a parent.

Joe and Suzi met in high school, got married and had two kids, but their marriage ended after twenty years. The demise of the marriage did not change their roles as parents. They would do their all, put aside their marital differences and cooperatively parent their two daughters, even if Suzi had another man come into her life.

I met Suzi long after the marriage to Joe ended. I was neither the reason nor the cause of their divorce. So, when Suzi and I announced our marriage, Joe was one of the first to congratulate us. He was an integral part of our married lives and our role as parents. And, along the way, he and I were blessed with a friendship that would last a lifetime.

It wasn't an easy transition for either of us. Suzi and I lived in Suzi and Joe's matrimonial home, so Joe never thought he wasn't part of the residency. Whenever Joe came to town, I would mow the lawn to make the place look good. Joe would drive in and mow the lawn again, and then trim the edges. If I cut back a hedge, Joe would prune a tree and transport the branches to the dump.

This territorial dispute went on for several months before I approached Joe about it. He said he was doing the yard work knowing that Suzi and I were working long hours, so that we would have more time for their daughters. I was not prepared to be humbled and would never question his motives again.

When there was a problem at the school, the principal telephoned Joe, telling him that he "needed to come and collect his daughter." Joe unleashed a tirade, pointing out that he lived seven hundred miles away, and that if the school hadn't telephoned me, who lived two blocks away, they should be ready for a fight. Then he drove through the night, and the three of us marched into school the next morning, a unified force.

The schools weren't the only institutions that struggled to understand the family dynamic. Joe had already moved back to California when one of the daughters was hit by a car. Joe was the first person I called, and we coordinated the response. Joe would be waiting for the ambulance at the hospital while I would collect Suzi and then make our way there. At the hospital, Suzi and I became separated as I circled to look for a parking spot, so I made my way directly to the daughter's hospital room. Suzi was denied access to see her injured daughter because "both the parents" were already in the room.

As the girls grew up, our relationship became more of brother/husbands. We socialized together, went metal detecting on the beach, and attended college football games. I introduced him as "my wife's ex-husband," and he introduced me as "his ex-wife's husband," as if everyone had the same family structure. At Thanksgivings, I hired a hall to seat all the extended family members around the table — my father, Suzi and her mom, Joe and his parents. The girls got to spend the holiday with multiple grandparents that way.

Joe and I went out for lunch one day. Joe always picked Mexican because he liked spicy food. "Burn on the way down, and burn on the way up," was his benchmark for tasty food. But on that day, he turned pale, burped after an especially spicy burrito, and then pushed away his plate.

"Joe, are you all right? I've never seen you leave any food behind."

Something was wrong, but Joe delayed going to see a doctor. Suzi took the initiative, made the appointment, and drove Joe to the doctor. She sat in on the consultation, and when Joe didn't comprehend the issue, advocated on his behalf.

The initial tests took a while to complete, and when the results came back, Joe shared them with us. Esophageal cancer. All the years of acid reflux had taken their toll and eroded the inside of his throat. Joe was going to need both radiation and chemotherapy.

I drove Joe to the chemotherapy appointments and went in with him, not only to support him but to shield him and protect his integrity. As the treatment continued, Joe withered, and eventually he was confined to a wheelchair or was carried by me. Suzi and I were there when Joe received the final prognosis.

"There's nothing more that can be done for you."

Suzi and I drove Joe home and sat with him as he delivered the news to his mom.

Joe deteriorated rapidly, but not once did I ever hear him complain. When the end was near, I would see it through, and I was with Joe when he took his last breath.

In the beginning, I never understood why Joe and I had such good rapport. He could easily have made the marriage difficult, but he chose to be the better man. He shared with me the joys and tribulations of the daughters, and I never considered that Joe had any ulterior motives. Joe only ever wanted to be a "girl dad," even if he was divorced and sharing it with another man. He taught me more about parenting, and I was blessed with a friendship that would last the lifetime of my wife's ex-husband.

— Grant Madden —

Kids Will Be Kids

94

The Truck Shirt

Early morning cheerfulness
can be extremely obnoxious.
~William Feather

On my son's third birthday, he received the Truck Shirt. Austin bounded out of his friend's house that day yelling, "Look, Mama! Look, Mama! LOOK! A Truck Shirt!" He wore a sky-blue T-shirt with row after row of trucks right there across his tummy. What more could a little boy want? He rambled on so excitedly about the Truck Shirt all the way home that his eighteen-month-old sister, Faith, looked down at her own plump belly as if to ask, "And where is my Truck Shirt?"

Just a week prior, my son had determined he didn't want to get dressed in the mornings. He figured out that if he didn't get dressed, I couldn't take him to preschool and then go on to my office. Mornings became stressful. As I struggled with Faith's own defiance about wearing clothes, Austin sat naked on his bed, refusing to get dressed. I begged, bribed and reasoned with Austin as Faith scurried about diapered, hiding the car keys and eating everyone else's breakfast. I had always been a prompt employee, but now I was arriving late to the office. I couldn't sleep at night thinking about the morning's pending showdown and my boss's growing displeasure.

Enter the Truck Shirt.

Austin wore the Truck Shirt as often as our laundry habits permitted, about twice a week. On the nights prior to a Truck Shirt day, I set his little shoes, socks, underwear, shorts and the Truck Shirt on top of his short dresser.

From the darkness of his bed, I heard him say excitedly, "Is that my Truck Shirt?"

I danced the shirt in front of him.

"Yay! It is my Truck Shirt! It is!"

The next morning, Austin stood in his doorway, fully dressed and proudly modeling the Truck Shirt. I arrived at work on time. My boss was happy. I was happy.

In order to keep the Truck Shirt clean and available, we increased the laundering to three times a week. Those launderings meant three seamless mornings that I relished. However, all the laundering was wearing the Truck Shirt's material thin. Plus, there were still those other two mornings that remained a challenge.

So, I put the word out: If you see the Truck Shirt, buy it in gross. Friends and acquaintances were told to be on the lookout.

A month of constant laundering went by without a single Truck Shirt sighting. Just when we were about to give up, a friend called to report that she had seen the Truck Shirt at a store in the mall.

I raced to the store, two-stepped up the escalator and landed in the middle of boys' T-shirts. Truck Shirt? Truck Shirt? Truck Shirt? There was no familiar blue. Not to be dissuaded, I snatched up a green shirt with a bulldozer, a gray shirt with a fire truck and a white shirt with a bus. "These are Truck Shirts," I tried to convince myself as I headed toward the cash register.

But there, right there! On a wobbly corner rack, there they were! The original Truck Shirts! I hugged them with glee. A maniacal laugh escaped my lips. Had a child approached me and asked for one, I might have growled. I had my Truck Shirts.

The next night, I felt a rush as I folded the two freshly laundered Truck Shirts. I almost giggled as I tucked them into the dresser. On top of the dresser was a Truck Shirt, ready for Austin to slip into the next morning.

I pulled out a pair of shorts to set next to it and heard from the darkness, "Those shorts don't match my Truck Shirt."

I pulled out a second pair of shorts that better matched the Truck Shirt.

"Not those either," I heard, followed by the padding of little feet behind me. Austin's small hand opened the hamper and pulled out the shorts he had worn that day. "These are the only shorts that match my Truck Shirt, Mama."

I didn't sleep well that night.

— MJ Lemire —

95

Underfoot

My therapist told me the way to achieve true inner
peace is to finish what I start. So far today,
I have finished two bags of M&M's and
a chocolate cake. I feel better already.
~Dave Barry

'm not sure if being the youngest of three siblings means you're the least sensible, but the entire family, including my parents, referred to me as the "crazy kid." When family or friends stopped by to visit, my dad started the conversation by saying, "Do you know what our crazy kid did?"

Dad had plenty of comic material to work with, but he only knew the half of it. Our home was ruled with an iron fist, but I was a kid-size conscientious objector. If they had used the catching-more-flies-with-honey approach, I might have toed the line.

Most of my battles were around bath time and meals. Once, I invented a way to skip baths altogether. I'd fill the tub with more bubble bath than water, and then splish-splash my dolls in the sea foam for sound effects. Afterward, I received a surprise inspection. My mother asked, "How come you're only clean from your hands to your elbows?" Not given a chance to explain the faulty soap, she sent me back to the tub — not once but twice for good measure.

I soon discovered that "Go wash up" was code for "Get out of my hair." A few nights a week, neighbors came by to visit while the kids played ball until dark. I was too young to mingle with the adults, and the older kids complained I was always "underfoot," which I took to mean I was one foot too short. One particular evening, I sat sulking amongst the adults when my mother suddenly commented about the dirt behind my ears. "Go wash up," she said.

It always amazed me how well she could spot dirt from three yards away while facing the opposite direction, but she did. After a thorough cleaning, she pulled and tugged at my ears. "You missed a spot. Go wash 'em again."

By the third scrubbing, my ears turned as red as a radish, and I sounded off, "Aren't you worried they'll rub clean off?" But she'd send me away as many times as she liked if it kept me from eavesdropping on their gossip.

Parents, including mine, didn't think we were as clever as they were. I may not have always won at their games, but I sure gave them a run for their money. I might have appeared silly to them, but I was extremely cunning.

Every evening, Mom made a meal of three basics: meat, vegetables, and mashed potatoes. After dinner, we'd have ice cream for dessert. I wasn't especially fond of peas so during one meal I slipped the bowl past me without putting the required heaping spoonful onto my plate. When the bowl came around again, Dad remarked, "Seems Cindy missed out on the peas. Now, she can finish the bowl."

Like many nights, I sat alone at the table long after everyone excused themselves. I stared down those forty-three peas swimming in green juice, trying to make them disappear with telekinesis. When that didn't work, I began to fiddle around, looking for an open crevice under our 1950s Formica kitchen table with its tubular-steel, chrome-plated legs. Bingo!

Who knew those table legs were hollow, open-ended like a funnel, and conveniently sealed at the base with a steel button? With just enough wiggle room for my seven-year-old fingers, I dropped each squishy pea down that hole without a sound. I managed to eat the last pea in case anyone wondered if I finished the bowl.

"Yes, I did," I'd reply truthfully, and then look for my reward. "Can I have dessert now?"

Just imagine all the things you can stuff into a table leg: lima beans, hominy, rhubarb, and liver cut into small pieces. Some items weren't feasible to shove down my new trash receptacle, like spinach, cottage cheese, or Mom's Depression Stew made up of bread pieces, her canned tomatoes, and sugar. I forced myself to eat those foods while holding my nose. But one time, I refused to eat her slippery creamed asparagus.

"You're not leaving this table until you eat your asparagus," Dad said, and then doubled down with a threat. "No dessert until you do."

An entire hour passed before that asparagus even tried to move. My sister was at the sink washing up dishes when she turned to pester, "You'd better hurry and eat that before I get done."

Another fifteen minutes went by before Dad called out from the living room, "Have you cleaned your plate yet, or do you plan on sitting there all night?"

I hadn't considered sleeping there but figured his first option sounded best. I scraped that snotty-looking asparagus right off my plate and packed it inconspicuously under the plate's rim. When it was pretty well cleared off, I yelled, "My plate's clean."

My sister lifted my plate off the table, and it made a suction noise. "Daaaaad," she bellowed, "look at what she's done!"

I stealthily edged my way for the exit as my dad entered the kitchen to see what all the fuss was about. I loved how parents always asked dumb questions when they obviously knew the answer. "Now, what do you call this?" he asked, pointing to a perfect, wreath-shaped asparagus ring.

"I cleaned my plate just like you asked."

"You think you're funny?" he cracked. "Here's a fork. Now start cleaning that up until it's gone."

I certainly didn't want to, but he left me no choice. Dejected and alone, I began clearing the plate as best I knew how. "One forkful for me, twelve for the table leg."

My bristly upbringing didn't hurt me any; instead, it gave me the means to be more resilient and adventurous. I've passed many of those rules down to my children, like finishing your plate before dessert. As luck would have it, they no longer make kitchen tables with open steel legs.

I'll never forget my dad's face when they replaced our 1950s dinette with a newer model. As a kid about to be found out, I stood nervously watching them jostle that chrome table upside-down and all around to haul it away. Petrified peas, dried meats, and fossilized asparagus began falling from the leg, making the same kerplunking noise a baby rattle makes when it's shaken.

At the next family gathering and each one after, my dad started every conversation by saying, "Guess what our crazy kid did now!"

— Cindy Horgash —

96

Greetings

*A lifetime is not too long to spend
in learning about the world.*
~Caroline Pratt, I Learn from Children

When my three oldest children were six, four, and almost twenty months, we took a trip that required a layover at the Atlanta airport. My four-year-old son, J.P., had been excited about the trip for weeks. He loved planes, space-ships, rockets, and anything to do with flying and outer space. When we boarded the plane in our hometown, J.P. had been jumping up and down with excitement. By the time we landed in Atlanta, his excitement had progressed to a full-blown state of exhilaration and delight. Eyes wide and head rotating in all directions, he stared at the gigantic jets taking off and landing, the swarms of people arriving and departing, and the beeping people-mover vehicles that darted back and forth. He was overwhelmed but totally thrilled.

Unfortunately, J.P.'s joyful state was counterbalanced by the aggrieved state of my twenty-month-old toddler, who desperately needed a diaper change. I should have changed his diaper on the plane, but there was so little room to maneuver in the plane's bathroom that I decided to wait until we landed. Now, this diaper was reaching critical mass, and catastrophe was imminent. I looked around for a bathroom but couldn't see any indication of one nearby. I noticed, however, a small table in a corner behind some cleaning carts, out of the way of the moving crowds of people, and I headed toward it. It was difficult to interest

J.P. in this diaper activity, but eventually, with a hand on his shoulder, I was able to maneuver him and his six-year-old sister through the traffic to the table. Once there, I asked my daughter to stand in front of the table to block the view, and I set about changing the soiled diaper.

Suddenly, I realized the noise level in the airport had decreased. Looking up, I saw that the crowds of moving people had slowed. Some groups had even stepped to the side and halted altogether. They were looking behind them, and I realized someone or something was coming down the corridor.

Then, I saw them.

It was a dignified procession of extremely tall, dark-skinned travelers. They were the tallest individuals I had ever seen. Their group was led by its tallest member, a distinguished-looking man who wore a long, intricately designed, yellow-and-white, beaded necklace around his neck. He was followed by eight beautiful women, who almost equaled him in height, but they walked in two rows of four behind him. These women were also adorned with colorful beads, but theirs were in more of a bodice style that featured beads draping over their shoulders. Their whole party wore long, floor-length, brightly colored robes. As they walked, their robes billowed out behind them, making it look as if they were floating down the corridor. The height alone of these individuals would have drawn attention, but with their colorful robes and beads, they made a striking and majestic appearance.

Seeing this amazing group, J.P. immediately darted away from the table in their direction. He ran out into the center of the corridor and stopped directly in front of this distinguished party.

Halting abruptly, the man and the women behind him looked down at J.P.

Much to my chagrin, I heard J.P. begin to speak.

"What… planet… are you… from?" he asked in a loud, clear voice, enunciating every word distinctly and carefully.

Several of the people who had stopped to watch chuckled. A few laughed outright.

Shocked and embarrassed, I felt like I was having one of those out-of-body experiences. I remember being torn between hiding under the table or simply walking away. Dumbfounded, I just stood there and didn't move.

Much to my surprise, the tall man smiled broadly and responded in an equally loud and clear voice.

"We are the Jieng or Dinka people… of Sudan." Then, looking directly at J.P., he added, "The Sudan planet."

"The Sudan planet," J.P. repeated, nodding in affirmation. "You must have a universal translator. Where is it?"

Without skipping a beat, the man pointed to his beautiful beaded necklace.

Staring at the necklace, J.P. continued, "It works well. I can understand you perfectly."

There was a small pause, and then J.P. lifted both his arms, stretched them out to the sides, bowed, and said in a loud, clear voice, "Welcome to our planet."

Laughing, the gentleman lifted his arms in the same manner, bowed, and said, "Thank you!"

By this time, I had completed the diaper change, albeit in a somewhat haphazard fashion. Quickly gathering up my youngest in my arms, grabbing our bags and my daughter's hand, I weaved our way through the people to stand behind J.P.

"I am so sorry," I began. "He just… J.P. just… loves space. He's never been in a big airport like this, and I think he just assumed…"

At this point, my newly diapered toddler started to cry out and squirm in my arms. Letting go of my daughter's hand, I tried to grab J.P.'s shoulder to move him out of the center of the corridor so we could get out of everyone's way and allow the group to move on. As I reached for him, J.P. ran off toward another group of arriving passengers. I knew I had to race after him before the incident was repeated, and as I backed away, I mumbled again to the tall gentleman, "I really am very, very sorry."

"Don't be," the man answered with another laugh. "I don't know when we've had such a genuine, warm, and friendly welcome."

Bowing again, he and his party continued down the concourse. Totally unsettled, extremely self-conscious, and completely embarrassed, I managed to reach J.P. just as he was eyeing a group of women wearing leis around their necks and flowers in their hair. Grabbing him by the hand, I pulled him away from these arriving passengers toward a group of seats where we could talk.

I did my best to explain to J.P. that only human beings used the Hartsfield-Jackson Atlanta International Airport. When he finally realized that the airport did not accommodate interplanetary travelers, J.P.'s face darkened in disappointment, but I think he had learned a lesson. I know I learned mine.

After this trip, I never stopped to change a diaper anywhere unless I absolutely had everyone corralled and confined in a secluded bathroom!

— Billie Holladay Skelley —

97

Out of the Mouths of Babes

I brought children into this dark world because it
needed the light that only a child can bring.
~Liz Armbruster

If there is one thing I am thankful I did as a parent, it was keeping all the beautiful, hand-scrawled notes and artwork that my three kids produced as younglings. Before you know it, they are adults, and you either forget about their accomplishments or mix up who did what.

Admittedly, I did recently cull the collection significantly because I was moving, but my kids still have one box of treasures each that I just can't part with.

The most cherished item is a notebook of all the funny things my kids said when they were small. I should have started it way sooner than I did because a lot is long forgotten and forever lost.

Although I would be risking my life — and their "faces" — if I shared all the pearls of wisdom, here are a few gems to make you laugh and inspire you to start your own The Darndest Things My Kids Say Journal.

We were in Québec City at a nice restaurant eating breakfast when my matter-of-fact son declared in a very loud voice: "Did ya see the big zit on his face?"

Unfortunately, the waiter in question was still in earshot. It was a crawl-under-the-table moment.

The same child was struggling to get his winter gloves on one particular day.

"Mummy, my gloves are in a funny mood today."

SOOOO cute!

My hubby — at the time — was teaching my older son how to play poker and asked him if he knew the suits.

"Hearts, diamonds, shovels and cauliflowers."

To boot, he was asked, "They are the four what?"

"Jackets!"

It's so hard to keep it together when they are being so serious! And in his defense, spades are like shovels, and a cauliflower kinda looks like a club. And a suit has a jacket, right?

My hubby had taken the boys out for the afternoon. When they arrived home, my son accidentally informed on his father. "We didn't go to Hurley's, Mummy. We just went shopping."

Hurley's was — and still is — a favourite bar that welcomed kids at the time. For him to even say it, I knew they had been there.

My kids were obsessed with *Star Wars*. One day, I had clearly yelled at my son about something, and he retorted back: "Mummy, you are on the dark side!"

I still taunt him with that one to this day.

Probably one of the purest and most beautiful statements was when we were doing a drive-through downtown to see all the Christmas lights. I said to my son, "Look at all the pretty lights on the wreath!"

His response: "Wow! A bagel!"

I'd never even thought of the similarity between the two. So sweet — and true!

I have a signed and dated statement by another child that I can't wait to show their offspring.

"I will never force my children to do anything."

I guess s/he was being asked to do something s/he absolutely abhorred at the time. Perfect future fodder for a grandparent!

One of my sons has turned out to be quite the comedian. It started early on. He was learning the human reproductive system at school and was studying for an exam. As every good parent does, I was reviewing his knowledge the night before and asked the question, "What are the functions of the prostate and seminal vesicles?" His answer:

"Produce semen, help sperm move, and provide male gametes energy to survive the genocide that occurs in the vagina."

I swear I was on the floor in tears. He knew at this stage he had a way with words — and I did, too. What "normal" child would come up with that?

This is just a snippet of hilarious yet innocent things my kids have uttered over the years. I should have kept the journal up as they still come out with some choice sayings, even as adults.

I thoroughly recommend you start writing down their declarations. We have been in tears sharing their honest, unfiltered words.

— Barb Dalton —

98

In a Bind

The difference between a mountain
and a mole hill is perspective.
~Al Neuharth

I married my husband when Mitchell was six and his little brother was five. Frank and I lived in different towns, so after the wedding, he and the boys moved in with me. My home was much closer to his work, and the school system where I lived was great. It was a big move for the boys because they had lived on the same street as their grandparents and great-grandparents.

I lived in a city, but they loved my home. It was a new adventure. There was a pool, and we were close to theaters, parks, museums, and shopping venues. To ease the transition, we visited the grandparents frequently, and those little guys seemed to settle in as if nothing had happened.

Then came school. Suddenly, Mitchell couldn't sit still in class. Not for five minutes, not for one minute. My husband and I were truly puzzled. He had been well-behaved at his last school. He clearly had not shown any signs of ADHD or any misbehavior at his previous school. This was a calm child. His brother still had a naptime, both at home and at school, and Mitchell insisted he needed one, too.

Had the changes affected his behavior in a way we hadn't noticed?

We were able to contact his former teacher. She felt it was maybe an adjustment phase. One week of not sitting was not that unusual. However, when he was in his second week and still up and down and fidgety, we knew we had to figure out the cause.

As the older child, Mitchell paved the way. We were always in new territory with him. Since he had finished kindergarten in one school district and moved to another, we had hoped there would be a smooth transition. Did this teacher have stricter rules? Was he unhappy? Was he being bullied? He assured us he liked his teacher, and no one was bothering him. So why was he acting out?

We sat him down for a talk. Are you happy? He assured us he was. Has the move upset you? He said he missed seeing his grandparents, but that wasn't the problem.

"Mitchell, can you tell us what's happened?" my husband asked.

Mitchell sighed. It had to be horrible.

I was ready for the worst. "You can tell us." I took his little hands in mine.

He looked up and then away as if the words were just too terrible.

"It's like this…" He shook his head.

My heart beat faster as he gazed at me with those big, blue eyes. What horrible thing was going to be revealed? He hated me? He was homesick, school sick. I leaned forward and waited for that oh-so-horrible truth.

He took a deep breath and blurted, "My underwear is just too tight!"

"Oh." Relief washed over me. "We can fix that." I glanced to Frank, who just looked puzzled.

"Yeah. We can fix that right now. Let's go to the store," my husband added. "And next time, tell us."

"Oh." He gave a nod and then sing-songed, "Okay."

That evening, we bought both boys larger sets of underwear. And that was it. Problem solved.

Mitchell went on to graduate high school and college. He is now thirty-seven, well-adjusted, and still wearing comfortable clothing. And he always reminds me that you shouldn't assume a problem is too big. It may just be something simple, like tight underwear.

— Lisa McCaskill —

99

Blueberry Pie

A sister can be seen as someone who is both
ourselves and very much not ourselves —
a special kind of double.
~Toni Morrison

Like most siblings close in age, my two older sisters were competitive. They bickered over everything and were always looking for ways to best one another.

One Saturday when they were young, my mother went grocery shopping. She left my father in charge of the kids. He served them a sandwich and a glass for milk for lunch. As they finished eating, he noticed a piece of blueberry pie on a plate in the refrigerator.

"Would you guys like some pie for dessert?" he asked.

"Oh, yes." On this point, they agreed.

So, he got out the pie and a knife to split it into two pieces.

My father was a chemist and highly skilled at measuring small amounts. Knowing the kids' predisposition to argue, he cut the piece into two halves with extreme precision, so no one would feel cheated. Then, he put the pieces on two plates.

"Okay, Cornelia," he said to the younger sister, giving her first choice, "which piece would you like?"

Cornelia took her time. She squinted at the pieces of pie. Leaned in closer. Studied them carefully from every angle. My father had done a good job, and she could not determine which piece was bigger.

Finally, she looked up at him.
"I want the piece that she wants."

— Christine Gross —

100

Seeing Red

Red hair, sir, in my opinion, is dangerous.
~P.G. Wodehouse

A s a parent of grown children, I have come to realize that many things occurred during those child-rearing years that I knew nothing about. Sometimes, I think it is better that way. With an almost ten-year spread between the first three children and the last two, there seems to be no end of the "remember when" stories that punctuate our family gatherings.

At one gathering, my third child, Shelly, began talking about her hair. She has always had beautiful hair, and she capitalized on that during her teen years. On this afternoon, she threw out the statement that, when she was younger, she had red highlights in her hair. We all remembered that, upon this discovery, she delightedly brought her hair color to our attention. Lots of attention. Shelly laughed with us at the memory and then mused aloud how interesting it was that she hadn't seen any highlights in many years.

Snickering broke out from across the room. We all turned to look at the source. My youngest two girls, then in their mid-twenties, were sharing wide-eyed looks and giggles.

"Okay, what is so funny?" I asked them, my look demanding an answer. Amidst guffaws, they traded off sharing the details of a story that had us all laughing heartily.

Alisha and Cynthia, my sweet babies, regaled us with a day from their childhood when two of their good friends had stayed at our house for a couple of days. The four girls, ranging in age from seven to ten years at the time, had decided to form a beauty business. The girls had gathered various things from the surrounding forest to combine, attempting to make a new perfume. They boiled pine needles, wild-flowers, and whatever they found in a pot of water.

At some point, they decided to put the perfume into a shampoo bottle — Shelly's shampoo bottle. Realizing that the strawberry-colored contents looked different after adding their concoction, they decided to add red food coloring. They told us how they rushed each morning to Shelly's shower in order to shake up the bottle and distribute the color throughout once again. They were terrified of discovery.

Shelly's face whitened with anger and then reddened with embar-rassment before softening into humor. "Well," she said, after a moment, "I guess that explains it."

— Marcia Wells —

A Cup of Tea

*The simplest toy, one which even the youngest child
can operate, is called a grandparent.*
~Sam Levenson

One day, my wife was out, and I was in charge of our youngest grandchild.

She was maybe three years old. Someone had given her a little tea set as a gift, and it was one of her favorite toys.

I was in the living room engrossed in the evening news when she brought me a little cup of "tea," which was just water. After several cups of tea and lots of praise for such yummy tea, my wife came home. I made her wait in the living room to watch her bring me a cup of tea because it was "just the cutest thing"! Nanny waited, and sure enough, Hanna came down the hall with a cup of tea for Papa and watched me drink it up.

Then my wife said (as only a grandmother would know), "Did it ever occur to you that the only place she can reach to get water is the toilet?"

— Kerry Pardue —

Meet Our Contributors

P.A. Alaniz received her MFA in Writing and Poetics from Naropa University in 2014. Since graduating she has worked as an adjunct writing instructor at Baker College and Jackson College. Peggy enjoys traveling with her family, is passionate about tea and is in the process of creating her own blog about tea, travel, and spirit.

Lisa Aldridge lives and writes in a 19th century church which she and her husband are renovating while carefully not disturbing the ghosts. She is the author of *The Knowing Ones* and *Dangerous Impressions*. She enjoys cultural anthropology, painting, teaching, and her family. She earned her MFA from Lindenwood University.

Suzanne Alexander is an award-winning writer of fiction and nonfiction for children and adults. Her recent short memoir, "Nature Is Always Open," was published in the anthology, *Voices from the Pandemic* (Headline Books, Inc., 2021), which has won multiple awards.

Donna Anderson is a wife, mom, and grandmother who lives in Texas with her husband, Tom, and dogs: a Border Collie who could rule the world if she had a smart phone and opposable thumbs, and a Golden Retriever who lives for tennis balls. Aside from writing, she enjoys genealogy, photography, and antiquing.

Katrin Babb has been published in *Boys' Quest* magazine, *Screamin Mamas*, and *GreenPrints*.

Barbara Wackerle Baker grew up in Banff, Alberta and spends her free time racing up and down the Rockies to keep up with an active family of outdoor enthusiasts. E-mail her at bbaker.write@gmail.com.

Peter Bana trained as a lawyer and holds a master's degree in law from the University of London. He abandoned law for the world of literature and works as an editor. When he is not at the editing desk, he occupies himself with career coaching. His hobbies are walking and cycling.

Sydney Bayne lives in Florida with her husband John. They have two children and two granddaughters in college nearby. When she isn't writing, she enjoys needlepoint and quilting. An avid reader, Sydney belongs to a book club and Florida Star Fiction Writers.

Brenda Beattie is a retired letter carrier and chaplain for the USPS. She has been writing for decades and has self-published four books. Her passion is to encourage others.

Marina Bee and her family live in Toronto, Canada. As a member of the Sandwich Generation, Marina writes a blog called "Living the Jam Gen," a light-hearted take on the topics of parenting, caregiving and life on the home front. To read more amusing tales, visit www.jam-gen.com/recent-posts or www.facebook.com/JamGenLife.

Pamela Kae Bender and Charlie, her husband of fifty-six years, are thoroughly enjoying retirement! While Charlie spends time with his friends at the nearby golf course, Pam enjoys photography and quilting. And even though their travel plans have been postponed, they're both extremely happy their favorite restaurants are open again!

Cate Bronson is an accountant turned author whose nonfiction work reflects her devotion to family and animal welfare. Cate lives in Florida with her husband and rescued racing dogs. She enjoys reading and writing in the sunshine while giant hounds lounge by her side.

BB Brown studied at University of Padua, Italy, graduated from UCLA, and taught in Hawaii and California. She lives on five acres with her family of fourteen. Her stories are published in five anthologies, a sixth in *Chicken Soup for the Soul: My Hilarious, Heroic, Human Dog*. She has completed a YA and an upmarket novel. Writing is like breathing — she writes daily.

Louise Butler is a retired educator with advanced degrees in administration and economics. She was a speaker at the Global Summit on Science and Science Education. She now enjoys the life of a writer. Louise is active in her community where she enjoys good books, bad golf, and great friends.

Jack Byron has worn several different career hats over the course of his life, including work as a freelance illustrator, gallery artist, and tattoo artist. His most rewarding work, however, was the ten years spent working as an activity director with patients suffering from Alzheimer's disease. He lives in Southern California.

Blanche Carroll received her Bachelor of Science, with honors, from Eastern Nazarene College in 2008. She has three grown children and lives in Massachusetts. Blanche enjoys traveling, reading, watching romantic comedies, and hiking. E-mail her at blanche68@comcast.net.

Eva Carter is originally from Czechoslovakia, raised in New York and now living in Dallas, TX with her Canadian husband and their two cats. Her background is in finance and telecommunications.

Gwen Cooper received her B.A. in English and Secondary Education in 2007 and completed the University of Denver Publishing Institute in 2009. In her spare time, she enjoys traveling, gardening, and spending time exploring the outdoors with her husband and Bloodhounds. Follow her on Twitter @Gwen_Cooper10.

Barb Dalton is a nursing instructor who dabbles in photography and writing in her spare time. A New Zealander by birth, she now resides in Montreal, Canada and is a proud mom of three humans and two cats. Her stories are centred around her photography, work, family, and life experiences.

Darcy Daniels is mom to two amazing daughters: Wendy and Penny. She is a historian, teacher, and writer. In the summer she's a tour guide on the Freedom Trail in Boston. The best thing she ever did was marry her college sweetheart, Michael. She still believes that people are inherently good.

Andy DeWitt is a retired oral surgeon. His first book, a missionary's biography, helped raise over a million dollars. He now empowers Christian leaders to convert their content into engaging books to release their inspirational teaching, raise their professional status, and boost their bottom line.

Margaret V. Doran lives with her husband of fifty-three years and their son and daughter-in-law in rural Northwestern Washington. She writes poetry, essays, occasional family stories, is a needlework and paper artist, and loves cooking and reading. She gains inspiration from the beauty of nature and her quirky family.

Renee Dubeau lives in Nashville, TN with her husband and four (mostly) grown children. A healthcare worker by day and writer by compulsion, Renee is obsessed with the human condition and the reasons why people do what they do. Renee enjoys yoga, hiking, gardening, cooking, baking, and playing with her tuxedo cats.

Pamela Dunaj has written a corporate parody newsletter and has been published in a university literary journal. She was awarded second place in the "Unknown Writers" contest hosted by the Denver Women's Press Club. Currently, she is working on new writing projects, including one with a companion multimedia facet to it. E-mail her at akos4@vfemail.net.

Award-winning author **Ellen Fannon** is a veterinarian, former missionary, and church musician. She and her husband fostered more than forty children and adopted two sons. She has published three humorous novels: *Other People's Children, Save the Date* (2022 Christian Indie winner), and *Don't Bite the Doctor*.

Gina Farella-Howley has taught special education in the Illinois Public School System for eighteen years. She stayed home for fifteen years with her amazing sons: Martin, Joe and Tim. She has enjoyed writing in freelance fashion, especially this story in addition to the four stories previously published in the *Chicken Soup for the Soul* series. Go White Sox!

Marianne Fosnow lives in South Carolina. She treasures her wonderful, wacky family and loves sharing laughs with them. She has been writing stories since the fifth grade, thanks to the encouragement of a wonderful teacher.

After teaching for twenty-six years, **Patricia Gable** retired and began writing. She has written over 300 education articles and short stories. Her first middle-grade book was published in 2021. She and her family have lived in Ohio, Michigan, Chihuahua, Mexico and now in Arizona.

Joan Gelfand received her B.A. in English from San Francisco State University and her MFA from Mills College. The author of six books, including the Amazon #1 best seller, *You Can Be a Winning Writer*, Joan enjoys hiking, yoga and kayaking and lives in San Francisco, CA.

Christine Gross grew up in Michigan. She enjoys learning languages and exploring foreign cultures. She writes both fiction and nonfiction, has contributed to cookbooks, and recently edited an art book. Currently she lives in Tucson, AZ with her husband and her cat.

Connie L. Gunkel received her criminal justice degree and Bachelor of Arts, with honors, and dental assisting certificate in 1982. She raised three children and as an empty nester enjoys camping, and playing keyboard in a band and at local retirement centers. She is learning Spanish and plans to begin writing a Young Adult novel.

Sharon Boerbon Hanson received her MFA from Hamline University. Recent publications include short stories in *Best New Short Stories 2021*, poetry in *Best New Poems 2021*, and "The Question," in *Northern Lights: 20 MinnSpec Tales*. Her fantasy novel, *The Straits of Allback,* is due out in February 2023.

A freelance writer and former piano teacher, **Wendy Hobday Haugh's** short stories, articles, and poetry have appeared in dozens of national and regional publications, Wendy lives with her husband, two frisky feline companions, and dozens of white-tailed deer in the Adirondack foothills of upstate New York.

Stephen Hecht is a retired newspaper writer and copyeditor. He is a graduate of Duquesne University.

Butch Holcombe hails from north Georgia and is founder/owner of Greybird Publishers and *American Digger Magazine*. When not working at the above, he pursues his hobby of freelance writing. Learn more at publishers@americandiggers.com.

Sylvia Garza Holmes is a native Texan. She enlisted in the United States Air Force and retired as a Chief Master Sergeant. Her husband of forty-six years proposed to her on the Golden Gate Bridge; the two have eight grandchildren. Sylvia keeps busy writing her memoirs so others can read about her blessed incredible life.

Since 1992, **Cindy Horgash** has invited all listeners and wanderers to sit a spell and enjoy the magic of storytelling. Whether on stage or in a classroom, Cindy holds her audience captive with really-truly, spun, and passed-down stories. She is a member of the Northwest Indiana Storytelling Guild and Write-On Hoosiers, Inc.

Cheryl-Anne Iacobellis recently renewed her passion for writing about her family in 2022, when her first grandchild, Ivy, was born. Her story "Our New Year's Eve Tradition" appeared in *Chicken Soup for the Soul: Christmas in Canada.* E-mail her at cherylanneiacobellis@gmail.com.

Roberta Beach Jacobson is drawn to the magic of words — poetry, puzzles, song lyrics, flash fiction, and stand-up comedy. Her stories, essays, and poems have appeared in seventy anthologies published on four continents.

Robin Jankiewicz attended Whitman College, in Walla Walla, WA. She is married with two boys, and every few years she attempts to write a novel.

Wendy Jones is a wife, mom, and stepmom. She is happy to report that her family is now blending nicely, and her stepson has learned to prepare food he — and his siblings — really enjoy. He loves to present his frozen chicken nuggets and tater tots as "Jason's Famous Poultry and Potato Souffle."

Mary-Lane Kamberg is co-leader of the Kansas City Writers Group and is the author of *The "I Don't Know How to Cook" Book*, as well as thirty nonfiction books for middle school and high school libraries. She also wrote *The I Love to Write Book* series for young writers. She has ridden an elephant and been kissed by a camel.

Jill Keller lives in a small town of Southern Indiana with her husband and two children. She enjoys writing novels, making desserts for her home bakery, being a reborn artist for therapy dolls, running a business helping those going through baby loss, and reading to her children. Learn more at kellerjf.wixsite.com/author.

Sky Khan lives in Texas Hill Country with her best friend Ben and their four children. Currently on her own journey battling cancer, Sky is reflecting deeply on the seasons of life, and how to capture pieces of the experience on paper and canvas for generations to come. Contact Sky at sky@ilikeu.com or on Instgram @ilikeu.

MJ Lemire is a CPA by day and a writer by night. From Michigan,

MJ graduated from college in Texas and moved to California, where she's the mother of two. With family life providing endless anecdotes, MJ's been published in *Lunch Ticket*, *Literary Mama*, *Minerva Rising* and others. She's working on a collection of essays.

A native of the Missouri Ozarks, **Annie Lisenby** has an MFA in theatre. She performed professionally and taught at the college level. As a writer, Annie's debut novel *A Three-Letter Name*, a young adult survival romance, released in 2022. She is a mom, wife, writer, and speaker. Learn more at www.annielisenby.com.

Barbara LoMonaco is the Senior Editor for the *Chicken Soup for the Soul* series and has had stories published in many titles. She graduated from USC and has a teaching credential. She lives in Southern California where she is surrounded by boys: her husband, her three grown sons and her two grandsons. Thankfully, her three lovely daughters-in-law have diluted the mix somewhat, but the boys are still in the majority.

Marie Loper-Maxwell is the mom of many, lover of learning and devourer of books. She spends most of her time with her husband, parents, siblings, and seven children reading, writing, and making memories.

Victoria Lorrekovich-Miller's essays are widely published and her first children's book, *If a Mantis Finds a Fly in the Sky*, is now out! When not writing, Victoria and her husband are riding their Vespas, exploring the wine regions of California, befriending dogs, and loving their four amazing kids. E-mail her at Victoria@VictoriaLorrekovich-Miller.com.

Australian born author **Grant Madden** immigrated to the USA in 2005 and resides in El Cajon, CA. Grant had had cover stories in *Sailing*, *Cat Sailor* and the *San Diego Reader*. This is Grant's sixth story published in the *Chicken Soup for the Soul* series. Learn more at www.grantmadden.com.

Mary Beth Magee's faith leads her to explore God's world and write about it. She writes in many genres and takes inspiration from her wonderfully wacky family. She speaks on a variety of topics. Learn more at www.LOL4.net.

Lori Carol Maloy is a writer and a retired counselor in Central

Florida. Proud to be the winner of the Writer's Digest 90th annual memoir/essay contest, winning with her essay, "Passions War." She has previously published under the name LC Helms. She writes to help herself and others find their way home. Learn more at www.loricarolmaloy.com.

Joshua J. Mark is an editor/director and writer for the online site "World History Encyclopedia." His work has also appeared in *Timeless Travels*, *Litro*, *History Ireland*, and other publications in print and online. He lives with his housemate Sammie the dog in Staatsburg, NY.

Deborah E. Martin is a retired probation officer, family history researcher, wreath maker, baby diaper gift creator and virtual journey walker. She is an encourager, supporter, helper, peace seeker, teacher, writer, friend, honorary mother, and happy GG. She writes to remember and to be remembered.

Karen Langley Martin lives and writes from Durham, NC. Learn more at karenthewriter.com.

Lisa McCaskill lives in North Carolina with her husband of thirty-plus years. They have four sons, two grandchildren, and many grand fur babies. She loves to spend time with family and friends, and whenever there's a free moment, she enjoys writing encouraging stories of faith, hope, and love.

Kat Mincz still has a scrapbook that contains a story she made up at the age of three. She is a retired children's librarian from the Henrico County Public Library system. She enjoys working with her church's card ministry, traveling, photography, storytelling, and collecting postcards. Kat's dream is to write a memoir.

Marissa Mitchell is a high school English teacher, Army veteran, and mother who lives in Southern Indiana with her daughter and two cats. When she's not grading papers, she enjoys reading, Taekwondo, and roller derby.

Amy A. Mullis lives in South Carolina where she keeps a nightlight on in the event she encounters another undead relative in the kitchen. Her writing has appeared in *The Christian Science Monitor*, *Sasee* magazine, several titles in the *Chicken Soup for the Soul* series, as well as on her blog, which can be found at MindOverMullis.blogspot.com.

Jenni Murphy is currently living in Arizona happily wrapped around the paws of a dog and a cat. Before they came into her life, she backpacked through Africa by herself, worked for a spine surgeon for twenty years, and followed Kenny Rogers around the country. Watch for her upcoming book *The Swear Jar*. E-mail her at jenni@bookjunkie.org.

Teresa Murphy lives in New Jersey with her husband and four children. She works at a women's shelter and enjoys hiking, traveling, biking, baking, and having lights on in her house.

Nell Musolf lives in Minnesota with her husband, three dogs, two cats and a large leftover wardrobe from the 1980s (but no leather). E-mail her at nellmus@aol.com.

Sandra R. Nachlinger enjoys quilting, reading, writing, lunching, spending time with her granddaughter, and hiking in the beautiful Pacific Northwest. She has written two novels (so far!) Her stories have appeared in *Woman's World*, *Northwest PrimeTime*, and several titles in the *Chicken Soup for the Soul* series.

Barbara Espinosa Occhino is an advertising and PR copywriter and co-owner of a marketing agency. She teaches entrepreneurship in college and volunteers as a student mentor. She serves as a music curator supporting local music/arts. Born in Cuba, her writing is inspired by the people and places that have colored her life.

Linda O'Connell, a retired preschool teacher, writes from St. Louis, MO. She finds humor in everyday situations. Family has given her many laugh lines. Linda, a frequent contributor to the *Chicken Soup for the Soul* series, enjoys dark chocolate, a hearty laugh, and walking on the beach. She blogs at lindaoconnell.blogspot.com.

Nancy Emmick Panko is a retired pediatric RN turned writer. She is the author of three award-winning books: *Guiding Missal*, *Sheltering Angels*, and *Blueberry Moose*. Nancy and her husband have two kids, four grandkids, and three grand-dogs. They love being on the water in their pontoon boat. Learn more at www.nancypanko.com.

Kerry Pardue has had three careers, from detective in Newport News, VA to letter carrier with the U.S. Postal Service in Virginia and Arizona to being a college recruiter for a very large vocational college in Phoenix, AZ. He completed his Bachelor of Arts in Political Science from Christopher Newport University in 1979.

Katrina Paulson lives in the Pacific Northwest where she wonders about humanity, questions with no answers, and new discoveries. Then she writes about them on "Medium" and in her two newsletters. Katrina loves to travel and explore the local forests and is currently working on her first novel.

Jillian Pfennig is a freelance writer, artist, and photographer. She is passionate about traveling and working on visiting every national park in the United States. Jillian also enjoys fashion, street art, and spending time with her family whenever she can.

Michael T. Powers, whose writing appears in thirty-five books (eleven in the *Chicken Soup for the Soul* series), is a youth pastor, international speaker, award-winning photographer and high school girls' coach. Preview his book, *Heart Touchers*, or join the thousands of world-wide readers on his e-mail list at HeartTouchers.com. E-mail him at Michael@faithjanesville.org.

Connie Kaseweter Pullen lives in rural Sandy, OR near her five children and several grandchildren. She earned a B.A., with honors, at the University of Portland in 2006, with a double major in psychology and sociology. Connie enjoys writing, photography and exploring nature. E-mail her at MyGrandmaPullen@aol.com.

Toya Qualls-Barnette holds a Bachelor of Arts in Communications/ Public Relations from Pepperdine University, Malibu. She is the mother of two wonderful sons and lives with her family in Northern California. Toya is a previous contributor to the *Chicken Soup for the Soul* series. Writing is her passion.

Lisa J. Radcliff is an author and speaker in southeastern Pennsylvania. She and husband, Doug, have been married thirty-seven years. They have three sons and daughters-in-law and nine grandchildren. Lisa loves spending time with her family, cheering for Philly sports teams, quilting, and shopping with a special group of friends.

Camille Regholec is a pastor who loves to inspire others. She is the author of two published historical romances, a memoir, and a children's picture book. Her articles have previously been included in numerous Christian magazines and in *Chicken Soup for the Soul:*

Messages from Heaven and Other Miracles.

Rachel Remick lives in Tampa, FL where she writes and works as a dog sitter. A previous contributor to the *Chicken Soup for the Soul* series, her stories have also been published in Rosebud, *Sasee* and *Pif*. An avid reader as well as road-tripper, you can find her on both Instagram and Twitter @tampawritergirl.

Donna L. Roberts is a native upstate New Yorker who lives and works in Europe. She is a professor who holds a Ph.D. in Psychology. Donna is an animal and human rights advocate and when she isn't researching or writing she can be found at her computer buried in rescue pets.

Laura Robinson is a talented singer-songwriter, actress and producer. She co-created the classic board game, *Balderdash*, bringing laughter to people all over the world! Robinson was nominated for an Emmy for her television game show, *Celebrity Name Game*. Learn more at www.laurarobinson.com.

Nan Rockey left her big-city lawyer job to return to her small hometown of Hope where she opened a bakery to sell organic, free-range cookies. She married the love of her life, Max Manly, and she spends her spare time swimming with mud mermaids and building her dog's film career. Children fear her.

Heather Rodin is a published and award-winning writer. As Executive Director for the mission Hope Grows Haiti she draws from her experiences to write of the joys and challenges in life. Mother to six married children and grandma to fourteen, she and her husband live on an acreage near Peterborough, Ontario.

Jeannie Rogers is the mother of three and the grandmother of four. A retired writer for a nonprofit organization, she is currently working on her own 365-page devotional book. Jeannie also creates artwork with colored pencils, reads a lot, and plays golf (enjoying the challenge of occasionally shooting her age).

Tyann Sheldon Rouw lives in Iowa with her husband and three sons. Her work has appeared in *Yahoo!Life*, *Huffington Post*, *Scary Mommy*, *The Mighty*, and several newspapers. In her spare time, she enjoys managing chaos, deep breathing, wearing her old blue robe, and advocating for those with autism. Follow her on Twitter @TyannRouw.

Tia Marie Ruggiero lives in upstate New York. She and her husband Jamie enjoy camping in the Adirondacks with their children Dustin, EmilyAnn, Dominick, and Elias. Tia has a private practice working with children and families as a psychotherapist, specializing in trauma. When free, she enjoys traveling, reading, and writing.

John Scanlan is a 1983 graduate of the United States Naval Academy and retired from the United States Marine Corps as a Lieutenant Colonel aviator with time in the back seat of both the F-4S Phantom II and the F/A-18D Hornet. He is currently pursuing a second career as a writer.

Marci Seither's writing career began after a family humor article was published in a small-town newspaper. Since then, she has written hundreds of articles as well as written for *Guideposts* and *Focus on the Family*. She is the author of three books and has mastered the art of baking Southern biscuits. Learn more at www.marciseither.com.

Billie Holladay Skelley received her bachelor's and master's degrees from the University of Wisconsin-Madison. A retired clinical nurse specialist, she is the mother of four and grandmother of two. Billie enjoys writing, and her work crosses several genres. She spends her non-writing time reading, gardening, and traveling.

Michele Sprague wrote hundreds of stories for corporate magazines and newsletters during her writing career in communications departments. Since retiring, published pieces include a story in *Chicken Soup for the Soul: Running for Good*, womensrunning.com, *INSPIRED* senior living magazine, and her book *Single Again 101*.

Steven Stampone is from Philadelphia, PA which means that he can say "yo" without shame or irony. He writes funny things, serious things, and even funny-serious things, and he loves all soups, not just chicken.

Dana D. Sterner is a retired registered nurse and a bit frugal herself. She has a "DIY Almost Anything" site where friends can share ideas and money saving tips and advice. This is her third story published in the *Chicken Soup for the Soul* series.

Allison Stiefel is a native of Chicago, IL. She has a grown son and a four-year-old rescue dog named Portia. She has cycled throughout the world, and when not writing works part-time at a boutique wine shop. Her stories are based on real life, love, and laughter.

Dani Michelle Stone is a previous contributor to the *Chicken Soup for the Soul* series and three-time published author. She lives with her husband Doug and two children (Jenna and Kade) in Kansas where she works full-time in marketing and part-time as a wedding officiant. Dani has a loud laugh and penchant for telling long-winded stories.

Nick Walker is a writer and voiceover artist, having worked forty years in television, twenty of those as an on-camera meteorologist for *The Weather Channel*. He performs educational weather programs for students, teachers, and parents and maintains the "Weather Dude" website at Wxdude.com.

Mary Hunt Webb is a recovering community college instructor, but her recovery is not going well as she continues to teach adults as a volunteer. Her written work has appeared in various publications since 1984. Mary and her husband, Morris, have been married for more than fifty years. Learn more at maryhuntwebb.com.

Marcia Wells has an undergraduate degree in English and history. She also has a Master's in Secondary Education. As a mother of five and grandmother of ten, life is never dull. She and her husband love snorkeling, kayaking, and skiing. The author of two novels, Marica intends to continue writing every chance she gets.

Holly D. Yount is an educator, writer and proofreader/editor all rolled into one. She has written for various publications including *Highlights for Children*. She resides in Texas with her son, twin daughters, husband, and Labrabull named Oscar.

Lori Zenker lives in small town Ontario in a big old house that is always under renovation. She is very grateful to the *Chicken Soup for the Soul* series for sharing so many of her crazy stories.

This is **Susan Zwirn's** second published story in the *Chicken Soup for the Soul* series. She is currently entertaining children (big and small) with her balloon art. In the past, she has worked as a singing messenger, event's clown, stand-up comic, and actress. She enjoys sharing stories of her wacky life with the public.

Meet Amy Newmark

Amy Newmark is the bestselling author, editor-in-chief, and publisher of the *Chicken Soup for the Soul* book series. Since 2008, she has published 186 new books, most of them national bestsellers in the U.S. and Canada, more than doubling the number of Chicken Soup for the Soul titles in print today. She is also the author of *Simply Happy*, a crash course in Chicken Soup for the Soul advice and wisdom that is filled with easy-to-implement, practical tips for enjoying a better life.

Amy is credited with revitalizing the Chicken Soup for the Soul brand, which has been a publishing industry phenomenon since the first book came out in 1993. By compiling inspirational and aspirational true stories curated from ordinary people who have had extraordinary experiences, Amy has kept the twenty-nine-year-old Chicken Soup for the Soul brand fresh and relevant.

Amy graduated *magna cum laude* from Harvard University where she majored in Portuguese and minored in French. She then embarked on a three-decade career as a Wall Street analyst, a hedge fund manager, and a corporate executive in the technology field. She is a Chartered Financial Analyst.

Her return to literary pursuits was inevitable, as her honors thesis in college involved traveling throughout Brazil's impoverished northeast region, collecting stories from regular people. She is delighted to have come full circle in her writing career — from collecting stories "from the people" in Brazil as a twenty-year-old to, three decades later, collecting stories "from the people" for Chicken Soup for the Soul.

When Amy and her husband Bill, the CEO of Chicken Soup for the Soul, are not working, they are visiting their four grown children and their spouses, and their five grandchildren.

Follow Amy on Twitter @amynewmark. Listen to her free podcast — Chicken Soup for the Soul with Amy Newmark — on Apple, Google, or by using your favorite podcast app on your phone.

Thank You

We owe huge thanks to all our contributors and fans. We received thousands of submissions for this popular topic, and we spent months reading all of them. Laura Dean, and Crescent LoMonaco read all of them and narrowed down the selection for Associate Publisher D'ette Corona and Publisher and Editor-in-Chief Amy Newmark. Susan Heim did the first round of editing, and then D'ette chose the perfect quotations to put at the beginning of each story, and Amy edited the stories and shaped the final manuscript.

As we finished our work, D'ette continued to be Amy's right-hand woman in working with all our wonderful writers. Barbara LoMonaco, Kristiana Pastir and Elaine Kimbler jumped in to proof, proof, proof. And yes, there will always be typos anyway, so please feel free to let us know about them at webmaster@chickensoupforthesoul.com, and we will correct them in future printings.

The whole publishing team deserves a hand, including our Vice President of Marketing Maureen Peltier, our Vice President of Production Victor Cataldo, Executive Assistant Mary Fisher, and our graphic designer Daniel Zaccari, who turned our manuscript into this beautiful, inspirational book.

Sharing Happiness, Inspiration, and Hope

Real people sharing real stories, every day, all over the world. In 2007, *USA Today* named *Chicken Soup for the Soul* one of the five most memorable books in the last quarter-century. With over 110 million books sold to date in the U.S. and Canada alone, more than 300 titles in print, and translations into nearly fifty languages, "chicken soup for the soul®" is one of the world's best-known phrases.

Today, twenty-nine years after we first began sharing happiness, inspiration and hope through our books, we continue to delight our readers with new titles, but have also evolved beyond the bookshelves with super premium pet food, television shows, a podcast, video journalism from aplus.com, licensed products, and free movies and TV shows on our Popcornflix and Crackle apps. We are busy "changing your world one story at a time®." Thanks for reading!

Share with Us

We all have had Chicken Soup for the Soul moments in our lives. If you would like to share your story or poem with millions of people around the world, go to chickensoup. com and click on Submit Your Story. You may be able to help another reader and become a published author at the same time. Some of our past contributors have launched writing and speaking careers from the publication of their stories in our books!

We only accept story submissions via our website. They are no longer accepted via mail or fax. Visit our website, www.chickensoup. com, and click on Submit Your Story for our writing guidelines and a list of topics we are working on.

To contact us regarding other matters, please send us an e-mail through webmaster@chickensoupforthesoul.com, or fax or write us at:

Chicken Soup for the Soul
P.O. Box 700
Cos Cob, CT 06807-0700
Fax: 203-861-7194

One more note from your friends at Chicken Soup for the Soul: Occasionally, we receive an unsolicited book manuscript from one of our readers, and we would like to respectfully inform you that we do not accept unsolicited manuscripts, and we must discard the ones that appear.

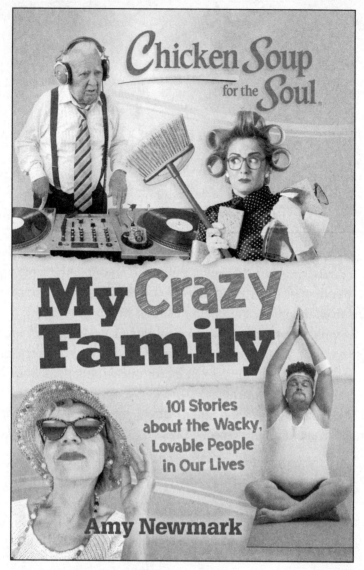

Paperback: 978-1-61159-977-0
eBook: 978-1-61159-277-1

More heartwarming shenanigans

Too Funny!

101 Hilarious Stories to Brighten Your Days

Amy Newmark

Paperback: 978-1-61159-089-0
eBook: 978-1-61159-327-3

and laugh-out loud tales

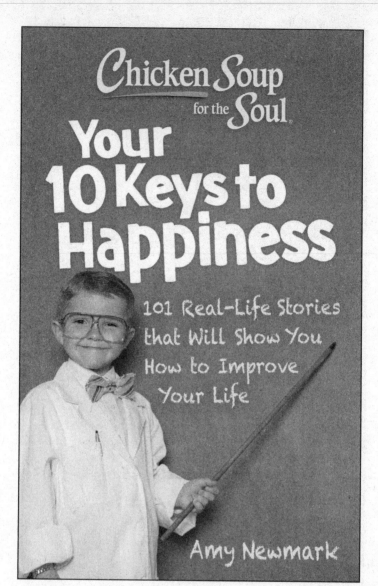

Paperback: 978-1-61159-091-3
eBook: 978-1-61159-330-3

Happiness is within your reach

Chicken Soup for the Soul

Attitude of Gratitude

101 Stories
About Counting
Your Blessings
& The Power of
Thankfulness

Amy Newmark

Paperback: 978-1-61159-093-7
eBook: 978-1-61159-331-0

and it starts with gratitude

Changing your life one story at a time ®
www.chickensoup.com